"Matt has provided a scholarly treatise for parents and professionals written in the engaging and invigorating style that he is so comfortable with. This book in my opinion is the most thorough and well written analysis of the history and application of disability law, and the impact on real life experiences for students, available in print to date."

—*Kathryn Dobel, co-chair of CAPCA*
(California Association for Parent-Child Advocacy)
and founding board member of COPAA
(Council of Parent Attorneys and Advocates)

"Matt Cohen brings his extensive knowledge of special education and his talent as a writer to this book, explaining complex legal matters relating to the education of children with special needs in a way that is clear and easy to understand. This is a book every parent, teacher, administrator or family member of a special needs child will want to read cover to cover."

—*Nancy Hablutzel, Ph.D., J.D., Chicago-Kent College of Law*

"Matt Cohen is one of the leading lights of special education law. He has an unmatched record of success in representing families in their efforts to obtain educational and support services for children with disabilities. This book is filled with insights and practical information drawn from his comprehensive knowledge of the law and his extensive experience in advocacy. I recommend it to everyone working in the field."

—*Mark C. Weber, Vincent dePaul Professor of Law,*
DePaul University, and author of Special Education Law and Litigation Treatise

"Wow! This book is like a "Mapquest" that puts the parent on a journey, making the process clear and concise. But more important, it is sensitive to the emotions a parent feels during very vulnerable times on the journey. As a parent, I would want to keep it within reach by day and under my pillow at night."

—*Ellen McManus, Wilmette, IL,*
whose daughter has been represented by Matthew Cohen

"Matt Cohen is a lawyer's lawyer and an advocate's advocate. His deep storehouse of experiences in special education are synthesized in this comprehensive, comprehensible, and compelling book. Cohen's insights and strategies have been ground-truthed through years of case work, policy work, and community and parent education. His lucid analysis of the law and his distillation of advocacy strategies that actually work will benefit anyone who is interested in the education of children. This up-to-date book, filled with useful references, will become the benchmark work in the field."

—*Dean Hill Rivkin, College of Law Distinguished Professor,*
University of Tennessee College of Law

"An excellent, very readable explanation not only of what IDEA requires, both substantively and procedurally, but how advocates and parents can make it work. From the convenient outline of the process provided by the table of contents, in the order most parents will encounter it and arranged to properly emphasize substance over process, to the practical pointers highlighted by his "E=MC^2" formula, Mr. Cohen has admirably achieved his stated purpose: to help parents (whose children are not experiencing success) identify points of potential conflict and ways to address those conflicts."

—S. James Rosenfeld, Founder and Director,
The National Academy for IDEA Administrative Law Judges
and Hearing Officers at Seattle University School of Law

"Matt Cohen's secrets of great special education advocacy are in this book, laid out in a user-friendly, understandable format. It's all here—tips at the end of each section with tangible strategies for parents and their advocates, forms and letters, and a glossary of the alphabet soup so critical to special education. This essential resource will empower parents, giving them and their advocates the tools necessary to enforce their children's special education rights."

—Aimee E. Gilman, special education attorney and parent,
co-founder and Executive Director, Special Education Services, Cleveland, OH

"Matt Cohen's background as a disability rights expert, attorney, and parent insures the practical grasp, sensitivity, and wisdom necessary to distill the substance of the laws and strategies involved in special education advocacy. His expertise is grounded in this brilliant and strategic treatise assisting families and professionals to acquire the best programs and services for children. Having an uncanny insight into the issues that families face on the ground, Matt Cohen's new *Guide* provides families and professionals alike the most reliable resource yet to navigate the special education conundrum."

—Barbara H. Dyer, Staff Attorney, University of Tennessee College of Law;
The CAN-LEARN Project; Children's Advocacy Network;
Lawyers Education Advocacy Resource Network

"*A Guide to Special Education Advocacy* is probably the most comprehensive publication yet to combine a thoughtful analysis of special education law and practice with effective advocacy strategies on behalf of children with disabilities. Each chapter contains "E=MC^2 Advocacy Strategies," which are sterling practical tips and insights for parents and advocates. This book is a must-read for all those that want to increase their knowledge and understanding of special education law and advocacy strategies."

—Torin D. Togut, Adjunct Professor of Law,
University of Georgia School of Law; Georgia Legal Services Program;
Council of Parent Attorneys and Advocates

A Guide to

Special
Education
Advocacy

of related interest

Guiding Your Teenager with Special Needs through the Transition from School to Adult Life
Tools for Parents
Mary Korpi
ISBN 978 1 84310 874 0

Alphabet Kids: From ADD to Zellweger Syndrome
A Guide to Developmental, Neurobiological, and Psychological Disorders for Parents and Professionals
Robbie Woliver
ISBN 978 1 84310 880 1

Fun with Messy Play
Ideas and Activities for Children with Special Needs
Tracey Beckerleg
ISBN 978 1 84310 641

Building a Joyful Life with Your Child Who Has Special Needs
Nancy J. Whiteman and Linda Roan-Yager
ISBN 978 1 84310 841 2

A Guide to Special Education Advocacy

What Parents, Clinicians and Advocates Need to Know

Matt Cohen, Esq.

Jessica Kingsley Publishers
London and Philadelphia

The following cartoons are reprinted with permission from Michael F. Giangreco: "Ants in His Pants" (p.58) and "Is Bigger Better?" (p.114) © 1998 from *Ants in His Pants: Absurdities and Realities of Special Education*; "Appropriate Labels" (p.77) © 1999 from *Flying by the Seat of Your Pants: More Absurditites and Realities of Special Education*; "Hazards" (p.199) © 2000 from *Teaching Old Logs New Tricks: More Absurdities and Realities of Education*. All published by Corwin Press, Thousand Oaks, CA.

Bell Curve (p.48) reproduced by special permission of the Publisher, Psychological Assessment Resources, Inc.,16204 North Florida Avenue, Lutz, FL 33549, from the Laminated Bell Curve Card. Published 2006 by PAR, Inc., originally developed by Dr. Lewis M. Terman in 1921. Further reproduction is prohibited without permission of PAR, Inc.

First published in 2009
by Jessica Kingsley Publishers
116 Pentonville Road
London N1 9JB, UK
and
400 Market Street, Suite 400
Philadelphia, PA 19106, USA

www.jkp.com

Copyright © Matthew Cohen 2009

Library of Congress Cataloging in Publication Data

Cohen, Matthew D.
 A guide to special education advocacy : what parents, clinicians, and advocates need to know / Matthew Cohen.
  p. cm.
 ISBN 978-1-84310-893-1 (pb : alk. paper)
 1. Special education--Law and legislation--United States. 2. Children with disabilities--Education--Law and legislation--United States. 3. Special education--United States. 4. Children with disabilities--Education--United States. I. Title.
 KF4209.3.C64 2009
 344.73'0791--dc22

2008030476

British Library Cataloguing in Publication Data

A CIP catalogue record for this book is available from the British Library

ISBN 978 1 84310 893 1

Printed and bound in the United States by
Thomson-Shore, 7300 Joy Road, Dexter, MI 48130

This book is dedicated to my two sons, Daniel and Nathan, who, each in his own way, has taught me much, has displayed unique talents and passion for life, and has brought me great joy and pride. I love them both dearly.

Contents

Preface

As a result of enactment of the Individuals with Disabilities Education Act (IDEA) in 1975, many children with disabilities have gained access to the educational system when they might have been previously excluded altogether or relegated to separate classrooms or schools with inferior education. Many excellent teachers, classes, and schools have made immeasurable contributions to increasing the success and self sufficiency of children with disabilities around the country.

Yet, despite these many accomplishments, the special education system has not fulfilled the sweeping promise it originally offered. Many children are passed through without receiving the quality and intensity of services that they require. These children are served in overly restrictive settings, not because their disabilities demand these settings but because the schools are unable or unwilling to provide the training and support necessary to facilitate the success of the children in less restrictive settings. Conversely, some children with disabilities are served in regular education without sufficient support, leading them to make less progress than would otherwise be possible or to experience avoidable problems that ultimately require more intensive intervention.

While there are many wonderful regular and special educators, as well as many schools where parents and staff work together in a positive collaboration in support of the children, many parents feel devalued and marginalized, excluded from meaningful participation, or even blamed for being concerned about their child's education or punished for speaking up on their child's behalf. While there are myriad success stories that deserve acknowledgment and many staff who merit commendation, there are also many horrible stories that go untold of mediocrity, incompetence, or even malice. As this foreword was being written in May 2008, a story was disseminated widely in the media of a kindergarten student in Florida who was having difficulty in his class related to his disability—Asperger Syndrome. According to the media reports, the kindergarten teacher had invited the other students in the (regular education) kindergarten class to express their feelings about the student in front of him and then had the students vote as to whether they wanted him to remain in the class, a vote that, tragically, was for the child to be excluded from the class.

While this story seems extreme, and may not accurately reflect what transpired, it highlights the struggles of many children with disabilities—with stigma, with exclusion, with scapegoating and hostility from other students, and with insensitivity and intolerance from staff. And it also highlights the ongoing struggles that parents face when they send their child with a disability out the door and entrust him or her to the schools. Will their special needs children be safe? Will the staff understand their disability? Will the staff have the skill to educate them adequately, let alone to educate them in a way that allows them to achieve their full potential? Will the child be able to tell the parents if something is wrong? Can the staff be trusted to raise concerns when problems develop? Can the parents share their concerns without fear of offending the school staff or provoking a defensive or hostile reaction?

Parents, clinicians, and advocates need to understand this complex system and to have as many tools as possible to work effectively within it. Unfortunately, many parents and those working with them have neither a full understanding of their rights nor of what they may reasonably expect from the schools. Further, there is all too often a huge gap between what the law appears to require and what schools actually offer. As a result, knowledge of the law is only one element for effective advocacy. It must be accompanied by awareness of the many real-world issues that may influence how the school educates the child, how it interacts with the parent, and how it responds to parental efforts to achieve the best possible education for their child.

This book provides information about the special education and disability rights laws in the United States that govern services to children with disabilities. It also describes some of the real-world issues that have an impact on how these laws are implemented. This contextual information is intended to help parents and advocates to navigate the system and to have realistic expectations about how the system works (and what may not work). Finally, it offers strategies for working within the system (and, where necessary, against the system) to promote the ability of parents to make the system work as well as possible for their child, despite the many challenges and constraints that the child and the parent may face as they pursue this goal.

The book focuses on *problems* within the system in order to help parents identify points of potential conflict and ways to address those conflicts. It is not intended as a scientific review of the regular or special education system. While there are frequent references to how the system works and does not work, these are based on my own experience and are not intended as statements of research-based statistical certainty. Given this, the observations contained in the book will likely resonate strongly for many, if not most, parents and advocates. Conversely, some readers, particularly educators and others working within the system, may vigorously object to particular observations or to the overall tone of dissatisfaction with the current system that is embedded in many of the observations and suggestions that are offered here. Yet, the book's purpose is not to focus on the system's successes, whatever or wherever they may be, but to help parents whose children are not experiencing success or who are encountering educators and schools that are not open to collaboration and mutual problem solving. As such, the focus is necessarily on ways the system fails children and families and strategies that parents, clinicians, advocates, and even educators can use to overcome these problems and achieve improved educational experiences for the children and improved working relationships among the parents, staff, and other professionals involved.

As an attorney and as a parent still traveling through the system, I recognize that there are many excellent educators of good will. But I also recognize that the system is enormously stressful, frustrating, and overwhelming for many parents. This book is my effort to assist parents so that the process is more manageable and their efforts to make a positive difference in their child's educational experience can be as effective as possible.

Acknowledgments

This book would not have been possible without the support of my staff, some of whom worked directly with me on the book, while others diligently carried on the work of the office on behalf of our clients in ways that gave me the time and freedom to devote to this project.

I thank my partner, Joe Monahan, for his commitment to the firm and to my practice. Thanks to Courtney Stillman and AnnMarie Robinson, for their ongoing dedication and phenomenal talent and effort on behalf of our clients and children with disabilities in general. I especially thank Tami Kuipers, my assistant, for her extensive help with the preparation of this book, while managing the many other elements of my day-to-day work and the needs of our clients. Appreciation is also due to the entire staff of Monahan and Cohen, for its support of our practice and my efforts, including the continuing work of Jane Vertucci, our office manager; Elissia Simmons, who efficiently and accurately transcribes much of our written material; and Marisa Renteria, Aubrey Rauch, and Bethany Relyea, who all contribute to the smooth operation of my special education practice and our entire firm.

My involvement in special education advocacy evolves from and has been continuously supported by my family, which has helped to shape my values, passion, persistence, and willingness to press on and fight for what I believe, even when at times it has seemed an uphill battle. They have also suffered the consequences of my many professional demands but have supported these efforts nonetheless. To all of them, but especially my parents and my children, I say a heartfelt special thanks.

And, finally, I acknowledge and thank the many families I have had the pleasure and pride to come to know, learn from, and represent. They show strength, courage, humor, resilience, persistence, and love, again and again, and inspire me to continue with what I do.

Introduction

All that's valuable in society depends upon the opportunity
for development accorded to the individual.

—Albert Einstein

*Tremayne, a seventh grade African-American student in a
racially divided urban school district, was being educated in
a special education classroom for children with emotional and
behavioral problems. Tremayne's behavior was deteriorating,
and he was getting very poor grades. His mother felt that he
wasn't learning anything, so she had him evaluated by a private
psychologist.*

*The psychologist concluded that Tremayne had attention
deficit/hyperactivity disorder (AD/HD), rather than an
emotional or behavioral disorder, and that he met the criteria for
mild mental impairment. Presented with this information, the
school district decided that Tremayne was too low functioning
to be regarded as having a learning disability, but too high
functioning to be labeled as mentally impaired. District officials
told Tremayne's mom that, if his behavior was being caused by
AD/HD, he shouldn't be labeled "emotionally disordered" and
that they didn't accept AD/HD as a disability that warranted
services. Therefore, Tremayne was declassified, and the school
district recommended he return to regular education without*

any support. Furthermore, because the school district now took the position that Tremayne didn't have a disability, it vigorously applied regular education disciplinary procedures, including calling the police for his minor behavioral infractions.

Shawn was a sophomore in high school. He was failing all of his classes and spent almost as many days on suspension as in school, primarily for behavior such as failing to get to class on time, failing to turn in his work on time or at all, and missing the detentions he received for these behaviors. Shawn's mother repeatedly asked school officials to help her son, but nothing was done. Finally, they told her that they thought Shawn had a drug problem and referred her to a drug clinic. Shawn was tested; the clinic ruled out any drug problem or even regular drug use and referred her to a mental health clinic. The results of that evaluation revealed that Shawn was mentally retarded and had AD/HD. He had never been tested by the school district.

Nora was a seventh grader with severe cerebral palsy and mental retardation. After she had lived in a group home in another community for a number of years, Nora's parents decided they wanted her to live at home and receive a regular education at a public school in her own community. Having never served a child with Nora's disabilities, the local school district enrolled Nora in a self-contained, segregated school for children with severe disabilities, while allowing her to attend some activities at her neighborhood school for a limited time each afternoon. Nora's parents objected to this program and sought her full time enrollment in the neighborhood school. A lengthy legal battle ensued and persisted for so long that Nora graduated from the junior high school. Her high school district, which endorsed the segregated placement, was then brought into the litigation.

Prior to 1975, many children with disabilities were routinely excluded from public education, while others were placed in inadequate segregated programs or left in regular education without any accommodations or support. The gross inadequacy of educational services for children with disabilities led to several class-action law suits, including *Mills v. District of Columbia Schools*[1] and *Pennsylvania Association for Retarded Citizens v. Commonwealth of Pennsylvania*.[2] Each of these landmark cases led to sweeping new standards for the public education of children with disabilities. These cases incorporated five bedrock principles that have become the cornerstones of special education law in the United States:

1. Children with disabilities have a right to an education.
2. This education must meet a standard of quality that is sufficient to allow the child to benefit from the education and that is individualized to meet the needs of the particular child.
3. Education must be provided to children with disabilities in the least restrictive environment appropriate to meet their needs.
4. Parents have a right to receive information about, and to participate in, decisions concerning their child's education.
5. Parents must be provided with procedural due process safeguards that ensure their access to information and their ability to participate in a meaningful way and that give them the ability to challenge the school district's decisions before a neutral decision maker.

These bedrock principles were subsequently incorporated into a new federal law, the Education of All Handicapped Children Act of 1975 (EAHCA), also known as Public Law 94-142 (PL 94-142). The EAHCA, which became effective in 1977, created a sea change in the education of children with disabilities in America. For the first time, all children with disabilities were entitled to receive an education. For the first time, all children with disabilities had a right to an education that had some relationship to their individual needs. For the first time, parents of children with disabilities were legally permitted, indeed required, to be allowed to participate in the decision making process concerning their children. For the first time, if the parents and school disagreed, the parents had legal recourse to challenge these decisions before an impartial hearing officer. These new rights were revolutionary. Indeed, they substantially eclipsed the rights of parents of children in regular education, a disparity that has increasingly become a political issue in the years since the law was enacted.

The promise and accomplishments of the system

In the year 2000, the U.S. Department of Education, members of Congress, and the disability and education community celebrated the 25th anniversary of the EAHCA, now renamed the Individuals with Disabilities Education Act (IDEA). The anniversary provided an opportunity for reflection on what had been accomplished in the special education field since the passage of the law in 1975. Neither effort nor exaggerations are required to acknowledge the enormous progress that has occurred in the education of children with disabilities since that time. With the possible exception of children displaying severe behavioral problems, a subject that will be addressed in detail much later in this book, it is now virtually unheard of for children with disabilities to be excluded from school. A vast new special education bureaucracy has been created, including special educators, evaluators, therapists, and paraprofessionals, who are charged, in conjunction with regular education teachers, with educating children with disabilities. Parents are generally more involved than they used to be in the review and planning of their children's education. Increasing numbers of children with disabilities are being educated for some or all of the day in general education classrooms, often in the school they would have attended if they did not have a disability. General educators are becoming more involved in the planning and education of kids with disabilities in their classrooms. Where disagreements between the parents and the schools occur, there are mechanisms that provide parents with mediation and/or an outside review of disputes.

These systemic changes can be seen on a day-to-day level in many classrooms, schools, and school districts across the United States. They are evident in the work of creative and inspired teachers who successfully individualize instruction for all students and in the truly individualized programs working well for particular children. These changes are especially present in aggressive training programs that keep staff on the cutting edge of new practices and techniques. They can be seen in schools that welcome parents as members of the school community, encouraging them to be involved not only in their own child's education but in the life of the school as a whole. They can be seen in increased access to technology for many children with disabilities that has profoundly impacted their lives. They can be seen in increasing numbers of classes, schools, and even entire districts that not only have children with disabilities present but also actively include them as accepted members of the class or school community. Now, teachers are finding that the techniques they are using with children with disabilities are often equally effective for all children. And they can be seen in the increasing number of children without disabilities whose educational experiences are enriched because children with disabilities as classmates are, for them, the norm rather than the exception. Parenthetically, my personal experience is that these things can occur in districts that are financially distressed as well as in districts that are wealthy (and, conversely, systemic problems may occur in wealthy districts as well as in poor ones).

Problems in the special education system

Despite the many important, positive changes that have resulted from the IDEA, its promise remains illusory for many children and families. The stories of Tremayne, Shawn, and Nora are renditions of actual stories with the names and some details changed to protect confidentiality.

Unfortunately, while the cases might seem extreme, many children with disabilities continue to encounter problems like those described in the anecdotes. For those with more mild disabilities, who may actually be able to function at a typical level if given aggressive intervention, such intervention is often denied on the grounds that the law does not require that services allow children to fulfill their maximum potential. Even for children with severe disabilities, intervention may be insufficient. Other children suffer milder forms of exclusion or mistreatment, through failure to receive accommodations, setting of irrelevant or unproductive goals and objectives, or using inappropriate or ineffective educational methods. Technology critical to a child's ability to communicate, move, participate, or learn is either not provided, or worse, not used due to untrained school personnel. Children with behavioral problems are often pushed into more restrictive settings or pushed out of school. Conversely, children with severe disabilities are too often physically present in regular education settings but denied the accommodations needed for them to participate in a meaningful way.

As an adjunct to these problems, the law's promise to parents that they can participate as equal members of the educational decision making team has sometimes been not only a hollow promise but a cruel hoax. It has raised parental expectations, while sometimes causing educators to circle the wagons in reaction to parent demands that are perceived as unrealistic and unwanted intrusions. The legally mandated individualized education program (IEP) planning meetings for students—intended to be forums for mutual sharing, collaboration, and brainstorming—instead often function as a procedure for rote recitation of written reports, for stonewalling, or even for outright hostility and contentiousness. Rather than serving as a forum for promoting communication, these meetings can become the battleground for conflicts over problems, real or imagined, big or small, between the parents and the school.

For all the progress resulting from the law, these problems are real. They are pervasive. They are borne out in my experience of over 25 years as an attorney and advocate representing families of children with disabilities. They are borne out in the experiences of many disability organizations, which consistently report that their members encounter these sorts of obstacles. They are borne out in my travels throughout the U.S. as a speaker and trainer and, as a result, a lightning rod for reports from parents of problems they are encountering. The presence of these problems does not negate the many successes of the law or the positive achievements of many educational professionals, schools, and school districts. But the continuing difficulties that some children and families face emphasize the need for better funding, more effective implementation, and informed advocacy by parents and clinicians.

Indeed, the problems are also borne out by the research and reports of federal agencies that gather data on these issues. Since the passage of the EAHCA in 1975, the U.S. Department of Education has submitted annual reports to Congress providing information about how the law is working. While these reports reflect some progress on a variety of measures concerning an appropriate education in the least restrictive environment for children with disabilities, they also document consistent gaps in performance between what should be occurring and what is. Most striking, a January 2000 report by the National Council on Disabilities (NCD), a federally funded agency charged with monitoring overall national disability policy, found that, while there was wide variation among the states in their compliance with the IDEA, not a single state was in *full* compliance with the law. Moreover, the NCD study, based on U.S. Department of Education data, found that, while the degree of compliance varied, there were essentially no requirements of the law that were being fully implemented.

Of great concern, federal studies continue to document the persistent reality that the educational outcomes for children with disabilities are dismal in relation to those of the regular education population. Both the drop out rates and rates of unemployment and underemployment remain disproportionately high for children with disabilities in comparison to the nondisabled population. The IDEA 2004 congressional findings concluded that implementation of the IDEA "has been impeded by low expectations and an insufficient focus on applying replicable research on proven methods of teaching and learning for children with disabilities."[3] These problems are real. They are pervasive.

The problems faced by people with disabilities and their families

Systemic problems confound the many challenges that families of children with disabilities face on a daily basis. First and foremost, individuals and families must come to grips with the fact of the disability and deal with the complex emotions it inevitably produces. Despite the assumption of people unfamiliar with disability, this process, like the grieving process, is not entirely sequential. Rather, it is an ongoing process in which the many different complex emotions may be triggered again by new events, accomplishments, challenges, insults, or disappointments. Indeed, the all-too-familiar refrain that "those parents haven't come to grips with their child's disability" is more often reflective of the simplistic judgments of people who haven't lived the reality than it is an accurate diagnosis of a family's problems.

But the challenges for children with disabilities and their families don't end there. Families are at once highly dependent on clinicians, educators, and other professionals—both to understand their child's disability and to know what to do about it—while simultaneously also needing to critically assess the advice they receive. They find themselves asking many questions: Does the diagnosis fit with our impression of our child? Do we understand what we have been told? Are we getting consistent opinions from different professionals? Do the recommendations make sense? Are they consistent with our desires and our values?

In addition, parents want to trust the educator, the doctor, the psychologist, the lawyer. Yet, they know the experts are not always right—or they may be clinically correct but seeing information through their own bias or prejudice. In my experience, it is not uncommon for children to be diagnosed with a disability that they don't actually have or to be diagnosed as not having a disability when they do. It is also not uncommon for parents to be told, in relation to a very young child, "Your child will never speak," "Your child will never be able to read," or "Your child will need to be in an institution," when those statements prove to be incorrect. Parents must simultaneously rely on experts, while becoming critical consumers and experts in their own right.

The complicated relationship parents have with private professionals plays out even more intensely with public school educators. Many of us grew up in an era when schools and teachers were revered. We trusted the schools and, short of where we chose to live, had a limited ability to have an impact on the education our children received. Educators, as is true of any professional, wish to be respected, and many prefer the autonomy with which they were historically vested. Yet, many parents in the special education world feel that they know more than the educators do about their child, about his or her disability, and about how their child should be educated. For some, this may actually be true. An inherent tension is built into the parent/school relationship because the law, according to the Supreme Court, requires the school only to provide an education that offers "some benefit," whereas parents naturally want the best education possible for their children.

These problems occur in the context of a society that has paid lip service to the rights of people with disabilities yet simultaneously perpetuates prejudice and separation at many levels. While we have done a good job of building curb cuts and installing Braille numbers on elevators, our society has not progressed significantly in our attitudes about people with disabilities and our willingness to provide accommodations that are active rather than passive. We have not moved from the stage of accommodation to the point of real inclusion. Can we expect the schools effectively to serve (and integrate) children with disabilities when the society at large does not? At one level, the schools are an important starting point in this effort, but, at another level, they also reflect what is (and is not) happening in the culture as a whole. People with disabilities and their families often feel disenfranchised—not necessarily entirely excluded but not fully included either. Worse, they may be the victims of overt hostility or discrimination due to disability, such as the bullying or harassment of a child, refusal of medical care ("I don't want to deal with someone like that in my practice"), or employment discrimination.

To add insult to injury, the shortcomings of the educational, medical, and human-services systems frequently mean that parents must serve as the ultimate case managers for the child. Most parents of nondisabled children can comfortably "turn their children over" to the schools, to doctors, to daycare, to camp, to summer jobs, and the like. They may choose to be more involved because that is their desire, but they often do not need to be more involved. By contrast, parents of children with disabilities typically must remain actively engaged in every activity in which their child participates; they must select providers, monitor progress, implement programs, check on communication, assure that other teachers or providers are told what the primary providers have agreed to, ensure that information follows the child from place to place and year to year, and more. A recent study from the University of Iowa highlighted this problem, finding that 48 percent of school nurses reported problems with consistent and correct administration of medications at school in the prior year.[4] Even with respect to something as obviously important as the precise and reliable administration of medication, there is evidence that parents cannot trust the professional providers to do the job right consistently—or do it at all.

The role of clinicians

As the comments above suggest, private doctors, evaluators, and therapists play a critical and often disproportionate role in influencing how children with disabilities are understood and perceived, both by parents and educators, and in shaping the direction of a child's treatment and education. Private clinicians are uniquely positioned to assist parents in obtaining a comprehensive understanding of the nature and extent of a child's disabilities. They can give the parents hope or cause the parents to feel hopeless. They can help to empower the parents and give them resources and options, or they can give the parents a sense that there are few or no options for their child. They can work collaboratively with the parents in charting a course for the child that maximizes the child's opportunity for independence or convey that the child will be dependent, so that fostering independence seems a waste of time.

Often, physicians, psychologists, speech therapists, and occupational or physical therapists may be the first professionals sharing information with the parents about the child's disability. They can impact how the parents understand the disability and help them work through the many complex reactions (of disappointment, grief, fear, anger, expectation, helplessness, and even denial) in order to help them reach more positive and productive reactions. Equally important, through their own efforts and by connecting parents with information and support groups, they can help parents feel that they are not alone, that there are other people out there with shared experiences.

In terms of a child's future educational career, private clinicians can also play a pivotal role. At times, they may reach a diagnosis that has implications for a child's education before the school has even evaluated the child. At other times, private evaluators may be following up on an evaluation that the public school has already conducted—and may reach a different conclusion. Evaluators might decide that the child has a disability when the school concluded that the child did not (or vice versa); they may also decide that the child has a different disability from the one identified by the school. Apart from reaching a diagnosis, the evaluator can often provide a wide range of recommendations, both to the parents and to the school, about the type of special education services that are needed, the methodologies that should be used to instruct the child, the amount of services the child should receive, and whether these services should be in regular education or special education. Evaluators can also recommend various accommodations or, for a child with behavioral problems, various behavioral intervention strategies.

Such findings and recommendations represent a critical starting point for parents. However, evaluators can often do even more. They can give the parents feedback about programs to seek out or avoid and strategies for working with the school. They can even go to the school meetings with the parents to assist them and the school staff in developing an appropriate program for the child.

Given the important contributions that private clinicians can and should provide for children with disabilities, it is critical that clinicians be aware of special education laws and how they work. If clinicians are not able to operate comfortably in the educational milieu and use the necessary special education terminology—a language all its own—their effectiveness may be diminished because they won't be able to express things in ways that get results. For example, as will be discussed in detail, if a clinician recommends what is "best" for a child, as opposed to what she feels is "necessary" for a child, she may be giving the school district license to ignore her recommendations. This simple difference of wording can make a significant difference in how the school staff or a hearing officer responds to the clinician's recommendations. Clinicians will do their clients an enormous service if they equip themselves with the knowledge needed to understand the special education system.

The purpose of this book

The purpose of enumerating these problems is not to introduce a polemic against the American special education system. Rather, it is to provide the backdrop for this advocacy manual. At its core, the law gives parents of children with disabilities and clinicians broad opportunities to influence the quality of education for a particular child and for the system as a whole. Yet, the people affected by the law can use the system effectively only if they have a clear understanding of how it is supposed to work, how it actually works, and what strategies will make it work more effectively. As many have already discovered, the laws are complex and subject to interpretation. The education system is also complex, and schools are often less than forthcoming in sharing with parents how the system works and what options are available. Strategies for working within the system range from the obvious to the subtle but are always dependent on the particular situation. For example, a parent's request for a one-on-one aide for a child may be obvious and noncontroversial in the case of a child with severe physical impairments, whereas it may be highly controversial and hotly contested in the case of a child with behavioral problems, autism, or AD/HD.

This book will provide a detailed overview of what the law says and how it works. It will identify sources of controversy or dispute between schools and parents and provide practical strategies for building successful relationships with schools and overcoming barriers to effective services. In order to understand the context of the conflicts that arise between parents and schools, a discussion of the politics and psychology of special education will also be provided.

Thus, the purpose of this book is to empower parents, clinicians, and advocates by giving them the necessary information to be effective partners with educators and other professionals and to help them, where necessary, be more effective advocates. The intent is not to promote conflict. Indeed, the information and strategies in the book will help people obtain what is needed without conflict. On the other hand, it is sometimes the case that, despite the parents' efforts or even mutual efforts between parents and schools to avoid conflict, aggressive advocacy and/or legal actions become the only means for obtaining the services to which a child is entitled. Teddy Roosevelt once said, "Walk softly, but carry a big stick." In the complex world of special education, parents and clinicians can navigate the walkway well (and softly) only if they have a good map. Often, the "big stick" need not be an adversarial proceeding but merely a display of knowledge and assertiveness that conveys an ability to use the adversarial process if necessary. This book is intended to give the reader both a good map, and the information necessary to choose wisely when to walk softly and when a stick is needed.

$E=MC^2$ Advocacy Strategies

Albert Einstein wrote that, "[i]n matters of truth and justice, there is no difference between large and small problems, for issues concerning the treatment of people are all the same."[5] As it happens, Einstein's theory of relativity provides a model for understanding the importance of individual action in the face of inequity, inadequacy, or discrimination in the treatment of children with disabilities, indeed in relation to unfair treatment and oppression of all types. In relation to the theory of relativity, Einstein stated, "It followed from the special theory of relativity that mass and energy are both but different manifestations of the same thing—a somewhat unfamiliar conception for the average mind. Furthermore, the equation $E=MC^2$, in which energy is put equal to mass multiplied by the square of the velocity of light, showed that a very small amount of mass may be converted into a large amount of energy and vice versa."[6]

Einstein's theory of relativity suggests that, in many situations an individual may appear to be relatively powerless, but, through the exertion of energy, he or she is capable of exerting enormous power on the circumstance he or she is struggling with. Dr. Michio Kaku wrote of Einstein's theory of relativity that, "[s]ince the speed of light was a fantastically large number and its square was even larger, this meant that even a tiny amount of matter could release a fabulous amount of energy."[7] Similarly, advocacy efforts by parents or others on behalf of children with disabilities, though difficult and perhaps at times overwhelming, can have an enormous impact on the quality of the child's education. Such efforts can even result in changing the systems that are providing services to the child.

Throughout this book, a variation of Einstein's theory of relativity will be presented. Rather than focusing on the equation as stated in physics (energy equals mass times the speed of light squared), a different formula will be used: Empowerment (E) = Making (M) Change for Children (C^2) ($E=MC^2$). Incorporated throughout the chapters, readers will be provided with "$E=MC^2$ advocacy strategies" to assist in utilizing the legal and practical information for effective action on behalf of children with disabilities.

An explanation of the contents

In Chapter 1, the book starts with a brief overview of both the IDEA and Section 504 of the Rehabilitation Act of 1973. Section 504 is a federal law that prohibits discrimination against persons with disabilities in any program or activity that receives federal financial assistance. Section 504 provides important legal protections and is often a basis for accommodations and services for children with disabilities, even if they are not covered by the IDEA.

The next chapters provide a detailed examination of the key components of the IDEA, accompanied by practical strategies for using them and, where appropriate, sample letters to be adapted as needed for particular cases. The discussion of the IDEA covers the following categories: eligibility (Chapter 2); evaluation, reevaluation, and independent evaluation (Chapter 3); free appropriate public education and the individualized education program process (Chapter 4); special education and related services (Chapter 5); least restrictive environment requirements (Chapter 6); private placement issues (Chapter 7); behavior management and discipline (Chapter 8); transition from special education and graduation (Chapter 9); and mediation and due process procedures (Chapter 10).

The full discussion of the IDEA is followed in Chapter 11 by a more detailed overview of Section 504 and how it works and a comparison of the relative advantages and disadvantages of Section 504 and the IDEA for children with disabilities.

Chapter 12 provides my thoughts about the political and psychological issues that contribute to the difficulties many parents and schools face in addressing the needs of children with disabilities and my final thoughts about the system, including how parents, clinicians, and advocates should use it so it works better.

In Chapter 13, I present an introductory explanation of the relationship between federal law and state law; the hierarchy of the different types of laws and regulations; and an explanation of the interplay between the law as written and how it is interpreted by the courts, the U.S. Department of Education, state education agencies, and school districts.

After the concluding chapter (Chapter 14), a number of appendices are provided, including important Web sites, a glossary of common acronyms used in special education, a list of disability groups and advocacy resources, methods for obtaining the necessary laws and regulations, and examples of sample letters for key communications with the school system.

Disclaimers

A number of disclaimers or cautions are necessary as an introduction to this book. First, as will be discussed in greater detail in Chapter 13, this book, by necessity, focuses on federal law for several reasons. The IDEA and Section 504 are the basis for all the state special education laws. State laws may provide rights to individuals that exceed federal rights, but they cannot erode or reduce the federal protections. State laws can fill in gaps that are not addressed by federal law—and there are many—but they cannot contradict federal law. In the special education domain, federal law is generally the ultimate authority.

In addition, because there are areas where the laws and mechanisms for implementing the laws may differ from state to state, it would be impractical to provide a detailed analysis of each state's statutes and regulations and how they compare to federal law. For example, in some states, a child may be labeled as developmentally delayed through age 9, while, in others, the child may carry that label only through age 6. In some states, a party appealing a due process decision will be required to file an appeal in court within 30 days of an adverse decision, whereas, in another state, parties may be able to file an appeal up to two years after the decision. Sometimes, the difference is not one of substance but one of wording. For example, different states use different terminology to describe the meetings that are legally required to develop an individualized education program (IEP). Thus, while this book provides a detailed framework for understanding special education law, *it is still essential that readers consult their state's special education laws and statutes to verify the details of how the system works in their area.* In some instances, I will highlight those topics or issues where checking state law or procedure is especially important.

It should also be recognized that special education law is ever-changing. Congress regularly considers and passes new revisions or amendments. The U.S. Department of Education periodically issues new regulations and interpretations. The courts are constantly refining our understanding of the law based on their judicial interpretations of its meaning. As a result, special education law is not a static mandate. The reader is always well advised to check information provided in any publication to make sure it is up to date and accurate, but this is especially true in relation to legal requirements. A number of resources are identified in the appendices to assist readers in this regard.

For a number of reasons, including the ones just described, readers must be absolutely clear that *this book does not provide legal advice.* If readers have a legal problem or a legal question, they are strongly encouraged to seek legal counsel and are directed to the Web sites listed in Appendix A, which provides resources for finding knowledgeable advocates and lawyers. Surely, no one would feel confident in a medical diagnosis made when the doctor had neither met the patient nor seen the results of tests that had been performed. Similarly, the reader should not substitute general information and strategy for the individualized information that would be provided by a knowledgeable special education advocate or attorney in response to a particular case. In fact, it cannot be stressed enough that every child is different, every case is different, and every legal and political interchange is unique. These facts create both opportunities and hazards, but the reader must exercise great caution in overgeneralizing from the suggestions of this book or from the advice given by other sources, particularly from the parent grapevine or the Internet. For example, just because your friend's child has the same disability label does not mean that your child is necessarily entitled to the same services.

The challenges facing children with disabilities and their families are daunting. In the face of these challenges, parents rise to the needs of their children and immerse themselves in learning about their child's disability, the educational system, and their legal rights. This book is about these systems, but it is also about the translation of this knowledge to the creation of successful relationships and, where necessary, the use of information to exert power in support of children. Unfortunately, while the special education system has dramatically improved, it still has many flaws. For many children, the promise that special education would promote their path to independence in adulthood has not been realized. This book is intended to empower parents, clinicians, and advocates to ensure that the system provides children with all that they are legally entitled to, in order to raise the bar in terms of what schools provide and children achieve.

Gaining knowledge is the first step in gaining power. The information and strategies described in this book will assist all of those involved with children with disabilities, improving the quality of individual services and the responsiveness of the system as a whole.

CHAPTER 1

An Overview of Legal Protections for Children with Disabilities

C hildren with disabilities may, depending on the circumstances, be eligible for the protections of the Individuals with Disabilities Education Act (IDEA), Section 504 of the Rehabilitation Act of 1973, both of these laws, or neither. In order to understand the special education system and the protections that are potentially available for children with disabilities, it is important to understand both laws, how they interact, and under what circumstances they are applicable. Also, both laws are used in very different ways, depending on the school system and the disability. Given three children with identical needs, one school system may address the child's needs under the IDEA, another under Section 504, and the third may refuse services or provide them through regular education. Depending on the circumstances, all of these options might be reasonable; but, in many instances, one option may be more appropriate, even if it is not agreed to by the school system. This chapter provides an introduction to these laws to provide a context for the more detailed discussion to follow.

A brief overview of the 1975 IDEA

The IDEA, originally called the Education for All Handicapped Children (EAHCA) or Public Law 94-142, is a statute that provides states (and local school districts) with federal funding on the condition that the states adhere to the special education requirements established by the U.S. Congress. The IDEA was intended to provide enough federal money to make special education services affordable for states and school districts. Congress promised that the federal government would provide 40 percent of the funds states need to deliver special education services. Unfortunately, since the law was passed, Congress has *never* provided that level of federal funding. In fact, in recent years, the federal funding is inching toward only 20 percent of the total cost, and promised increases seem illusory.

Adopting the five benchmark principles of the Pennsylvania and District of Columbia court cases (discussed in the introduction), Congress incorporated into the IDEA sweeping and detailed requirements for how special education was to be delivered, including requirements for parental participation and for outside review.

The provisions of the IDEA were further clarified by U.S. Department of Education regulations that became effective in 1977. The IDEA has been amended several times since 1975, most recently in 2004, and will be due for review in 2009, though this review will more likely not occur until 2010 or beyond. The Department of Education regulations have, as a result, also been modified several times to make regulations conform to the new provisions of the law. This occurred most recently in 2006.

Throughout this book, where references are made to specific provisions of the IDEA or Section 504, the references will be to the federal regulations interpreting the law, as they are more detailed. The federal regulations for the IDEA begin at 34 Code of Federal Regulations (CFR) 300. The references to the Section 504 regulations begin at 34 CFR 104.

At its core, the IDEA requires that, in order to be eligible for special education services, a child must meet the criteria for at least one of the categories of disability specified by the law. The disability has to affect educational performance adversely and require special education services. The judgments about whether a qualifying disability exists must be made based on a comprehensive, multidisciplinary evaluation, carried out by professionals trained to conduct the necessary testing and using nondiscriminatory tests created for the specific purposes for which they are being used. Equally important is that parental consent is required both prior to the initiation of testing and prior to the initiation of special education services. The law also calls for periodic reevaluation and requires schools to consider and, under some circumstances, pay for independent educational evaluations. In addition, on December 1, 2008, the U.S. Department of Education issued final regulations amending several important rules relating to special education and the Individuals with Disabilities Education Act. These regulations took effect on December 31, 2008. Two changes are of particular importance for all parents and for educators.

First, for the first time in the history of special education, parents now have the right to revoke consent at any time to their child's participation in special education. The revocation must be provided to the school district in writing. The parent must be provided with a notice from the school district indicating that the revocation constitutes a change of placement/ status and explaining the parents' rights. The parents or the school may at a subsequent date request that the child be reconsidered for special education again. However, if the parents revoke the consent for special education, the school is not responsible for the failure to provide a free appropriate education. The new regulation addressing this issue is 34 Code of Federal Regulations 300.300(b). If the parent revokes consent, the school district may not pursue a due process hearing or other legal measures to overturn the parents' decision.

The second major change involves representation at due process hearings. Previously, prevailing interpretation of the IDEA provided that the parents could be assisted at due process hearings by non-lawyers, regardless of the state's rules regarding unauthorized practice of law by non-attorneys. Under the new IDEA regulations, the rules as to whether a non-lawyer may represent either the parent or the school at a due process hearing will now be governed by state law. It will now be necessary for parents to investigate the rules in their state regarding unauthorized practice of law.[1]

The most fundamental requirement of the law is that children with disabilities who are eligible for special education services are entitled to receive a "free appropriate public education" (commonly referred to as FAPE). While this term continues to be the source of controversy and litigation to this day, it is unquestionable that Congress, in using this language, intended to set a floor of opportunity—a minimum standard of educational quality that the schools are required to meet in providing services to children with disabilities. The law specifies that, in order to receive an FAPE, children with disabilities must be provided with special education and related services necessary for them to benefit from their education. These services are to be provided pursuant to an individualized education program (IEP) that is tailored to meet the unique needs of the particular student. In a dramatic departure from regular education procedures, these IEPs must be developed with the full participation of the parents and must be reviewed and revised as needed, but at least annually.

Hand in hand with the requirement that an FAPE be provided, the IDEA also requires that the special education program be delivered in the least restrictive environment appropriate for the child. The schools are obligated to provide support to children with disabilities to help them be successful in regular education where possible. Even where a child with a disability is to be educated for part or all of the day in an environment other than a regular education setting, such as a special education class, the law requires that the child be "mainstreamed"—or included with typically developing peers—to the maximum extent appropriate. This means that the child should still be able to participate in regular education as much as possible, even if his or her primary educational programming is being delivered outside of regular education.

The IDEA also sets out a broad array of legal protections for children and parents, again beyond those of regular education. Parents have the right to access their child's educational records, including all results of testing. They have the right to be notified of any proposal to initiate, change, or terminate programs or services and to participate in the decisions surrounding those proposals. They have the right to be informed in advance of any formal IEP meetings, including receiving information about who will be invited and what will be discussed, and to have the meetings occur at a convenient time. There are also extensive rules relating to how schools should respond to children with disabilities who are having behavioral problems, including procedures for promoting positive behavioral intervention strategies to respond to problem behavior and detailed procedures for what schools may do in response to serious behavioral difficulties.

In order to ensure that all of these requirements are fully carried out and recognizing the importance of parental participation and empowerment, the law also gives parents (and school districts) the right to request an impartial hearing to resolve disputes concerning a school district's proposals, action, or even failure to act. Parents may request hearings for a wide array of reasons, including a school district's refusal to evaluate a child or make the child eligible for services, a school district's proposal to place the child in a program or setting parents disagree with, a school's failure to provide sufficient or effective services, a school's decision to discipline a child in a way the parents disagree with, or a school's decision to terminate services or even graduate a child when the parent feels the child needs more help. Schools may also request hearings against parents, for reasons including the parent's refusal to consent to have their child evaluated.

The IDEA also sets forth rules for how these impartial hearings must be conducted. The rules include the rights to have a hearing within a specified time frame, to have an attorney involved, to receive all written evidence at least five days prior to the start of the hearing, to present written evidence and oral testimony and to cross examine any witnesses presented by the opposing party, to receive a written or electronic transcript of the proceedings, and to receive a written order from the hearing officer. Either party may appeal the decision of the impartial hearing officer to a court if they are dissatisfied with the outcome. (State laws specify the statute of limitations period or deadline for filing a due process request or an appeal in court.) Some states also provide a second level of administrative review prior to appealing in court.

In an effort to avoid where possible due process and court proceedings, the law also provides for a voluntary mediation procedure. In this procedure, the parents and the school district can meet with an independent and impartial mediator in an effort to reach an agreement about their particular dispute. Mediation can occur only if both parties agree to participate. However, mediation is not like binding arbitration. The mediator has no power, and, if the mediation is unsuccessful, the parties retain the ability to go forward with a due process hearing if needed. In my own experience, as will be described in detail, mediation is a very valuable process that often resolves disputes that appeared impossible to resolve.

In 2004, Congress added an alternative to mediation, prior to a due process hearing, called a "resolution session." This meeting is intended to provide the parties an opportunity to resolve the dispute prior to proceeding to a hearing, but does not include a mediator.

The IDEA, in short, provides sweeping and detailed requirements for the provision of appropriate educational services to children with disabilities, as well as broad mandates for parental involvement in decision making. If anything, the several rounds of revisions of the law, most recently in 2004, as previously stated, have led to even more prescriptive rules regarding school conduct, in recognition of a persistent lack of compliance by the schools with existing procedures. This has set up a paradoxical situation in which noncompliance begets greater regulation, which, in turn, precipitates greater tension but not necessarily improved compliance. In some circumstances, Section 504 may then come into play as a mechanism to address a dispute that is not resolvable within the parameters of the IDEA.

A brief overview of Section 504 of the Rehabilitation Act of 1973

Unlike the IDEA, Section 504 is a civil rights law, rather than a funding statute. Its requirements are simple and direct:

> No otherwise qualified individual with a disability in the United States . . . , shall, solely by reason of her or his disability, be excluded from the participation in, be denied the benefits of, or be subjected to discrimination under any program or activity receiving Federal financing assistance.

Section 504 does not provide any federal funding. Rather, like several other civil rights laws, it attaches civil rights protections to any federal funds provided to a public or private organization. Because all states and school districts receive federal funds for a wide variety of activities, they are all governed by the Section 504 requirements. While the IDEA contains clear directives with respect to the special education procedures schools must follow if they elect to accept federal money, Section 504 contains only the language cited above. The specific rules implementing Section 504 are either contained in the regulations adopted by the federal government or have been established by virtue of court rulings and the Department of Education's interpretations of its requirements and limits. This means that the rules governing implementation of the IDEA are clearer than those of Section 504.

Under Section 504, a person is covered if he or she has a physical or mental impairment that substantially limits a major life activity, if he or she is perceived as having such an impairment, or if he or she has a history of having such an impairment. The law offers no specific categories of disability and no specific criteria for eligibility. But, under the law, learning itself is considered a major life activity. Thus, children with disabilities are protected by Section 504 if they have a disability that substantially limits learning and/or other major life activities.

Like the IDEA, the decision about whether a student qualifies must be made based on an evaluation that utilizes nondiscriminatory testing procedures. Unlike the IDEA, however, these procedures are described only in a general way. If it is determined that a child does have a physical or mental impairment that substantially limits learning or other major life activities, the school must also determine whether the child needs special education, related services, or accommodations in order to benefit from education. This is a key difference from the IDEA, which is aimed solely at children who require special education in order to be educated successfully.

For example, consider the case of a child with severe asthma. If the child receives medication for the asthma at school, he or she may still have some difficulty at school but is able to function there. However, if the child does not receive the medication at school, he or she can become severely ill and cannot remain at school. The child is thus considered to be disabled and in need of related services (i.e., the administration of the medication). If the services allow the child to participate in school, he or she is eligible for protection under Section 504. Because special education instructional services are not needed to address the asthma problem, the child is not likely to be eligible for the IDEA special education services. (The distinctions surrounding eligibility, including the impact of medication and other mitigating measures on application of Section 504, will be discussed in greater detail in Chapter 11.)

Once it is determined that children meet the criteria for the disability protections of Section 504, they must be protected from discrimination based on that disability. In order to assure access to an appropriate opportunity for education, the Section 504 regulations provide that the child is entitled to receive a "free appropriate public education," similar to that required by the IDEA, though the terms are not interpreted entirely the same way under the two laws. This education may include the special education and related services that are needed for the child to benefit from education. Many people mistakenly assume that Section 504 provides only accommodations that can be delivered in regular education, whereas special education services are available only through the IDEA. While this assumption accurately describes how many schools operate, it does not accurately reflect the Section 504 regulatory mandate for provision of a FAPE.

However, in contrast to IDEA, the Section 504 regulations neither spell out the procedures for development of a Section 504 plan nor spell out the content or structure of the plan. In addition, in most areas, there is no Section 504 bureaucracy comparable to the one established under the IDEA. Depending on the circumstances, this can be a good or bad thing, but it generally means that services are more likely to be delivered by regular education staff, as opposed to special education staff.

Like the IDEA, Section 504 also requires that services be delivered in the least restrictive environment appropriate for the child. Further, Section 504 provides that those children who are not primarily based in regular classroom settings should still be mainstreamed to the maximum extent appropriate. The Section 504 regulations also provide that children must be reevaluated before schools decide whether to place them in special education settings or make "any subsequent significant change" in their placement.[2]

In addition, Section 504 allows for parents to request an impartial hearing to challenge a school's actions or its failure to act. Unlike the IDEA, however, Section 504 regulations allow the school district to determine the hearing procedure and, unless directed otherwise by the state, to appoint the hearing officer. Again, the regulatory provisions here are far less detailed than those under the IDEA. On the other hand, unlike the options provided for by the IDEA, parents who feel a school district is violating Section 504 can also file a complaint with the Office for Civil Rights of the U.S. Department of Education, which is charged with enforcing Section 504. This can be done without involvement of an attorney and at no cost to the parent.

The Americans with Disabilities Act of 1990

Many people are familiar with the Americans with Disabilities Act. The ADA is a sweeping law that protects people with disabilities from discrimination in employment and requires that they have equal access to state and local government services and to places of public accommodation, including private businesses. The ADA substantially tracks the requirements of the Section 504 regulations, but goes even further in a number of areas because it applies to most private programs and businesses, regardless of whether they accept federal funding. In many ways, however, the ADA and Section

504 protections are similar. Because Section 504 protections were already in place in relation to public schools when the ADA was adopted, this book will not deal with the ADA in much detail.

The interplay of the IDEA and Section 504

Unquestionably, the IDEA and its implementing regulations—combined with the Department of Education and judicial interpretations of the IDEA—provide far more detail about how the IDEA is supposed to operate than the level of detail provided under Section 504. This increased level of regulation provides for greater accountability but can also limit the flexibility of parents and schools alike. As will be discussed in depth in Chapter 11, each statute has advantages depending on the circumstances of the particular case. It would be a mistake to assume that either is inherently better under all circumstances. In fact, creative use of both can sometimes provide opportunities for addressing a child's needs in ways that would not otherwise be contemplated. On the other hand, a lack of awareness of the pitfalls of each can mean that a child's needs may not be adequately addressed and/or that parents are unable to avail themselves fully of the legal protections to which they are entitled. To help clarify what these legal protections mean and how they can best be used, Chapter 13 provides an explanation of the hierarchy and interaction of federal and state laws, regulations, judicial decisions, and agency interpretations.

CHAPTER 2

Eligibility

The Individuals with Disabilities Education Act (IDEA) covers a wide range of children with disabilities. However, to qualify for special education services, the child must meet the criteria for at least one of the 13 categories of disability that the act encompasses. In some cases, the federal criteria are reasonably specific. In other instances, the criteria for a particular disability are very general. To complicate matters further, the IDEA gives the states discretion to set the criteria for some of the disabilities.

The 13 categories of disability are the following:

- ■ mental retardation
- ■ hearing impairments including deafness
- ■ speech or language impairments
- ■ visual impairments, including blindness
- ■ emotional disturbance
- ■ orthopedic impairments
- ■ autism
- ■ traumatic brain injury
- ■ other health impairments
- ■ specific learning disabilities
- ■ deaf-blindness
- ■ deafness
- ■ multiple disabilities.[1]

In addition to these categories, there is a special category of "developmental delay" for children who are 3–6 years of age. The statute gives states the discretion to allow children up to the age of 9 to be labeled as "developmentally delayed." The states vary whether to limit the use of "developmental delay" to the minimum ages allowed by the statute or to extend its use up through the age of 9.[2] This category was specifically adopted for younger children because of the difficulty of accurately diagnosing many disabilities when children are very young. Thus, the "developmental delay" category focuses on the child's developmental progress, without regard to whether the child has been given a specific diagnosis in relation to a particular disability.

In some instances, a child may meet the criteria for more than one disability category. Some states and school districts designate a particular disability as the primary disability, while any additional disabilities are identified as secondary disabilities. However, once a child is determined eligible for special education, the particular label—and/or the designation of a particular label as primary or secondary—should not impact the special education and related services the child needs.[3] Rather, the child's evaluation and program are supposed to be based on his or her individual needs, regardless of disability label.[4] Further, once a child is determined to be eligible for special education, the school is supposed to address not only the direct symptoms of the child's disability but also the indirect or collateral consequences of the child's disability. For example, a child may be identified as having a learning disability but suffer low self esteem as a consequence of that disability. The school should not only address the learning disability, but the self esteem problem as well.[5]

It is important to note that to qualify for special education services, the child must not only meet the criteria for one or more of the disability categories, but the disability must also cause an adverse effect on his or her educational performance. Further, the child must require special education intervention to ameliorate the disability's adverse effect.[6]

The phrase *adverse effect on educational performance* has been the source of much controversy, confusion, and litigation. Some schools interpret the phrase to mean that the child must be experiencing problems with academic functioning as reflected in low grades and/or low achievement scores. These schools often take the position that a child is not eligible for special education if he or she is passing and making some measurable academic progress.

The latter interpretation, however, flies in the face of the spirit, intent, and language of the IDEA. The law was written to encompass a wide range of areas of functioning, with the intent to assist children with disabilities to be as independent as possible upon graduation from high school.[7] The skills measured by grades and achievement test scores do not address many of the life skills needed for independent functioning. It would make little sense for the law to have such a broad purpose and yet have its implementation limited to skills related solely to academics. In fact, the law goes well beyond academic skills, requiring evaluation of the child's functioning in a wide variety of domains and the provision of special education and related services to address a wide variety of needs.[8]

That the law requires a focus on overall development as a basis for determining eligibility was settled early in the life of the IDEA, in the *Timothy W. v. Rochester School District* case, which adopted a zero reject position in relation to eligibility for special education, holding that even a child suffering from cerebral palsy, seizure disorder, and cortical blindness— and who had limited awareness or ability to communicate—was entitled to special education services. According to that ruling, schools may not require that children demonstrate that they can benefit from traditional education to be eligible for special education.[9]

The IDEA's requirement that eligibility be based on factors beyond academic performance is even more clearly borne out by its 2004 amendments. The 2004 act made repeated references to the need to assess and remediate not only academic deficits but developmental and functional deficits as well.[10] The inclusion of this broader language, which is repeated throughout the amendments in relation to the individualized education program (IEP) and transition planning as well, makes it clear that eligibility cannot be denied simply because a child is making progress as measured by grades or achievement test scores. The services must be offered as long as the disability is adversely affecting educational functioning in some significant way.[11]

E=MC² Advocacy Strategies

(1) Schools sometimes contend that a child's behavioral, social, organizational, or other areas of difficulty (such as hygiene) are not evidence of the child's disability's adverse effect on educational

performance. If this happens, consult the child's report card, which almost always contains ratings or comments that address these issues. It would make little sense that the school would evaluate these characteristics on report cards if they are not part of the school's educational program.

(2) Most schools and school districts have mission statements. Typically, these mission statements make reference to the goal of promoting each child's growth, with the desire that each child become a self sufficient and productive citizen to the extent possible. A focus exclusively on academic growth would be contrary to the school's mission statement.

(3) States now have statewide performance standards for schools. These standards often incorporate not only academic attainment but also social, communication, vocational, and emotional development. Again, to predicate eligibility for special education exclusively or even predominantly on academic performance would be contradictory to these state standards

Historically, some schools have also interpreted the "requires special education" tenet very narrowly. In some instances, parents may be discouraged from pursuing or accepting special education eligibility because they fear that the law's requirement that their child "needs special education" to qualify for special education means their child will have to receive instruction in a segregated special education classroom. Unfortunately, this misperception is sometimes encouraged by school administrators who are trying to dissuade parents from pursuing services.

In fact, the law is clear that special education is a service, not a place. The IDEA requires that schools provide a continuum of special education services, ranging from support for the child within the regular education classroom to provision of support in a special education class for a limited part of the day to placement in a self-contained special education classroom for a majority of the day, up to and including placement in separate special education day schools or residential treatment centers.[12] Further, the IDEA defines special education as specially designed instruction including adapting, as needed, the content, methodology, and mode of delivery of instruction.[13] The definition says nothing to suggest that a child may receive special education instruction *only* in a special education classroom. The law requires quite the contrary: that children be educated in the least restrictive environment to the maximum extent appropriate.[14]

E=MC² Advocacy Strategies

Some children may not meet the IDEA eligibility requirements for receiving specially designed instruction to address the adverse impacts of their disability. For example, a child who requires that a nurse administer medication at school or a special air conditioning system to address allergies may not need specially designed instruction. However, children whose disabilities require accommodations or the provision of related services—but not specialized instruction—can still qualify for the protections of Section 504 of the Rehabilitation Act of 1973. Section 504 protections are addressed in Chapter 11.

To put this in other terms, the IDEA requires that children be made eligible for special education if they have a disability that meets the criteria of one or more disability category, if the disability adversely affects the child's functioning at school, and if the child requires specially designed instruction to address the adverse effect of the disability. The six disability categories with the majority of identified children are emotional disturbance, specific learning disability, other health impaired, autism, speech/language impairment, and mental retardation. These eligibility categories are discussed in detail below. The remaining categories are briefly referenced along with Web resources relevant to that category that can be found in Appendix A at the end of the book.

Emotional disturbance

The category of disability called *emotional disturbance* (ED) actually covers both emotional and behavioral disorders. In fact, for better or worse, eligibility under this category is based primarily on problematic behavioral characteristics rather than on the presence of symptoms that meet the criteria for mental illness. Under the IDEA, the definition of emotional disturbance is the following:

a condition exhibiting one or more of the following characteristics over a long period of time and to a marked degree that adversely affects a child's educational performance: (A) An inability to learn that cannot be explained by intellectual, sensory, or health factors; (B) An inability to build or maintain satisfactory interpersonal relationships with peers and teachers; (C) Inappropriate types of behavior or feelings under normal circumstances; (D) A general pervasive mood of unhappiness or depression; (E) A tendency to develop physical symptoms or fears associated with personal or school problems.[15]

Not only does the child have to exhibit at least one of the behavioral characteristics listed, but the behavior also has to be present chronically, which means over a long period of time, and to a marked degree, which means it is present in a severe form. For example, a child who refuses to come to school for a prolonged period of time due to school phobia might be eligible based on the chronic nature of the phobia, whereas a child who wants to cut school to go on a one-time trip with his buddies would not be eligible based on that one event, even though the behavior violated school attendance policies.

While the criteria are behaviorally focused, rather than based on diagnosis of mental illness, they do specifically reference schizophrenia as a qualifying condition. A further compromise can be seen in the language relating to social maladjustment. Congress created an exception to the ED category for kids who are "socially maladjusted." This language provides that "[t]he term [emotional disturbance] does not apply to children who are socially maladjusted, unless it is determined that they have an emotional disturbance."[16]

This exception is a tautology: a statement that means nothing because of the way it is phrased. Put simply, it says children with a certain behavior are emotionally disturbed unless the behavior is due to a social maladjustment—unless the social maladjustment is due to an emotional disturbance. As such, the social maladjustment exception is little more than a bone thrown to those who wish to distinguish between children whose behavior can be clinically diagnosed as a mental disorder and those whose behavior is perceived as simply "bad." The exception is fundamentally flawed for a number of reasons. First, Congress provides neither a definition of *social maladjustment* nor the means to determine under what circumstances a child should properly be labeled as ED versus socially maladjusted. Second, because the social maladjustment criterion is based on societal norms of behavior, rather than on clinical assessment, it is more likely to be used selectively based on prejudice or subjective judgment.

In addition, the circular nature of the social maladjustment exception invites confusion and leads to haphazard applications based on the particular behavioral problem and the biases of the particular evaluators. For example, the use of the social maladjustment exception allows school officials to apply regular educational discipline to some students they are eager to remove from the school, who would otherwise remain entitled to services if found eligible under the ED category. This may result in disproportionate application of the exception based on race, economic status, social status, etc. Recall that the criteria for ED include "inappropriate types of behavior or feelings under normal circumstances" and "an inability to build or maintain satisfactory interpersonal relationships with peers and teachers."[17] These criteria are an invitation for decision making based on prejudice, stereotypes, and other improper factors, as there is little in the way of objective assessment that could possibly distinguish behavior due to an unspecified emotional disorder from behavior due to a social maladjustment. The author litigated this problem against the Broward County schools and the state of Florida in the early 1980s, in a class action law suit, *Lavon M. v. Turlington*, which resulted from a pattern of eligibility and placement decisions in which white children with behavioral problems were almost exclusively labeled ED and placed in a treatment program, while African American children with behavioral problems were typically labeled socially maladjusted and placed in a program on the grounds of the juvenile detention center.

Compounding this problem, research has shown that school IEP teams that are asked to assess the origins of problem behavior are often ill equipped to do so. Frequently, the teams lack mental health professionals as participants. Even when the teams include social workers or psychologists, they often lack appropriate training and criteria for making these sorts of complex judgments.[18]

Both the ED category and the social maladjustment exception are often misused as a mechanism for either segregating or excluding children with behavioral problems. The ED category is also problematic in another sense. The ED criteria cover children whose behaviors have different targets—external and internal. Some kids, for example, have problems with disruption, aggression toward others, destruction of property, and the like. Others may be withdrawn, depressed, isolated, and even self-injurious. (While some children display both types of behaviors, other children with emotional and behavioral problems tend to display one or the other predominantly.) Due to the inappropriate breadth of the ED label, children in both categories can end up in the same segregated classes or programs. This sometimes means that the most vulnerable children are grouped together with the most aggressive children—a potentially disastrous mix.

Compounding matters further, because the ED criteria are behaviorally based, a child may be determined eligible under the ED category for behavior that actually is caused by a disorder that better falls under a different special education label. For example, some of the characteristics of attention deficit/ hyperactivity disorder (AD/HD) overlap with some of the characteristics of ED. There is no clarity for schools on when to make a child eligible under the "other health impaired" category for behavior resulting from AD/HD or when to make the child eligible under ED. Similarly, a child with autism may display behavior that meets criteria for ED. Again, the broad and vague language of the ED criteria invites confusion and misuse because of the difficulty of distinguishing the symptoms from the cause.

E=MC² Advocacy Strategies

(1) Investigate whether the school has provided non-special education interventions prior to referring the child for special education eligibility.

(2) If the child is receiving outside mental health services, check with those practitioners as to whether the child would benefit from, or be harmed by, special education (ED) eligibility and/or placement. Whether you are seeking or opposing eligibility, the opinions of outside clinicians may be very useful in establishing your position.

(3) Suggest that a functional behavioral assessment (FBA) and behavior intervention plan (BIP) be done prior to seeking eligibility. The new emphasis on early intervening services, response to intervention (RTI), and prespecial education intervention supports this approach. Early intervention services and RTI are discussed in more detail in the next section of this chapter.

(4) If you are trying to avoid ED eligibility, carefully review the school's behavioral reports, progress reports, and report cards. Often, the school's records indicate that there is not a problem that is chronic and severe. On the other hand, if you are seeking eligibility to obtain services or to avoid regular discipline, or both, the records may contain important information substantiating the chronic nature of the child's behavior problems.

(5) If you are seeking eligibility, immediately request in writing that the school conduct an evaluation to determine if the student qualifies for special education. This may also trigger some of the special education procedural safeguards. These issues are discussed in more detail in Chapter 8 on behavior management and discipline.

Specific learning disability

Specific learning disability is the eligibility category with the largest number of students. The term *specific learning disability* may also be the most misunderstood. In my experience, many parents who are new to special education assume that the term *learning disability* is synonymous with *disability*—in other words, that any child having trouble learning must have a learning disability. Many other parents, and some educators, also seem to confuse the term *learning disability* with the term *dyslexia*. Some assume the terms mean the same thing; others assume they are mutually exclusive. Neither of those positions is correct. In the meantime, controversy over the learning disability (LD) label abounds because of the growing number of kids who are being given the label and because of concerns about how the diagnosis is made.

Under the IDEA, a specific learning disability is defined as "[a] disorder in one or more of the basic psychological processes involved in understanding or in using language, spoken or written, which disorder may manifest itself in the imperfect ability to listen, think, speak, read, write, spell, or do mathematical calculations."[19]

Several things about this definition are important. First, it focuses on the presence of a processing disorder as the critical element in whether a child has a learning disability. A processing disorder refers to a reduced or impaired ability to receive, perceive, interpret, and understand information.[20] Second, it indicates that the child's learning deficit cannot be better explained by some other condition, such as an emotional disorder, a health problem, or an economic or cultural disadvantage. (These are called *exclusionary factors*.) Third, it allows states to determine the specific extent to which a child's processing must be impaired and the criteria for determining a processing impairment. This leads to considerable variability in relation to the criteria for eligibility, based on where a family lives.

Prior to the 2004 IDEA amendments, something called a *discrepancy formula* was used as the basis for determining the presence of a learning disability. The discrepancy formula used a combination of IQ test scores and achievement test scores to determine whether a child was underperforming. The first step was to measure the child's intellectual potential using an IQ test, which purportedly establishes intellectual functioning within a certain margin of error. The IQ score provides a predicted level at which the child should be able to perform academic tasks, as measured by achievement tests. For example, if a child has an IQ of 100 (statistically average), he or she should be able to achieve average academic achievement test scores. If the child's achievement test scores fell more than a certain level (typically 15–20 standard score points or 1.5 to 2.0 deviations on the scaled score) below the predicted level of achievement, the child was regarded as having a learning disability. The bell curve below illustrates how test scores are used

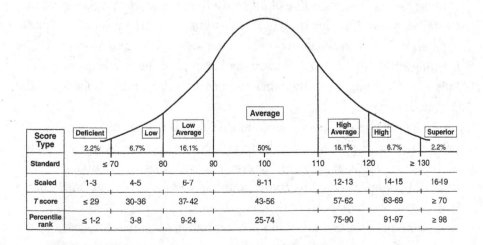

Score Type	Deficient	Low	Low Average	Average	High Average	High	Superior
	2.2%	6.7%	16.1%	50%	16.1%	6.7%	2.2%
Standard	≤ 70	80	90	100	110	120	≥ 130
Scaled	1-3	4-5	6-7	8-11	12-13	14-15	16-19
T score	≤ 29	30-36	37-42	43-56	57-62	63-69	≥ 70
Percentile rank	≤ 1-2	3-8	9-24	25-74	75-90	91-97	≥ 98

P4R Psychological Assessment Resources, Inc. · 16204 N. Florida Avenue · Lutz, FL 33549 · 1.800.331.8378 · www.parinc.com

to compare an individual student's performance on a particular test to the average (or "norm") of students in the general population.

In theory, the decision about whether or not students had a learning disability was made using a combination of test results, anecdotal data, and the judgment of the IEP team. Thus, a child whose test results were close to the line could be ruled in or out based on the team's judgment. In practice, my experience has been that schools placed great reliance on the statistical data, with children on the border being ruled in or out of eligibility based on a number of factors, some of which were unrelated to the child's functioning or needs—such as whether the LD program had room.

As the number of children determined to have learning disabilities has grown, there has been increased attention to whether the discrepancy formula is an accurate assessment tool. Clinicians, educators, and politicians generally now agree that the discrepancy formula is not reliable as a means of diagnosing an LD. In fact, much of the blame for the alleged over identification of children with learning disabilities is laid on the discrepancy formula because the formula is most useful in identifying underachievement. It does not, however, provide accurate information as to the presence of a processing disorder or other potential causes for a student's underperformance. As a result, some students have been identified as having a learning disability simply because they were underperforming, not because they had been accurately diagnosed as having a processing disorder or true learning disability. A wide variety of factors could cause underperformance other than a processing disorder, such as the presence of depression, other psychological problems, attention difficulties, a seizure disorder or other neurological problem, a short term illness, or family problems.

According to one theory, some children underperform because the regular education they've received has not been effective. In this view, some children are being labeled as having a learning disability not because they have a processing disorder but because they have not been taught properly. It is out of this theory that the RTI was created in the 2004 IDEA. Under this provision, states and schools are no longer required to use the discrepancy formula; indeed, its use is implicitly discouraged.[21] At the same time, schools are given the option to use research based regular education interventions to determine if children who are at risk of being identified as having a learning disability due to academic problems are able to display greater academic progress when provided with more intensive, research based teaching methods: "In determining whether a child has a specific learning disability, a local educational agency may use a process that determines if the child responds to scientific, research based intervention as a part of the evaluation procedures."[22]

Under the RTI model, schools have the option of offering intensive regular education instruction to children suspected of having a learning disability, rather than immediately referring them for a special education evaluation. Under RTI, the child is to be provided with research based instruction for an unspecified time period with an unspecified level of intensity. Children who respond positively to the regular education intervention presumably are not in need of special education, since the positive response demonstrates that the child's problem was one of inadequate education, rather than due to a disability.

Obviously, there are potential advantages to this strategy. If, as a consequence of the regular education intervention, the child's skills accelerate to such an extent that he or she is no longer at risk of needing special education, the child has clearly benefited academically. If this positive response occurs, the school system is spared all of the bureaucracy and expense associated with special education evaluation procedures, documentation, staff time, and other demands; and the child is able to remain in the regular program without special education programming. At a general level, the use of research based intensive remedial programs also should expand the range and quality of instruction available within regular education.

Although RTI offers promising possibilities, it also has many potential drawbacks in relation to identifying children with disabilities—and as a broad educational policy. First and foremost, RTI was not intended as a diagnostic process but as an additional educational intervention. There appears to be limited research about its use as a diagnostic procedure. Further, while its use may be widely mandated, many public schools do not have sufficient teachers who are trained in the scientifically based techniques that are a critical element of the RTI approach. As such, schools will be asked to implement a program without the capacity to do so. Indeed, if schools today had this implementation capacity, there would be no need for RTI as a preliminary step to identify children with problems—since children with academic problems would presumably already be getting the regular education reading intervention they needed.

Beyond this, there are a number of other downsides with the RTI approach. First, the 2004 IDEA amendments did not address how children should be evaluated when they do not respond to the scientifically based reading interventions. Given that the discrepancy formula has been somewhat discredited, the absence of an alternative evaluation process when a child fails to respond to intervention creates a statutory void. If the intervention doesn't work and no alternative evaluation procedure is specified, what are the schools to do? How should they determine that the lack of response is due to a learning disability? Indeed, many factors may account for the child's lack of response to intervention, including, but not limited to, a learning disability. Thus, the absence of an alternative procedure for evaluation leaves parents, clinicians, and educators in a state of confusion.

The 2006 regulations to IDEA 2004 provide more detail in relation to the RTI methods and establish the progression of events that should be used in making assessments. The new regulations provide that a child may be determined by the eligibility team to have a learning disability if two conditions are met. The first is that the child is not making adequate scholastic progress or reaching state approved grade-level standards in at least one of the following areas: oral expression, listening comprehension, written expression, basic reading skills, reading fluency skills, reading comprehension, mathematics calculations, and mathematics problem solving. The second condition is that the child is not making

> sufficient progress to meet age or state approved grade-level standards, . . . even after scientific, research based interventions have been provided in a regular school setting; or the child exhibits a pattern of strengths and weaknesses in performance, achievement, or both, relative to the age, state appropriate grade-level standards or intellectual development if it is identified by the group to be relevant to the identification of the specific learning disability, using appropriate assessments consistent with Section 300.304 and 300.305 and . . . the group determines that its findings . . . are not primarily a result of (i) visual, hearing or motor disabilities; (ii) mental retardation; (iii) emotional disturbance; (iv) cultural factors; (v) environmental or economic disadvantage; or (vi) limited English proficiency.[23]

It should be noted that the regulation goes on to require that, when making these judgments, the school district *must* consider data demonstrating that "prior to, or as part of, the referral process, the child was provided appropriate instruction in regular education settings, delivered by qualified personnel." In addition, the regulation requires that schools make repeated assessments of student progress at reasonable intervals and provide those assessments to parents. This provision is significant in several respects. First, it makes clear that the intervention process prior to evaluation for LD eligibility must include documentation that the child has been provided appropriate regular education instruction. However, it does not indicate that the child must have been provided a scientifically based, specialized intervention. Second, the provision requires the school to have utilized some formal process for objectively assessing the student's progress at reasonable intervals and sharing that information with the parents. On the other hand, although it does not require research based RTI strategies, it does allow the team to determine that, prior to or as part of the evaluation process, the child must be provided with some form of appropriate education before the eligibility decision. In other words, the determination of whether a child has a learning disability may include whether the child has already received appropriate regular education instruction, including intense research based instruction. Thus, even if a child has been clinically diagnosed as having a learning disability, the child may, under some circumstances, be determined by the school to be ineligible if he or she has not first received research based intervention in regular education.

However, the regulations and subsequent U.S. Department of Education Office for Special Education Programs policy statements indicate that the parent retains the right to request a special education evaluation at any time. When a child is referred for such an evaluation, the school must respond within the appropriate time frame even if regular intervention strategies have not yet been employed or are currently being implemented.[24] This is an important option for parents if they feel that their child's needs warrant immediate evaluation, prior to use of RTI methods, or that the RTI process has gone on too long or isn't working.

As will be discussed below, the language providing for eligibility based on "a pattern of strengths and weaknesses in performance, achievement, or both, relative to age, state approved grade-level standards, or intellectual development"[25] appears to reflect a compromise in relation to the statutory void in how to determine the presence of a learning disability in the absence of these discrepancy formulas. This language suggests that the discrepancy formula may still be used as one of the means of determining whether a child has a learning disability but also expands the scope of the discrepancy formula. Previously, the discrepancy formula was tied to the difference between the child's expected performance based on his estimated intellectual potential as measured on an IQ test and his actual performance on achievement tests. Under the new language of the IDEA 2006 regulations, the determination of a learning disability can be based on a pattern of strengths and weaknesses in a number of areas, and based not only on a discrepancy between IQ test scores and achievement scores but also on discrepancies in relation to the child's age, grade-level standards, and intellectual development.

In addition, by focusing on a pattern of strengths and weaknesses, the regulations appear to allow for a determination of eligibility that may not require below average functioning but that instead is based on variability in the student's functioning.

Under some circumstances, it could be argued that this expands the pool of children who may be eligible for services based on a learning disability, including children who are gifted yet may be performing only at an average level in some areas.

This problem is compounded by the absence of any timeline in the law for how long a child should receive regular education intervention before being referred for special education evaluation. The law provides no direction for resolving these disputes. It is likely that these various problems with RTI will lead to conflict among educators and between educators and parents.

There are two other points of conflict in relation to the evaluation and identification of children suspected of having learning disabilities. First, the educational criteria for LD historically have sometimes been different from the criteria used by some private clinicians. Often, private psychologists have identified children as having a learning disability based on wide range within the child's IQ scores. Similarly, private clinicians may diagnose learning disabilities by using a particular component of the IQ score (typically the verbal IQ score) to compare to the child's achievement test scores. In some instances, psychologists may even rely on specific processing tests that do not look at discrepancies at all but only examine delays in specific processing skills. By contrast, school psychologists were typically expected to adhere more rigidly to the discrepancy formula and to compare the child's full scale IQ score to the child's overall achievement test results.

Second, private psychologists may diagnose a child as having a learning disability based on the presence of a significant discrepancy between IQ and achievement, even when the achievement scores are in the average range. This occurs most often in relation to children who are regarded as "gifted/ learning disabled." By contrast, school psychologists and school IEP teams sometimes refuse to identify a child as having a learning disability unless the child's achievement scores are below average. Thus, some kids may be given the LD label by private evaluators but are denied eligibility by the school districts because the different evaluators are using different criteria to make their diagnoses. This is an area of frequent conflict between educators and parents. In some instances, the LD diagnosis seems unwarranted, as the child is, by available measures, performing well, despite the tested discrepancies. In other instances, however, the child may experience great frustration because of the presence of drastically different abilities in various areas of processing. These may directly impact the child's ability to complete expected work or may have an indirect impact arising from the child's inability to perform across the board at the level of his or her apparent intellect. For example, a child may have strong conceptual and analytical skills and strong vocabulary and comprehension but have great difficulty with decoding or fluency. Imagine having the intelligence to handle higher level work but also having a reading ability at a much lower level. The higher level work becomes taxing because of the reading problem, but the lower level work is very boring because of the absence of sufficiently challenging content. These problems are real but are sometimes unrecognized by schools. As described above, the IDEA 2006 regulations may be interpreted possibly to encompass children who display this sort of pattern of strengths and weaknesses.[26]

It is likely that these problems will persist even with the advent of RTI as a step in the evaluation process for children with learning disabilities. In effect, the presence of differing criteria and different ways to analyze available data will still inevitably lead to confusion and conflict over which children should be made eligible.

As will be discussed in further detail in Chapter 3, the new law also contains new language that may expand opportunities for learning disability services. Under the new law, schools are required to address a child's developmental and functional progress, as well as his or her academic progress, both in the evaluation and IEP process.[27]

This new language broadens the focus from academic performance to include also functional performance. As such, it should be interpreted to expand the criteria for determining whether a child has an impairment and also the standards for the services to be provided. In relation to kids with a possible LD, this should mean that greater consideration is given to things such as the child's reading, writing, or math fluency, including how quickly the child is able to read, the amount of time the child spends completing expected work, the child's accuracy, and other factors that may be masked using some of the historical evaluation tools and criteria. For example, the child who is a slow reader but doesn't quite display below average functioning may now qualify for services based on the child's functional reading problems as opposed to his or her "clinical" problems.

E=MC² Advocacy Strategies

(1) Identifying a learning disability sometimes requires getting a more in-depth evaluation than schools provide. Elements of an in-depth evaluation may include specific testing by a clinician or neuropsychologist, testing of specific areas of academic processing, or periodic testing over a period of time to assess whether the difficulty is chronic. To rule out causes for a child's performance difficulties, other types of evaluations may also be required, such as those that examine neurological status, emotional state, vision, hearing, motor skills, and general health.

(2) Whenever psychological test data are used to assess a possible learning disability, it is very important to be aware of the evaluator's assessment criteria. As indicated, there are many different approaches to diagnosing learning disabilities. Use of a more appropriate standard may lead to a different outcome.

(3) Some of the tests used to diagnose learning disabilities include both overall scores and subtest scores. Always pay attention to the subtest scores. Wide subtest scatter may be an indicator that a learning disability is present, even when the child's overall performance is adequate.

(4) Real world information about how the child performs is especially important under the 2004 IDEA. Parents and clinicians should keep track of how a child completes assignments; the child's functional reading, writing, and math skills; the child's ability to accomplish tasks under a variety of circumstances; and the amount of effort it takes the child to perform a particular task. For example, a child may be able to read but require three times as long as most children to read a passage. A child may be able to do equations in a test environment but may be unable to do the same equations when in a restaurant or the school cafeteria. The new emphasis on functionality makes such data especially important in assessing how the child actually does in the real world.

Other health impaired

The "other health impaired" (OHI) category covers children with health impairments that adversely affect their educational performance. The law provides a list of impairments as examples of health conditions that may warrant eligibility. However, the list is not all inclusive. Any child with any diagnosed health condition that meets the additional criteria for eligibility may be able to receive special education services. The IDEA regulations define OHI as follows:

> Having limited strength, vitality or alertness, including a heightened alertness to environmental stimuli, that results in limited alertness with respect to the educational environment, that is due to chronic or acute health problems such as asthma, attention deficit disorder or attention deficit hyperactivity disorder, diabetes, epilepsy, a heart condition, hemophilia, lead poisoning, leukemia, nephritis, rheumatic fever, sickle cell anemia and Tourette Syndrome; and adversely affects a child's educational performance.[28]

In order to meet the criteria for this category, the student's medical condition must result in limited strength, vitality, or alertness, which adversely affects educational performance. Many students have health conditions that impact educational functioning, due to symptoms such as fatigue, inability to sit in a chair for prolonged periods of time, or inability to sustain attention. In some instances, these symptoms result from a health problem that is also listed as one of the major disability categories. However, for those students whose impairment is not listed as one of those major categories, the OHI category provides a catchall that may provide a basis for services. In the following paragraphs, I discuss specific disorders and the OHI designation.

Attention deficit/hyperactivity disorder (AD/HD) and OHI

Ever since the IDEA was originally enacted in 1975, there has been confusion and controversy over whether AD/HD qualifies children for services under the OHI category. Because AD/HD was not specifically listed as a disability category in the IDEA statute itself, many school districts took the position that it was not a covered condition, regardless of its impact on a child's performance. The confusion led to considerable conflict.

In an effort to clarify matters, the U.S. Department of Education in 1991 issued an unusual joint policy memorandum from both the Office of Special Education Programs and the Office for Civil Rights. The memorandum stated that children with AD/HD could be made eligible for services under the OHI category of special education and could also be protected as children with disabilities under Section 504.[29] Subsequently, in response to a request for clarification from this author—which resulted in a statement referred to as the "letter to Cohen"—the Department further expanded its position, indicating that children with AD/HD could be covered under the OHI category based on displaying "limited alertness to educational tasks due to heightened alertness to environmental stimuli."[30]

While the 1991 policy statement, the letter to Cohen, and other policy statements helped to clarify and expand the special education rights of children with AD/HD, they did not resolve the controversy. Many schools continued to regard AD/HD as an uncovered condition, in some instances even questioning the legitimacy of AD/HD as a disorder. In response, in the 1999 IDEA regulations, the U.S. Department of Education amended the definition of "other health impaired" to list AD/HD and attention deficit disorder (ADD) explicitly as covered conditions. In addition, the department added the language from the letter to Cohen, stating that children could qualify if they displayed limited alertness to educational tasks due to heightened alertness to environmental stimuli.[31]

Even with the new amendment, however, AD/HD continues to be a condition that is disputed by some schools—and there continues to be disagreement over whether particular children qualify. The issue arises with children who are displaying symptoms of hyperactivity or impulsivity, rather than explicit inattentiveness. It also comes up in relation to children who may be inattentive but are getting passing grades and/or showing progress as measured by academic achievement tests. It should be noted that the Department of Education incorporated both AD/HD and ADD in the list of covered conditions in the OHI category. Since the American Psychiatric Association lists only AD/HD in its diagnostic manual—and places subtypes of the disorder, such as inattentive type, hyperactive type, or combined type, under that main category—it appears that the department wanted to make clear that children diagnosed with every variety of AD/HD were covered.

Both the American Academy of Pediatrics and the American Academy of Child and Adolescent Psychiatry have issued practice guidelines stating that a medical evaluation is a necessary component of AD/HD assessment.[32] In addition, the medical groups stress the importance of obtaining extensive family and school histories, verifying that the symptoms are not caused

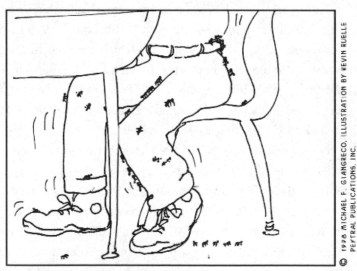

© 1998 MICHAEL F. GIANGRECO. ILLUSTRATION BY KEVIN RUELLE PEYTRAL PUBLICATIONS, INC.

AFTER A HASTY SPECIAL EDUCATION PLACEMENT FOR BEHAVIOR PROBLEMS, SCHOOL OFFICIALS WERE EMBARRASSED TO LEARN THAT MARTY REALLY DID HAVE ANTS IN HIS PANTS.

by other medical conditions, and determining whether they have persisted since early childhood and are present in various settings, such as at home, at school, and in the community.

Despite this, the Department of Education has stated that, when school districts evaluate children suspected of having AD/HD, they do not necessarily have to include a medical evaluation, as long as the evaluators are qualified and experienced in evaluating the disorder.[33] Some school districts, however, continue to require that a child suspected of having AD/HD be evaluated and diagnosed by a physician to qualify for special education services. When a school district believes that a medical evaluation is needed, the evaluation must be performed at no cost to the parent.[34]

$E=MC^2$ Advocacy Strategies

(1) AD/HD is a disability that cannot be diagnosed by a blood test or x-ray. Diagnosis relies on assessment and documentation of symptoms and/or behaviors. It is important for parents to keep track over time of any information that documents symptoms such as inattentiveness or impulsivity/hyperactivity. Report card narratives and behavior reports often reflect teachers' concerns with these behaviors. Notes home from teachers may also be useful in establishing the presence of symptoms over time. Such documentation should be saved.

(2) When a child is suspected of having AD/HD, it is often important to get both a psychiatric or neurological evaluation by a physician and a psychological evaluation by a school or clinical psychologist. These diagnoses may help confirm the presence of AD/HD or rule out other contributing conditions.

(3) AD/HD symptoms may be present in differing degrees depending on the time of day, the activity, and other factors. Some people mistakenly assume that, because children can pay attention properly under some circumstances—such as watching television or playing a video game—they do not have AD/HD. This reflects a misunderstanding of the symptoms of AD/HD, which may be affected by a wide variety of environmental factors.

(4) Schools sometimes assume that AD/HD should be recognized as a disability for special education purposes only if the child is getting

poor grades or achievement test scores. Some children with AD/HD may be able to demonstrate academic progress or even success but may suffer a wide variety of other problems resulting from their AD/HD. For example, they may misbehave, get into trouble for talking out of turn, have difficulty complying with deadlines, or have social problems. These issues may provide a basis for eligibility if they adversely impact the child's functioning at school—even if the child's academic performance is adequate.

(5) Remember that, under the 2004 IDEA, the evaluation process and the IEP must address not only the child's academic progress but also the child's developmental and functional progress.[35]

(6) Not all children with AD/HD or other health impairments require special education services or the accommodations or supports of an IEP. Remember that a child may also qualify for a Section 504 plan even if he or she does not require special education or an IEP but does require accommodations or other supports. Some children with AD/HD or other health impairments may be able to function adequately at school without an IEP or a Section 504 plan.

Tourette Syndrome and OHI

When it comes to special education eligibility, many children with Tourette Syndrome (TS) have encountered difficulties similar to those encountered by children with AD/HD. Like AD/HD, TS is often misunderstood by educators and by the public because children may display a wide variety of symptoms, with varying intensity depending on the situation and the child. Because a child with TS may be able to display appropriate behavior for various periods of time, some may question whether the child actually has a disability. As with AD/HD, it is not uncommon to hear people say in relation to children with TS that they "can control it when they want to, so it can't really be a disability." Further, because TS is often portrayed in a stereotyped way in the media, substantial confusion and misunderstanding exist about the disorder. In addition, and again like AD/HD, because TS can cause symptoms that result in inappropriate or rule breaking behavior at school, children with TS are vulnerable to punishment and disciplinary exclusion, particularly if they are unprotected by a well developed IEP or Section 504 plan.

Adding to the controversy has been the absence of TS as a listed condition in the eligibility categories or subcategories of the IDEA. Because it was not listed as a disability, some educators contended that TS was not covered. For some children, this produced a horrible catch-22, in which the child was denied eligibility for special education services because TS wasn't listed but was also refused eligibility under other categories, such as "emotional disturbance," because the behavior was attributable to the TS, rather than to some other emotional or behavioral condition.

In the new 2006 IDEA regulations, the Department of Education rectified the situation and added TS to the list of health conditions covered under the OHI category.[36] This change, which parallels the action the department took in 1999 in relation to AD/HD, should produce a significant improvement in the ability of children with TS to obtain appropriate special education and related services. At the same time, many of the problems described above in relation to AD/HD are likely to persist for children with TS as well. While the explicit listing of TS as a covered condition is a significant step in the right direction, ongoing training about the diagnosis, evaluation, treatment, and programming for children with TS will remain a high priority. Further, families of children with TS will still need to advocate aggressively for their children to overcome the lack of knowledge and the ongoing resistance to addressing the needs of children with these types of complex neurobehavioral disorders.

Medication disputes and OHI

In addition to disputes over eligibility, parents of children with AD/HD, TS, and other health or behavioral conditions sometimes face pressure from schools in regard to medication. Because the symptoms of AD/HD, TS, and other neurobiological disorders, such as bipolar disorder, are sometimes helped by medication—allowing children to maintain more appropriate behavior—educators may place subtle or explicit pressure on parents to place their child on medications. Nevertheless, the decision to use medication is a private one between the family and a medical professional. *Schools may not require the use of medication as a prerequisite to receiving special education or other educational services.*[37] Language in the 2004 IDEA explicitly prohibits school staff from requiring medication as a prerequisite for evaluation, services, or even the right to attend school, but school staff may discuss the potential benefit of evaluation for special education services, based on observation of the student's performances or behavior.[38] When a child does require medication to be administered at school, it is often helpful to include this directive in the child's IEP or Section 504 plan, including the specific procedure used to administer the medication. The plan should ensure that the child receives the medication in a manner that safeguards the child's privacy and that the medication is taken consistently and at the prescribed times. It is helpful for such plans to provide for documentation of the date and time of administration and to ensure that the medication itself is kept in a secure setting. Because of concerns regarding liability issues, some schools have insisted that parents sign a waiver of liability as a precondition for administering medication at school. The Office for Civil Rights has ruled that such waivers are an illegal requirement and cannot be used as a prerequisite for the administration of medication, if the medication is medically necessary for the child to participate successfully in school.[39]

Other disorders and OHI

Some other potential situations where children have problems involve the ability of children with asthma to access nebulizers or steroid medications; the ability of children with allergies to be provided a safe, allergen-free (and potentially air conditioned) environment and to have access to medications in the event of an emergency; and the provision of appropriate staff monitoring for children with diabetes who have to be monitored for low or high blood sugar levels. Similarly, children with diabetes or sickle cell anemia may have a variety of symptoms that require special monitoring at school. For children with these and other health issues, the key to receiving services is that the condition results in limited strength, vitality, or alertness; manifests itself over time; and adversely affects educational performance.

In some instances, a child may have a psychiatric condition, such as bipolar disorder, that has a neurological or biological component. The OHI category may be an option for eligibility, instead of the more typical use of the "emotional disturbance" category. As with AD/HD and TS, any child with a health impairment that doesn't meet the criteria for OHI may still be entitled to protection under Section 504.

Autism

Historically, autism was such a rare and misunderstood disorder that, like AD/HD, it was not included as a disability category. However, in the last 15–20 years, the number of children being diagnosed with autism has increased dramatically, as has our understanding of appropriate interventions. The American Psychiatric Association's *Diagnostic and Statistical Manual* (fourth edition), known as the *DSM-IV*, lists autism as a subcategory of what are called "pervasive developmental disorders" (PDD). The *DSM-IV* also lists Rett Syndrome, Asperger Syndrome, and pervasive developmental disorder–not otherwise specified (PDD–NOS) under the PDD umbrella.[40] However, many people use the term *autism* as a broad label for these different "spectrum" disorders.

All of the disorders on the autism spectrum have some characteristics in common. However, children may display a wide range of symptoms, the severity of which can vary greatly. The range of symptoms, coupled with the differing criteria for diagnoses, is a cause of much confusion. For example, many people use the term *autism spectrum disorder* interchangeably with PDD, without distinguishing the nature of the person's specific disability or level of severity. Causing further confusion, in 1997, Congress amended the IDEA to add autism as a specific category of disability, without specifying whether the intent was to address autism only or to address any PDD.[41] As a result, schools often use the autism label regardless of which category of PDD a child has been diagnosed with.

Although the IDEA requires that children's educational programs be based on their needs, not their labels, the confusion over diagnostic categories and the propensity to lump together all children with a PDD or spectrum disorder, both diagnostically and programmatically, are highly problematic. Some children with autism may have very limited intellectual ability or limited or no verbal communication skills or engage in severe self injurious behaviors. Conversely, a child with Asperger Syndrome or high functioning autism may be of average or above average intelligence, have considerable language ability, and display few or no self-injurious or aggressive behaviors. For these latter children, the predominant symptom may be difficulty with social relationships, including trouble with pragmatic language, nonverbal communication, and social relatedness. These children present more subtle symptoms, requiring careful individual diagnosis, and have vastly different programmatic needs than do children with more severe forms of autism.

The tendency to lump together all forms of autism spectrum disorders is reflected in the statement of the National Research Council's Committee on Educational Interventions for Children with Autism: children with autism spectrum disorders may be more likely to obtain special education services through use of the educational label of autism by the schools.[42] Many professionals and parents have embraced this suggestion, assuming that an educational label of autism was the preferred and perhaps only ticket to eligibility and services. In fact, children who meet criteria for a PDD may be appropriately labeled under the autism label but may also meet eligibility criteria for other disorders in addition to or instead of the autism label.

For example, children with one of the spectrum disorders may meet criteria for a speech and language disorder (since the autism spectrum disorders impact the ability to communicate appropriately). Children may also meet criteria for OHI (since spectrum disorders may impact the ability to maintain appropriate alertness for educational tasks); for "mental impairment" (for children who have severe intellectual delays); or for "emotional disturbance" (for children who have severe mental illnesses or inappropriate behavior concurrent with their autism).

Another problem in diagnosing and labeling children with autism spectrum disorders involves higher functioning children who are labeled as autistic or as having Asperger Syndrome. For these children, symptoms may not be recognized as a result of a disorder but may be attributed instead to social awkwardness, or being odd, unmotivated, or just "strange." Many children functioning at the higher end of these disorders may have severe social difficulties that are ignored or misinterpreted by parents, educators, or even clinicians. Public and professional awareness of all these disorders must be improved, as failure of appropriate diagnosis and treatment may delay the necessary interventions or might ultimately cause the less severe disorders to be as debilitating as those that are more severe.

Accurate diagnosis of these disorders requires the involvement of highly trained and experienced professionals. The addition of autism as an educational label for the special education system is very recent, and some schools lack personnel who are adequately equipped to make the assessments. Consequently, the process is often based on identifying symptoms that fit the characteristics of autism contained in the IDEA definition, which actually may be the result of a different disorder. Parents are advised to thoroughly investigate the professional experience of anyone who is charged with evaluating autism in their child. If in doubt, outside evaluation by an autism specialist is strongly advised.

E=MC² Advocacy Strategies

(1) If it is suspected that your child may have autism, a thorough evaluation, including consultation with a psychiatrist or neurologist, is advised. Because of the range of symptoms and severity levels, as well as the overlap of symptoms present in other conditions, it is imperative that an expert be involved and that other possible conditions be ruled out.

(2) If your child is diagnosed with a PDD or autism spectrum disorder, you should assess whether the educational label of autism is the best fit or whether some other special education label is more appropriate.

(3) In general, early identification of children with autism is very important, to initiate intensive interventions as soon as possible. Parents should investigate the benefits of intensive, research based treatment programs, such as the Lovass method or Applied Behavioral Analysis. They should ensure that the school is using appropriate methods, with sufficient intensity, delivered by staff with adequate training in the specialized method.

(4) Children on the autism spectrum may display behavioral symptoms that can be more effectively treated based on the use of an FBA and the implementation of a BIP rather than through school disciplinary procedures. FBA is a procedure in which the child is observed to determine, through careful data gathering and analysis, the causes or triggers for his or her behavior. A BIP is then developed to address the causes of the behavior, including modifying the child's environment, training the child in behavior skills, or using different strategies to reinforce appropriate behavior positively. In regular school settings, disciplinary policies often must be modified and exceptions made to accommodate children with autism disorders.

(5) Children with autism often have multiple disabilities or coexisting disorders. It is important that these be fully addressed in addition to the autism symptoms.

(6) Because some children with autism are nonverbal or have limited conventional speech, it is important to introduce, as early as possible, alternative means of communication, such as sign language; the use of picture exchange or other communication systems using symbols; or the use of assistive technology for purposes of communication, such as a touch screen that allows the student to select or type questions, answers, or comments. Further, it is important to recognize that an inability to communicate does not necessarily reflect a cognitive delay. When evaluating a child with autism, or other children who are nonverbal, it is important to ensure that adequate means of communication are provided, particularly when it comes to assessing intellectual ability. Evaluators should also be cautious when making judgments about cognitive ability based on low IQ scores, since these scores may be partially due to limited verbal, language, motor, or attention skills.

Speech/language impairment

The speech and language disorder category covers wide territory but is sometimes applied by schools and school speech and language therapists more narrowly than intended. The IDEA regulations define speech or language impairment as "a communication disorder, such as stuttering, impaired articulation, a language impairment, or a voice impairment, that adversely affects a child's educational performance."[43]

These criteria incorporate both children with speech impairments and children with language delays. Typically, speech impairments are much more easily identified and, in the author's experience, are more frequently the basis for speech/language services than are language deficits. However, language deficits can be every bit as debilitating as speech delays. In some instances, language delays can have a profound impact on the child's ability to function. Language delays may manifest themselves in deficits involving receptive language, expressive language, pragmatic or social language, or all of the above. These skills are critical to learning and interacting with others. In fact, a child with a language disorder may appear to be cognitively delayed or to have a learning disability due to problems understanding or expressing language. As there is an overlap between the development of language skills and academic functioning in general, this disability can have a massive impact. Further, some children may have adequate articulation and expressive and receptive language skills but have severe deficits in pragmatic language. These deficits could have a severe impact on the child's ability to function at school, even though the child does well on academic or achievement tests.

All disability categories other than "speech/language impaired" require that a student need special education services to qualify for special education eligibility.[44] In contrast, to qualify under the "speech/language impaired" category, it is sufficient that the child require speech or language therapy, without needing special education instruction of any kind.[45]

In some school districts, eligibility under this category is restricted to students whose speech or language delays are documented to be substantially below their overall level of functioning. This position assumes that there must be a discrepancy (similar to the discrepancy used in diagnosing a learning disability) that is significant in comparison to to the child's developmental level. Thus, children with mental retardation might not qualify as having a speech or language impairment unless their speech or language abilities were substantially below their cognitive abilities. Paradoxically, the ability to perform well on an IQ test is impacted by one's speech and language skills, so the use of this "developmental ceiling" to avoid provision of speech and language services creates a self fulfilling prophecy, one that is both inhumane and unwise, as it deprives students of services that may allow them to develop critical skills. In my view, the position that the criteria for speech and language eligibility should be linked to one's tested intellectual potential is not consistent with the IDEA.[46]

E=MC² Advocacy Strategies

(1) If your child has trouble communicating or is having difficulty with reading, writing, or understanding directions, it may be important to get a comprehensive speech/language evaluation. Speech therapists sometimes evaluate the child's articulation without evaluating the child's language development. As a result, many serious problems

may be overlooked. This problem is critical because language development impacts the ability to do well on IQ tests and may result in an inappropriate diagnosis of mental retardation when the child's problem, in whole or in part, may be the result of a language delay.

(2) If your child is suspected of having a language delay or is being evaluated for a language delay, make sure the speech and language pathologist has experience with evaluating language delays. Some speech pathologists are more experienced in evaluating speech problems.

(3) Sometimes a child will be made eligible under the speech/ language disability category without an evaluation of the child's overall functioning. At times, the speech/language problem may be the tip of the iceberg, and the child may also have a learning disability or other learning problem that cannot be diagnosed by a speech and language evaluation alone. If the child is having broader problems, a full educational evaluation should be considered.

(4) Some children with severe disabilities may also have problems with eating or oral motor issues, such as chewing or swallowing. Speech/language pathologists are sometimes the most appropriate professionals to evaluate these problems, but specialized training and experience in assessing these problems are needed for the pathologist to be able to conduct an appropriate evaluation. Make sure that the proposed professional is familiar with these issues.

(5) Speech and language problems are sometimes related to hearing problems. The child may need an appropriate audiological evaluation to determine whether a hearing problem may be contributing to the speech/language problem.

(6) Some children have a condition called speech apraxia, a disorder that makes it difficult for people to say consistently or correctly what they want to say. It is also known as verbal apraxia. The condition may be difficult to diagnose and often requires evaluation by a speech/ language pathologist who has specialized training or experience in diagnosing apraxia.

(7) For information on the components of an appropriate speech and language evaluation, go to www.asha.org/top-searches and click on Guidelines for the Roles and Responsibilities of the School-based Speech-Language Pathologist.

Mental retardation

Throughout the history of the IDEA, the terminology for the category of mental retardation has changed several times, but the criteria for eligibility have remained the same. In terms of diagnosis, meanwhile, the standard is set by the American Association of Intellectual and Developmental Disabilities (previously known as the American Association for Mental Retardation). The diagnostic process calls for a number of assessments, including an assessment of intellectual ability that typically uses standardized IQ tests, in conjunction with other means of assessing intellectual ability, along with an evaluation of the individual's developmental functioning. To assess developmental functioning, evaluators typically use adaptive rating scales, such as the Vineland Adaptive Behavior Scales and the Inventory for Client and Agency Planning. Evaluators also use social history, an interview with the student, and an interview with the parents to make the diagnosis. Generally, the child must display below average IQ scores as well as developmental delays in relation to life functioning to be diagnosed as mentally retarded. The American Association of Intellectual and Developmental Disabilities states that limitations in intellectual functioning are generally thought to be present if an individual has an IQ test score of approximately 70 or below. The association further explains that IQ scores must be considered in light of appropriateness, consistency with test administration guidelines, and the standard error of measurement. Because the standard error of measurement for most IQ tests is approximately 5, the diagnosis ceiling may go up to 75.

Children are sometimes identified as being mild, moderate, severe, or profound in their level of retardation. Other labels that have been used include mentally handicapped, mentally impaired, or cognitively impaired. These are all essentially variations on the label "mentally retarded" but have been employed at different times to address the accepted or politically correct terminology at the time.

Within school systems, there is often a correlation between the identified level of severity and the educational program that is offered. As a general rule, children identified as mildly retarded are more likely to receive a mix of academic programming and life skills curricula; children in the moderate range often receive more limited academic instruction, with more emphasis on life skills; and children in the severe/profound range are more likely to receive little or no academic instruction, with substantial emphasis on life skills.

This tendency to link instruction based on the perception of severity of mental retardation is problematic for several reasons. First, as discussed above, the IQ tests are not always accurate in measuring a child's cognitive ability. Performance on IQ tests is impacted by language, motor skills, and attention abilities, as well as by the academic instruction and other life experiences the student has received. A child may obtain lower scores on an IQ test for reasons unrelated to cognitive ability. Children with mental retardation can still benefit from academic instruction. The determination that academic instruction is not appropriate may create a self fulfilling prophecy, in which the lack of instruction aggravates or even causes further delay. Further, some schools may take the position that children with mental retardation should not be educated in the regular education environment or should only be in regular education for nonacademic activities such as gym, recess, or lunch. As will be discussed in far greater length in Chapter 6 on least restrictive environment, a blanket placement policy based on label or severity would be inconsistent with the least restrictive environment (LRE) requirements of IDEA and the LRE mandates of Section 504 and the Americans with Disabilities Act.

Further, children with disabilities are sometimes diagnosed with mental retardation or PPD at a very early age, when the child is still changing both physically and mentally. It can be dangerous to apply the mental retardation label too early, as it may limit the child's access to age appropriate instruction and peer models. Congress adopted the developmental delay category for children aged 3–5 (or, depending on the state, up to age 9) in order to allow schools to avoid prematurely labeling students as having a specific disability when it was too early to determine the specific nature or cause of those delays.

$E=MC^2$ Advocacy Strategies

(1) Make sure the child is old enough for psychological testing to be accurate before relying on psychological testing to be used as the basis for determining cognitive ability or whether the child is mentally retarded.

(2) When there are wide discrepancies among scores, discuss whether it is appropriate to avoid using a full scale IQ score, which may provide an inaccurate impression of the child's strengths and weaknesses. For example, a child might have verbal IQ scores in the 100s but nonverbal IQ scores in the 60s. A full scale IQ score in the low 80s or high 70s by itself might give parents and educators a false impression of the child's intellectual strengths and difficulties.

(3) Make sure that IQ testing adequately accounts for the child's other difficulties and that the IQ test doesn't inadvertently measure the child's other disabilities rather than his or her intelligence. For example, there are verbally based IQ tests, which rely heavily on language ability; nonverbal IQ tests, which rely more on abstract thinking; and motor free IQ tests, which are not dependent on the ability to write an answer. Obviously, given the presence of other disabilities, selecting the right IQ test and avoiding reliance on any one test may result in a more accurate picture of the child.

(4) Some children simply cannot be accurately tested using standardized IQ tests. Where this is the case, the child should not be given those tests. Even when evaluators put qualifying or cautionary language in their reports, scores take on a life of their own. It may be better to find non-standardized means of assessing the child in this situation than to use standardized tests that yield inaccurate results.

(5) Avoid the IQ glass ceiling. Like all children, children with mental retardation have a wide variety of interests, skills, and aptitudes. Decisions as to placement and program content should be individually driven, not based on the child's scores. Expectations also influence performance. It is important to push the system and the child to achieve as much as possible.

Low incidence disabilities

There are a number of disability categories covered by IDEA that impact smaller numbers of children. Although these categories are not discussed in detail in this book, many of the strategies that are presented in the book are relevant in relation to all disability categories. The categories not covered in detail are deaf-blindness, deafness, hearing impairment, multiple disabilities, orthopedic impairment, traumatic brain injury, and visual impairment including blindness.

Deaf-blindness means concomitant hearing and visual impairments, the combination of which causes such severe communication and other developmental and educational needs that they cannot be accommodated in special education programs solely for children with deafness or children with blindness.[47] See the National Consortium for DeafBlindness for more information at www.nationaldb.org. *Deafness* means a hearing impairment that is so severe that the child is impaired in processing linguistic information through hearing, with or without amplification, which adversely affects a child's educational performance.[48] For more information, see the National Institute for Deafness and Other Communication Disorders at www.nidch.nih.gov and the National Association of the Deaf at www.nad.org.

Hearing impairment means impairment in hearing, whether permanent or fluctuating, that adversely affects a child's educational performance but that is not included under the definition of deafness in this section.[49] For more information, see the National Institute for Deafness and Other Communication Disorders at www.nidch.nih.gov and the National Association of the Deaf at www.nad.org.

Multiple disabilities means concomitant impairments (such as mental retardation–blindness or mental retardation–orthopedic impairment), the combination of which causes such severe educational needs that they cannot be accommodated in special education programs solely for one of the impairments. Multiple disabilities do not include deaf-blindness.[50] See the National Information Center for Children and Youth with Disabilities at www.nichcy.org/pubs/factshe/fs10.pdf for more information.

Orthopedic impairment means a severe orthopedic impairment that adversely affects a child's educational performance. The term includes impairments caused by a congenital anomaly, impairments caused by disease (e.g., poliomyelitis, bone tuberculosis), and impairments from other causes (e.g., cerebral palsy, amputations, and fractures or burns that cause contractures).[51] For more information, visit the National Association of Parents with Children in Special Education at www.napcse.org/exceptionalchildren/orthopedicimpairments.php.

Traumatic brain injury means an acquired injury to the brain caused by an external physical force, resulting in total or partial functional disability or psychosocial impairment, or both, that adversely affects a child's educational performance. Traumatic brain injury applies to open or closed head injuries resulting in impairments in one or more areas, such as cognition; language; memory; attention; reasoning; abstract thinking; judgment; problem solving; sensory, perceptual, and motor abilities; psychosocial behavior; physical functions; information processing; and speech. Traumatic brain injury does not apply to brain injuries that are congenital or degenerative or to brain injuries induced by birth trauma.[52] See the National Institute of Neurological Disorders and Stroke at www.ninds.nih.gov/disorders/tbi/tbi.htm for more information.

Visual impairment including blindness means an impairment in vision that, even with correction, adversely affects a child's educational performance. The term includes both partial sight and blindness.[53] For additional information, see the National Association of Parents with Visual Impairments at www.spedex.com/napvi.

The implications of labels

Tremayne, the 12 ½ year old African American discussed in the introduction, had historically been labeled by his school district as mentally retarded but had been shifted to the label of emotionally disturbed, due to behavior problems he had at school. After the school placed Tremayne in a program for children with emotional and behavioral problems, his mother obtained a comprehensive outside evaluation. The results of the evaluation indicated that Tremayne had both AD/HD and a learning disability.

When presented with the findings of the private evaluator, the school district took the position that, if Tremayne's difficulties were due to AD/HD, he was not eligible for services because the school did not recognize AD/HD as a disability. Simultaneously, the school said that Tremayne was too low functioning to have a learning disability but too high functioning to be mentally impaired. Instead, he was just a slow learner, the school declared. As a result, the school district recommended that all special education and related services be terminated. When Tremayne misbehaved at school, the police were called, and Tremayne was prosecuted by the school district.

After a lengthy due process and federal court battle, Tremayne was awarded educational placement in a private special education school for children with learning disabilities. Tremayne attended the private school for all of high school and graduated several years ago. By failing to identify Tremayne's disabilities appropriately and by mislabeling him, the public school had set him up to fail. By declassifying him altogether, the district had effectively abandoned its responsibility to meet his educational and behavioral needs.

Tremayne's school district improperly used the labeling process as a way to drive educational services for him. Under the IDEA, the child's unique needs are supposed to be addressed through an *individualized* education program based on those needs. It should not have been necessary for the district to relabel Tremayne in order to provide services to address his behavior. The district was reluctant to address his AD/HD for fear that recognizing the AD/HD as a disability would require the school to develop different strategies for dealing with his behavior and would open the floodgates for other children to be labeled as "other health impaired" due to AD/HD. Further, because Tremayne was having behavioral problems, declassifying Tremayne allowed the school to discipline him using regular education disciplinary procedures, rather than through the far more rigorous special education disciplinary procedures.

Mara was nonverbal and had significant motor problems. Her school district believed she was mentally retarded, based on IQ tests she had been given. Her parents wanted her to be included in regular education in her neighborhood school. The school district proposed a satellite program in a different school district, offering opportunities for participation in regular education in classrooms that had both students without disabilities and those receiving special education. The school district's rationale was that the teachers in the "inclusive" program were more experienced in working with children with disabilities and that there were more supports in place in that school. The parents argued that Mara should be able to attend the school her siblings and neighborhood peers attended.

In the process of trying to work things out with the school district, the parents had Mara privately tested. Based on this more comprehensive evaluation, it was determined that, although Mara was nonverbal, she was not mentally retarded. Despite this, the district insisted that Mara be placed at the "inclusive" program at the non-neighborhood school. In testimony during the hearing, the teacher of the "inclusive" class described her classroom, in which there were approximately 15 children without disabilities and ten "inclusion" kids. When asked to whom she was referring, she said that the "inclusion" kids were all of the kids with disabilities who came into her class.

Even in this "inclusion" class, designed to normalize as much as possible the educational experience of the children with disabilities, the labeling process still occurred. Even though each child was different and all were participating in the regular education class, the teacher still viewed the children with disabilities differently and had a need to group them. Not surprisingly, the students with disabilities did not have full status in the classroom; instead, it appeared they were viewed more as if they were visitors.

Labels are a shortcut for describing a group based on a common characteristic. As such, the focus is inherently on the similar feature, rather than on the individual differences or unique qualities. Labels strip away individuality and cause us to assume things about people that are often inaccurate. This is true whether the label is "autistic," "inclusion kid," "504 kid," or Democrat or Republican. Not surprisingly, because the labels we use impact our perceptions, they also impact our expectations for what an individual can or will do.

In some school systems, labels are also enormously important in relation to the child's educational placement and in determining the kind and intensity of services offered. Some school systems use labels in explicit rating systems to determine aspects of placement and services, while other systems do this more covertly. For example, one school district used a matrix that determined eligibility for extended school year services based on the disability category and severity codes for each student. Because programming is supposed to be individually determined, such matrices are inherently suspect, if not outright illegal. On the other hand, some parents may be told things such as "Only children with physical disabilities can qualify for a one-to-one aide" or "If you want x service, you have to have the x label" or "All our children with y label are placed in that classroom—you don't want that, do you?!" These informal conversations are used to pigeonhole children to correspond to the particular programs, classes, or services that are available. Further, these conversations fail to take into account the potentially negative ramifications of both labeling and tracking by label.

Another major consequence of labeling concerns children with behavioral problems. The special education system provides that children with disabilities who engage in behavior that violates school rules are entitled to greater protections and procedural safeguards than children without disabilities. This is especially so when there is a determination by the school system that the child's behavior was caused by the child's disability (through a process called a *manifestation determination*). When a child is labeled emotionally disturbed, it is far more likely that the school will acknowledge a relationship between the child's disability and the behavior. Conversely, if a child is not labeled emotionally disturbed, school staff will sometimes rule out the possibility of a relationship between the child's disability and the behavior.

This seemingly neat distinction may result in a refusal to find a causal relationship in situations where the disability did, in fact, contribute to the child's behavior. Consider the impact of an auditory processing disorder on the ability of a child to understand and respond to instructions shouted at the child by a school lunch monitor in a noisy cafeteria or the impact of impaired social perception for a child with Asperger Syndrome on the child's reaction to another student's joke.

For better or worse, the special education system operates based on categorical eligibility even though the IDEA does not require that children with disabilities be certified by disability category as long as they are made eligible for services under the act.[54] Once eligibility is determined, the regulations require that the IEP be based on consideration of the academic, developmental, and functional needs of the child.[55] The law does not mention the child's label as a basis for determining the child's individualized education program. Labels are the door into the system. Unfortunately, the labels also sometimes determine what happens once the child is through the door.

To complicate matters, the labeling process is also significant outside the school environment. Labels are relevant when it comes to qualifying for accommodations on college achievement tests such as the ACT and SAT. They are relevant when it comes to getting accommodations in college or in a job, to qualifying for social security and other government benefits, and for qualifying for or being denied private insurance benefits (in terms of pre-existing condition issues). They also influence whether a person can be admitted to the military. And, in some instances, it is important to have been given a label while in public school in order to obtain appropriate services, funding, or accommodations post high school. The decision as to whether

THE MOST APPROPRIATE LABEL IS
USUALLY THE ONE PEOPLE'S PARENTS
HAVE GIVEN THEM.

to accept special education services, and via which label, is complicated in itself, but is all the more so given the need to think ahead to the significance of the labels when the child leaves public school and enters the community.

Labels are inescapable, both in special education and in our society at large. At best, we need to be aware of the significance of the various labels and the criteria for assigning them and ensure that they are applied accurately and strategically—recognizing who the child really is and taking into account the pros and cons of the particular label in relation to obtaining what the child needs, now and in the future.

3

The Evaluation and Reevaluation Process

The important thing is not to stop questioning.
—Albert Einstein

Tommy was a sophomore in a small, rural high school. He was failing all of his courses and was constantly being given detentions and suspensions for coming to class late, being unprepared, and missing work. During his freshman year, Tommy was suspended for more than 50 days for these types of behaviors. When Tommy's mother asked the school to do something to help him, she was repeatedly told it was a motivational issue. Finally, the school suggested that Tommy's mother take him for a drug abuse evaluation at her own expense. The evaluation indicated that Tommy did not have a drug problem, but the drug clinic suspected that Tommy might have attention deficit/hyperactivity disorder (AD/HD) and referred Tommy to a clinical psychologist for an evaluation. It turned out that Tommy did have AD/HD, but equally importantly, the testing also revealed that Tommy was mildly mentally retarded. Until this private psychological evaluation was completed, Tommy had never been evaluated by the school district.

This chapter focuses on the public schools' responsibility to identify and evaluate all children with disabilities who reside in a particular district, to ensure that any evaluations are appropriate, and to conduct timely reevaluations to ensure an up to date and accurate understanding of the child's functioning and degree of progress. In fact, identification and accurate evaluation are among the cornerstones of the entire special education system.

Identification is significant in ensuring that children with disabilities do not fall through the cracks, resulting in either academic failure within regular education, exclusion from school, dropping out, or involvement with the justice system. Evaluation is a key measure in ensuring the quality and appropriateness of instruction and in verifying that the instruction being provided is effective. It seems obvious that to provide appropriate and effective services, the school staff must, at the outset, have a clear idea of the child's needs and performance levels. Thus, there is a critical need for full evaluation at the front end. Ongoing evaluation is needed to assess whether the child is making appropriate progress and to allow for retooling of the individualized education program (IEP) if evaluation data suggest progress or lack of progress.

Evaluation is also needed to ensure that changes in the child's functioning are identified in a timely way and incorporated into the child's educational planning and services. On the positive side, a child may make sufficient progress and no longer require special education. Conversely, a child may require intervention owing to new problems that were hitherto unidentified or that may not have previously existed. These can result from changes in a child's health, from injury, or from the progressive worsening of a previously mild condition. Because the demands of school increase from grade to grade, some children experience greater difficulties as they progress through school simply because the gap between their abilities and those of their peers is growing over time due to the heightened demands of the upper grade levels. This chapter will address the referral process, the rules regarding parental consent, initial evaluations, reevaluations, independent evaluations, and some of the issues to be aware of in making sure that evaluations are appropriate.

The referral process

By law, the parents or the school district can make a referral requesting an evaluation for a child suspected of having a disability. If the student is eligible for special education, the parent, the school district, or the child's teacher may also request a reevaluation.[1] The reader should consult state law, as some states may allow for a broader range of individuals to initiate the referral and will specify to whom requests for evaluation should be directed. Any time an evaluation is sought, the request for it should be made in writing. Each state has its own procedures specifying to whom the request for referral should be made, but generally these requests should be directed to the school district's director of special education. Although the IDEA does not require that an explanation be given for why a referral is being made, it is generally advisable for the referring party to provide an explanation for why the child may require special education.

Once a referral is made, the school staff must determine whether it believes an evaluation is needed. This determination may be made based on existing information or the school may engage in some limited review of the child's functioning to determine whether an evaluation is needed. If the school staff determines that an evaluation is needed, the staff must provide the parents with written notice of the request for evaluation, as well as describe the proposed testing and the reason for the testing. The parents must give written and *informed* consent to the testing before it may go forward; if the parents refuse to consent, the district may request a due process hearing to overrule their refusal.[2] On the other hand, if the district decides not to pursue an evaluation, it must provide the parents with notice that an evaluation has been requested, that the district has decided not to pursue the evaluation and give the reason for refusing the request, and that the parents have the right to request a due process hearing to obtain an evaluation if they disagree with the district's decision.[3]

When a school wishes to evaluate a child and the parents refuse to give consent, the school is often successful in overcoming the parents' refusal at a due process hearing. In other words, parents who object to a school's conducting an evaluation are more likely to be unsuccessful if the school decides to take them to a hearing. By contrast, when parents seek to have a child evaluated for special education and the school refuses, the parents' chances of success are more dependent on the facts of the specific case.

Some parents mistakenly assume that if they obtain a private evaluation prior to the school's doing its testing, the school will automatically accept the private testing instead of doing its own. This is often not the case. Whether the parents sought testing to determine that the child does have a disability or to prove that the child does not have a disability, many school districts will insist on doing their own testing anyway. While they are legally required to consider the findings of the outside evaluation, they are not bound by those findings.[4] For a variety of reasons, many school districts prefer to use their own evaluation team, even when the outside evaluators are well regarded. Much of this reaction relates to the district's desire to control the process, but it may also have to do with concerns that private evaluators might not understand the nature of the evaluation process or the differences between the educational criteria for eligibility and the clinical criteria for diagnosis.

The 2004 Individuals with Disabilities Education Act (IDEA) does not have a timeline by which the school must respond to the referral for evaluation. Rather, the school must complete the evaluation within 60 calendar days from the date that the parents sign a written consent, unless state law provides otherwise.[5] As a result, it is important that parents seeking an evaluation for their child not only make a request for the evaluation but also give written consent for the procedure. In some instances, parents may wish to include a written consent in their referral request. The purpose of this strategy is to get the clock ticking earlier, setting things in motion from the date of the referral request rather than letting weeks pass while the school seeks the written consent it needs. While this strategy may not be recognized as legitimate by the school district, it does create a basis for arguing that the deadline for completing the evaluation runs from the original referral date. The downside of this strategy, even if the school accepts the consent as valid, is that it deprives the parents of the ability to exercise control over the specific tests that will be administered because the parents are effectively giving blanket consent in advance.

Further complicating the timing issue is the increased emphasis on early intervening services (EIS) in the 2004 IDEA. For the first time, the 2004 IDEA overtly encourages school districts to develop programs to address the needs of children who are having problems at school but who have not yet been identified as having a disability.[6] Although the statute was silent about how the use of EIS affected the referral process and evaluation timelines, the 2006 IDEA regulations make clear that parents retain the right to seek an evaluation even if the school is recommending or providing EIS, and that referral for EIS or response to intervention (RTI) services is not a basis "for delaying appropriate evaluation of a child suspected of having a disability."[7]

Unfortunately, there seems to be an inherent conflict here. When children are receiving EIS or RTI services, it would appear that the regulatory provision preserving the parents' right to seek an evaluation is undercut by the school district's open-ended option to deny the evaluation on the grounds that the child's EIS or RTI experience has not lasted long enough to provide sufficient evidence to evaluate whether special education is necessary. Parents may need to be aggressive about pushing for evaluation in the face of this kind of deflection. They can legitimately argue that the law provides support for evaluations being conducted even while EIS or RTI services are being provided. In fact, this could well be the best outcome—the child gets more intensive interim services through the EIS or RTI in the short run, while waiting for the school district's evaluation to be completed within the 60 calendar days. This combination can provide a useful service bridge for children who are ultimately found eligible and may even provide information that is useful in documenting the impact of the child's disability. On the other hand, it may also provide data to demonstrate that a child doesn't need special education if the child responds well to the EIS or RTI.

Child find

Independent of the referral process described above, the school district has a legal obligation to identify, locate, and evaluate all children aged 3–21 who have disabilities, to determine if the children require special education. Schools must take steps to identify children suspected of having disabilities whether the children are homeless or wards of the state and whether they attend private schools or public schools or are home schooled.[8]

Evaluation process

Once the school has decided to conduct an evaluation and written parental consent has been obtained, the school district must go forward with the evaluation. In deciding what the evaluation will consist of, the school is obligated to consult the parents and obtain their input about what testing or evaluation is needed.[9] The law sets forth certain minimum components for an evaluation. It also requires that any evaluation that is necessary to identify whether the child has a disability and requires special education must be conducted at no cost to the parents. In conducting the evaluation, the school district is required to follow a number of standards to ensure accuracy and lack of bias. Overall, it must "[u]se a variety of assessment tools and strategies to gather relevant functional, developmental, and academic information about the child, including information provided by the parent."[10]

Most importantly, the 2004 IDEA strengthened a prior requirement that the evaluation and planning process consider all of the child's needs—not just the child's academic needs.[11] The new evaluation language is important for a number of reasons. First, it expands the emphasis on the child's developmental, behavioral, and functional progress, as well as academic progress. Second, it requires that the evaluation be conducted in the "language and form most likely to yield accurate information,"[12] which appears to require that evaluators take into account the child's learning style and means of receiving and expressing information. In some instances, this may mean that standardized testing is inappropriate for particular children.

The new language is also important due to its requirement that the school evaluate what the child "knows and can do." This language is significant because it requires evaluation of the child's ability to generalize what the child is learning by looking at what he or she "can do," rather than evaluating learning in isolation from the child's ability to use the knowledge outside the test situation. In addition, the language appears to require assessment of the child's strengths as well as deficits.

The IDEA continues to have a variety of other important evaluation rules. First, the test procedures used to establish whether a disability exists must be nondiscriminatory.[13] Many evaluation tests are based on "norms" or standardization. This means the test makers have identified how the typical person would perform. The test measures to what extent the person being tested performs above or below this norm or average. However, in order for the test to be nondiscriminatory, the control or norm group must be sufficiently diverse to account for performance differences that may be due to variables other than disability. For example, on a particular test, girls and boys may perform differently. If the test doesn't take this into account, its scores can't fairly be used. Other variables that could lead to distortions or bias in the test results include socioeconomic status, income level, age, race, where the child lives, and whether the child's primary language is used in the test. A review of the IDEA's legislative history indicates that Congress was concerned with the misclassification of children through discriminatory testing procedures. Consequently, Congress mandated that "positive action be taken against erroneous classification of poor, minority and bilingual children and against the invalid use of testing."[14]

A second important requirement is that the test be designed to assess accurately the suspected disability. If the evaluator wishes to evaluate a child's intelligence, it would make little sense to use a vision test. Similarly, it would make no sense to use an adult level IQ test to evaluate a 6 year old or to use an IQ test that requires vision to evaluate someone who is blind. The law requires that the test instrument be suitable for use with the person who will be tested.[15]

The IDEA also requires that the person conducting the evaluation be competent to administer it. Although the law is not specific in defining what level of competency is required, it does require that evaluators meet general licensing or certification requirements in their field. Beyond this, the person should have specific training and experience in administering and interpreting the results of the particular tests that will be given.[16] Many test makers have standards that specify the type of training and experience that the evaluator should have. Information related to this type of training can often be obtained from the test publisher's Web site or by contacting the test publisher or author.

Finally, the law requires that the evaluation instruments be administered in a manner that is consistent with the standard procedures of the test.[17] Under some circumstances, there is great value in adjusting how a test is administered in order to get data that would not be available otherwise. When the evaluators deviate from the test rules, however, they should make sure to disclose this in the evaluation report, as it may affect the validity of the results or the ability to compare the results to national norms.

> *Bethany is given a timed test in social studies and does very poorly. However, the evaluator notices that Bethany did fairly well on the questions she answered but ran out of time before she could answer all the questions. In order to assess Bethany's knowledge, the evaluator gives Bethany extra time to complete the test. As a result, Bethany gets a much higher score.*

The higher score would not be valid because Bethany was given extra time. However, Bethany's ability to do well when given extra time would be useful information to report. It would demonstrate that Bethany's problem was not that she didn't know the material but that she either had trouble reading the questions quickly or had trouble retrieving her answers or accurately marking them down. Reporting this data, with the nonstandard circumstances mentioned, could help the evaluation team recognize that Bethany might require time accommodations or might have a processing problem that had not otherwise been addressed.

Reevaluations

Once children have been made eligible for special education, the IDEA requires that they be reevaluated under a number of different circumstances. First, either the parents or school staff may request a reevaluation if they believe circumstances warrant it.[18] When this occurs, the school district must determine whether a new evaluation is needed. If it determines that a reevaluation is indeed required, it must obtain written informed consent from the parents, including input from the parents on what testing is needed.[19] If the school determines that additional testing is not warranted at the particular time, it must advise parents that there has been a referral, provide the reason for the referral, and state that the school has refused the request for an evaluation and the reason the request is being refused. The school must also advise parents that they may request a due process hearing in order to overturn the district's refusal to reevaluate.[20]

Under the 2004 IDEA, if an evaluation by the school district has already been performed in a particular school year, either party—the school or the parents—has the right to block the school district from conducting another evaluation during that same year.[21] While there may be some circumstances where this rule protects children from overtesting, there are other circumstances when the rule may prevent children from getting the reevaluations they need. This could be the case, for example, if there has been a change in the child's functioning, health, or environmental situation. The child may have gotten severely ill since the first testing, may have changed placements or may have experienced a change in performance (for better or worse) that would suggest the need for new testing. This regulation does not affect the rules regarding the use of independent evaluations or the parents' right to request an independent evaluation at the school district's expense.

The law does, however, require that all children with disabilities be evaluated at least every three years.[22] When a three year evaluation is due, the school district must convene a meeting, with a parent in attendance, to determine what testing will be performed. The school district must also obtain the parents' written informed consent to the testing. The school district may decide that a full reevaluation is not needed and choose to conduct only a partial reevaluation or a review of available records. However, if the school wishes to conduct less than a full reevaluation, it must inform the parents that the parents have the right to a full reevaluation if they wish it.[23] If the parents wish to have a full reevaluation, the school is obligated to conduct it, even if the school does not feel it is necessary.

Independent educational evaluations

The IDEA requires school districts to consider all independent educational evaluations that are obtained by the parents.[24] Parents obtain such evaluations for a variety of reasons and under many different circumstances. They may obtain an outside evaluation because the school district has refused to conduct one or because they disagree with an evaluation performed by school staff. Sometimes, parents obtain an independent evaluation because they are concerned about their child and are unaware that the school could do an evaluation or prefer to have the evaluation done by someone they have selected. Although referred to as independent *educational* evaluations, the right to have independent evaluations considered by the school applies to any type of evaluation that the parents obtain, so long as it is relevant to the child's disability or functioning at school. This can include psychological testing; speech and language evaluation; occupational or physical therapy evaluations; and specialized diagnostic testing such as psychiatric evaluation, assistive technology assessments, or any other testing that is relevant to school issues.

Although schools must consider the independent evaluations, they are not bound to follow the evaluation's findings, conclusions, or recommendations. However, if they choose not to adopt the independent evaluation results, in whole or in part, they must offer a legitimate reason for not doing so. Schools give many reasons for rejecting findings of a particular evaluation.

These could include that the person is not qualified to administer the tests; that the testing was done improperly; that the person used different criteria or standards than the school uses; that the person was unfamiliar with the factors that the school uses in determining eligibility; that the person was unfamiliar with the programs the school uses to provide services; or that the person does not meet the state's requirements for that type of evaluation.

> *Chuck's mother, Tammy, believed that her son was having difficulty at school and suspected he had a disability. The school conducted an evaluation and concluded that Chuck was functioning at an acceptable level. Because Tammy was unconvinced by the school district's evaluation and disagreed with the decision, she arranged for an intensive neuropsychological evaluation by a private evaluator. The evaluator identified problems that the school had not and wrote a lengthy report, presenting data, explaining his conclusions, and making recommendations.*
>
> *At the IEP meeting, the special education director, who was not a psychologist, provided a lengthy critique of the private report in order to justify the school's decision to deny Chuck's eligibility for services. Her critique gave the impression that the school staff had seriously considered the private report, which the director indicated had nothing accurate or useful to contribute to the IEP team's considerations. However, at the resulting due process hearing, the school psychologist acknowledged that he had no disagreements with the accuracy of the private psychologist's data; he had not even done testing in some of the areas that the private psychologist tested; and he agreed with most of the report's recommendations. On this basis, the hearing officer concluded that the director had not seriously considered the report but had only looked for reasons to criticize it. The hearing officer ordered that the child be declared eligible and that the parent be reimbursed for the private evaluation.*

Sometimes, a private evaluator may diagnose a child and determine that the child has a disability, but the school disagrees with the conclusion, even though it accepts the evaluator's data as accurate. This can occur because private clinicians sometimes use different diagnostic criteria than the school team uses. In other words, under some circumstances, the child may meet one set of criteria but not another, leading to confusion and conflict. On the other hand, schools sometimes reject an outside evaluator's conclusions simply because they are trying to avoid providing special education services. This can happen because the school doesn't have a program or space for the child, because the school doesn't want to be bound by the rigorous IDEA procedural safeguards, or because the school wants to send a message that parents can't bypass the school process by getting a private evaluation. In any event, once an independent evaluation has been shared with the school, the school can't simply ignore it.

If the school has conducted an evaluation and the parents do not feel it was competently administered or do not agree with the results, they can ask the district to provide an independent evaluation at district expense.[25] This request must be made in writing and should be directed to the school district's director of special education or to whomever the state special education law specifies. The request should include the basis for why the new evaluation is being requested. It will not be enough, for example, that the parents simply disagree with the findings. Instead, they might point out that the evaluation was improperly performed, had inaccurate data, reached incorrect conclusions, or that there were other problems with the process.

Once the parents submit a written request for an independent evaluation at district expense, the district has several options. First, it can agree to pay for an independent evaluation. If the district agrees to do so, it can impose reasonable limits on who the evaluator is, the credentials/license of the evaluator, and on the cost and scope of the evaluation. If the parents disagree with the limitations imposed by the district, this becomes an issue for further negotiation or due process.

Second, the district may refuse to pay for the independent evaluation. In this case, the district must request a due process hearing to prove that the evaluation its staff conducted was appropriate.[26] The district is required to request the due process hearing without unnecessary delay. At this point, parents may need to get their own evaluation to provide evidence at the hearing that the school evaluation was inadequate. Presumably, if the district fails to show that its evaluation was appropriate, the parents should be entitled to reimbursement for their evaluation costs.

In some cases, a district may ignore the parents' request for an independent evaluation. In other cases, it may inform parents that it will not agree to an independent evaluation—and then fail to request a due process hearing to prove that its evaluation was appropriate. When this occurs, the parents must either decide to abandon their request for a private evaluation at district expense or request a hearing to enforce their right to an independent evaluation at district expense. Parents in this situation might be able to combine the district's failure to follow the rules with other issues they are unhappy about, in a combined due process proceeding. Under these circumstances, if the parents are able to afford it, they may want to obtain an evaluation at their own expense, to use the evaluation at the hearing, and pursue reimbursement for the cost of the evaluation as one of the remedies they are seeking. Alternatively, if parents do not have sufficient funds to pay for an evaluation up front, they can ask the hearing officer to order an evaluation as a preliminary matter before the main issues in the hearing are decided. Hearing officers have the power to order an independent evaluation at district expense, either at their own initiative or in response to a parental request.[27] If the parents ask for an independent evaluation and the district ignores it—or rejects the request but fails to initiate a due process hearing— there is a strong argument that the school district is in default and that the parents are entitled to an independent educational evaluation due to the district's failure to follow proper procedure.

$E=MC^2$ Advocacy Strategies

A school's evaluation may be considered inappropriate in a number of situations, including when

(1) data is not properly calculated;

(2) information in the report is inaccurate;

(3) tests were inappropriate for the child's age, gender, race, etc., or given what is already suspected or known about the child's disabilities;

(4) tests were administered under circumstances that invalidate results or call them into question. For example, the child may have been sick, the test environment may have been excessively noisy, or there may have been a problem in the rapport between the evaluator and the child;

5) parts of the school's evaluation are contradicted by other data or testing;

(6) an evaluator did something improper during the evaluation, such as making racial comments, insulting the child, asking improper questions, or refusing to recognize that the child needed to use the bathroom.

Sammy was a 5 year old boy with autism. He was extremely distractible and was receiving home schooling. Sammy was evaluated by a school speech pathologist and psychologist at the school building, in a test room with windows. He was so distracted by the wind blowing leaves from the trees outside the building that he couldn't complete the speech evaluation. The psychologist was also unable to get Sammy to cooperate with her and finish the tests she was trying to administer. Neither evaluator asked that Sammy's testing be changed to another location or that he be retested on another day. The hearing officer ruled that the school's evaluation was inappropriate and ordered the school to implement an outside evaluator's recommendations.

Haley was a 10 year old with asthma, speech and language problems, and suspected learning disabilities. The school's speech and language pathologist failed to test Haley in a number of areas related to her suspected disabilities. The private speech pathologist did more comprehensive testing, on which the school relied in developing its IEP. The school district was ordered to reimburse the family for the cost of the private speech evaluation.

$E=MC^2$ Advocacy Strategies

If parents are already in dispute with the district about other issues, it may make sense to seek reimbursement for the costs of the independent evaluation, in addition to the other financial relief they are pursuing. However, my general view is that it makes little sense to go to a due process hearing solely over payment for an independent evaluation. The cost of litigation may exceed the cost of the evaluation and will substantially delay the process of obtaining the evaluation. On the other hand, if the parents cannot afford to pay for an independent evaluation but have access to pro bono legal representation or choose to represent themselves, it may be necessary to seek a hearing to obtain an independent evaluation at district expense.

Independent evaluations as a mediation strategy

Under a number of circumstances, independent evaluations may come into play through the mediation process. When parents request an evaluation at district expense—and either the parents or the district request a hearing over the issue—it is often possible to negotiate for an independent evaluation through mediation. Just as it is prohibitively expensive for most parents to litigate over an evaluation, it is equally expensive for a school district to do so. Both parties have an incentive to resolve the dispute without expending lots of time, effort, and money on legal battles.

In addition, where the parents and district have a dispute over the child's disability, level of functioning, or special education needs, an independent evaluation can often resolve or narrow the dispute without resorting to a hearing. If an outside expert who is trusted by both the parents and the district can provide a fresh view of the child and the child's needs, this can often help both parties reach a mutually acceptable resolution.

A number of cautions are necessary, though. The parents must make sure that the evaluator is truly independent of the school district and has the requisite expertise to complete the evaluation adequately. It can actually make the situation worse for the parents if they agree to an independent evaluation by someone who is somehow connected to the school administration and produces an ostensibly independent report that is not really independent.

It is also important that the parties agree in advance about the referral questions being asked and the specific answers being sought.

$E=MC^2$ Advocacy Strategies

Referral questions might include the following:

- *Does the child have a disability? If so, what is it?*

- *Does the child have additional disabilities beyond those that have been identified?*

■ *What is the level of severity of the identified disabilities?*

■ *Does the child appear to be making appropriate progress in light of his/her disabilities?*

■ *Does the child require more/less/different services or intensity of services than the child is currently receiving?*

■ *Is the educational setting appropriate, too restrictive, not restrictive enough?*

■ *Are there helpful intervention strategies or methodologies that the staff is failing to use that should be implemented?*

■ *Is the IEP appropriate, or are there parts of the IEP that should be changed?*

■ *Are there any concerns with prior evaluations?*

■ *Are there are any concerns with how the staff is working with the child? Does the staff require any additional supports or training to meet the child's needs effectively?*

An example of the importance of these questions can be seen in a situation where parents feel their child's behavior is due to AD/HD and the school believes the behavior is due to poor motivation or an emotional disorder. If the evaluator is not asked specifically to evaluate the child for AD/HD but only to evaluate whether the child has an emotional problem, it may skew the results and defeat the evaluation's effectiveness in addressing the parents' concern.

$E=MC^2$ Advocacy Strategies

(1) If possible, it is important to agree on what test instruments will be used and what prior information will be shared with the evaluator in advance of the evaluation. For example, some ratings scales are designed to evaluate autism, some to evaluate AD/HD, some to evaluate "executive function skills," some to evaluate independent living skills, and some to evaluate various behavioral or emotional conditions. The type of tests or assessment tool used can influence

how the child's performance is assessed and the conclusions that are reached.

(2) At times, it may be important to share the child's records in advance. Under other circumstances, the parties may want to have the evaluator assess the child with no prior information in order to avoid prejudicing the evaluator about the child.

(3) Generally, it is useful to structure the evaluation to include an opportunity for the evaluator to interview both the parents and the school staff, but this has potential pitfalls, depending on the circumstances.

(4) It is also important to clarify among the parties and the evaluator what is desired in the way of recommendations. Some evaluators will reach clinical conclusions but will avoid offering recommendations about the types, intensity, and location of services. If this is something that is in dispute, it may be useful to spell out exactly what types of recommendations are being sought.

It is also important for parents to clarify whether the parties to a mutually endorsed independent evaluation will be legally bound by the evaluator's findings or whether they retain the right to disagree with the results. If they may still disagree with the independent evaluator's findings or recommendations, they should recognize that their involvement in selecting the evaluator will still give the report added weight. Thus, if a school district suggests an independent evaluation, it is very important that the parents thoroughly investigate the evaluator to make sure they have confidence in his or her competence and independence. Sometimes, it may even be helpful to negotiate a continuing role for the evaluator. This might include participation in IEP meetings (and certainly can include the meeting at which the evaluator's report will be considered). It might also include periodic reassessment of the child; periodic observation of the child in the school environment; and/or ongoing consultation with the parents and staff to troubleshoot problems as they arise.

In sum, a mutually negotiated independent evaluation has enormous potential for creating a positive resolution to the dispute but also holds risk for both parties.

E=MC² Advocacy Strategies

Here are important questions to ask an independent evaluator:

(1) What training and experience do you have in evaluating children with this type of suspected disability?

(2) What training and experience do you have in evaluating children of this age?

(3) How many children have you evaluated with this type of suspected disability?

(4) In addition to your graduate education, have you received any specialized training or attended any special workshops related to evaluating children with this disability?

(5) Are your evaluations accepted by school districts and/or the state (i.e., do you meet the criteria that schools use for independent evaluators)?

(6) How long does it take to get an appointment? How long does it take to get the report after the evaluation is done?

(7) Are you hired by both parents and school districts to do evaluations?

(8) How many evaluations have you done for parents? For school districts?

(9) How much time does the typical evaluation of this sort last?

(10) How do you decide what tests to use? Do you discuss this with the parents in advance?

(11) What information do you need in advance of evaluating the child?

(12) Do you seek information from the school staff, as well as the parents? How do you do that? What information will you want from the parents? What do you do if you feel other testing is also needed? Do you work with or refer clients to other evaluators? If so, who are they?

(13) Do you ever observe the child in the school or home setting? Under what circumstances?

(14) Do you meet with the parents before the evaluation? Do you meet with the parents to share the results before writing your report?

(15) What role will the parents' concerns play in the evaluation process?

(16) What does the typical evaluation cost? Is it covered by insurance? Do you bill insurance directly or is that the parents' responsibility?

(17) Do you attend IEP meetings to discuss your findings? Do you make recommendations that can be used in the IEP process? What do you see as your role at the IEP meeting? How would you describe your approach or style in working with parents and/or the school district—as an advocate, neutral party, facilitator, consultant?

(18) If there is a dispute with the school district, are you willing to testify at a due process hearing? Have you done so before? How often for parents? How often for school districts?

(19) What procedure do you use if you are mutually selected by the parents and the school district to do an independent evaluation?

(20) If the parent is working with an attorney or advocate, are you willing to discuss the testing process with them?

Specific issues for children with AD/HD, bipolar disorder, Tourette Syndrome, learning disabilities, and other neurological or neurobehavioral disorders

By virtue of the more subjective nature of the evaluation of AD/HD, bipolar disorder, Tourette Syndrome, learning disabilities, and similar disorders, parents and clinicians should keep in mind several considerations. In some instances, the criteria by which a private clinician may evaluate a child for these conditions are different from those used by the school district. Thus, a child may legitimately qualify under the *medical/clinical* criteria while not qualifying under the *educational* criteria. Often, this issue can be overcome by using more extensive evaluation procedures that provide the necessary data in both categories. In some instances, however, schools are using excessively rigid criteria that don't take into account the more subtle areas of difficulty the child is experiencing, but instead focus on the child's overall performance. For example, the child may be a competent reader on a general reading test but may have great difficulty reading efficiently or fluidly in a real world environment. The 2004 IDEA places greater emphasis on functional and developmental impairment, making it especially important that consideration be given to the child's actual performance in school and at home, and not just to standardized test scores.[28]

Sometimes, parents and schools get into disputes over who is qualified to perform particular evaluations. This can play out in two different ways. On the one hand, schools may claim that only evaluators who are specifically credentialed by the school district or the state education agency are qualified to evaluate children for purposes of educational eligibility. Thus, a school district may choose to disregard the findings of a highly experienced private psychologist because that person is not credentialed as a "school psychologist" by the state. In general, however, school districts should take into account all evaluations performed by competent professionals, even if those professionals don't have the requisite state certification.[29]

On the other hand, the school district may insist that certain conditions can be diagnosed only by a medical doctor. This often occurs with AD/HD, bipolar disorder, Tourette Syndrome, and some other neurobehavioral disorders. In some instances, this is unquestionably the correct position. For example, only a physician can diagnose epilepsy. However, there is some controversy as to whether nonphysicians can diagnose some disorders. For example, in many instances, clinical psychologists diagnose AD/HD. While the best practice standards indicate the importance of medical assessment for the purpose of ruling out other disorders, the U.S. Department of Education has indicated that, as long as school districts use clinicians who are appropriately trained and experienced in the evaluation of AD/HD, there is no federal requirement that a physician be involved.[30]

In situations where a school district, by policy or in a particular situation, does require that an evaluation be conducted by a physician or by some other specialized evaluator who is not on the school's staff, the law requires that the evaluation be conducted at no cost to the parent.

Referrals to private physicians or other outside evaluators are sometimes made by school staff informally, or "off the record," because the school staff wishes either to (1) avoid responsibility for the cost of the private evaluation or (2) avoid getting in trouble with the administration because the school might be held responsible for the cost. In some instances, districts may have formal or informal policies against their staff's making such suggestions. Informal or secret referrals, in any event, do not relieve the district of responsibility for testing. School staffers, moreover, cannot pick and choose when to wear their official hats and when their suggestions are off the record. To avoid confusion, it is always preferable that school personnel openly share concerns about the need for outside evaluation. Unfortunately, because of the tension over financial responsibility, school employees may be inhibited about honestly expressing their views, fearing that they either will be dragged into a dispute by the parents or blamed for the dispute by the school.

It should be noted that the 2004 IDEA provided specific guidance on this issue. It declares that school staff may share information about the need to evaluate a child for a suspected disability but that the staff may neither recommend medication nor set a condition of eligibility for services on the parents' obtaining medication for the child.[31]

Another area of dispute regarding independent evaluators is that they sometimes do not have full information about the educational criteria or language used for evaluation, eligibility, and programming. For example, an evaluator might identify a child as potentially in need of special education services but may fail to evaluate or describe the precise problems that cause "a specific adverse educational impact," as required by law. Again, the IDEA has expanded the requirement for assessment of functional and developmental performance, and this should result in expanded assessments by all evaluators, whether public or private. Often, however, the private evaluator does not incorporate sufficient information about school performance.

In some instances, this may be because the school refuses to give access to such information. At other times, it may be because the evaluator was not aware of the need to obtain—or did not know how to obtain—such information, despite its importance.

E=MC² Advocacy Strategies

As a general matter, it is very important that private evaluators obtain as many different sources of data about school functioning as possible. These may include the following:

(1) use of behavior rating scales, including scales from school staff

(2) review of school records, including school evaluation reports, IEPs, report cards, and behavioral or incident reports

(3) observation, where possible

(4) interviewing school staff by phone, even when direct observation isn't possible

(5) a review and summary of prior testing by the school district, including both individualized assessment and the results of school wide assessments.

When it comes to private evaluations, school districts are sometimes penny wise and pound foolish. First, by refusing to pay for a private evaluation or by making an off the record or "informal" recommendation for private evaluation, the school district loses control over the process of selecting the private evaluator and may end up with an evaluation that has wide implications for the child's eligibility and education but which the school has no ability to influence or control.

Second, by refusing to pay, schools often trigger angry responses from parents, sparking conflicts that escalate far beyond the cost of the evaluation, when agreement on the evaluation may have allowed the parties to move forward in a far more collaborative manner.

Third, in the absence of specific guidance from the school district, the parent may indeed obtain a medical evaluation that doesn't follow accepted standards for evaluation. Nonetheless, based on that inadequate evaluation, the parent is likely to expect the school to recognize the child as eligible for special education or Section 504 protections. For example, it is not uncommon for doctors to provide a one paragraph diagnostic statement that the child has condition X (often AD/HD) and needs service package Y, without describing (or conducting) an appropriate evaluation process or the clinical basis and data that resulted in the diagnosis and recommendations. The parents—despite being armed with an inadequate evaluation—are likely to be angry if they're told services can't be provided. Given the expense of independent evaluations, the fact that insurance companies don't always cover the full or even partial costs, and the difficulty many families have in accessing affordable and competent evaluators, schools that refuse to pay for in depth evaluations (and then refuse to offer services) may find themselves at war with parents—a situation that almost never benefits the school, the family, or the child in question.

In general, schools could avoid many battles if they could reach advance agreement with parents about the need for outside testing and the nature and extent of such testing, while also deciding who will pay for the evaluation and who will conduct it. In the realm of diagnosis of AD/HD, autism, and other complex disorders, the subjective nature of diagnoses makes conflict especially likely and highlights the value of mutually agreed upon independent evaluators.

4

Free Appropriate Public Education and the IEP Process

O nce a child is determined eligible for special education, the Individuals with Disabilities Education Act (IDEA) provides that the student is entitled to receive special education and related services designed to meet his or her unique needs, based on an individualized education program (IEP), in the least restrictive environment appropriate for the child.[1] The critical terms in this general statement of rights and services are *the right to a free appropriate public education* and *the right to services in the least restrictive environment appropriate to the child's needs*. Perhaps the most significant and controversial word in the entire special education statute is the word *appropriate*. When Congress enacted the special education law in 1975, it was unclear whether the intent was for children to receive the maximum level of services possible to ensure that they make the highest degree of educational progress or whether the law intended to provide some lower level of services. This question came to a head in the *Hendrick Hudson School District v. Rowley* Supreme Court decision issued in 1982. The *Rowley* decision has been widely interpreted to mean that children who are eligible for special education services are entitled to receive only services based on an appropriately constructed and legally compliant IEP that provides some educational benefit. This standard has been widely described as entitling children with disabilities to a Chevrolet rather than a Cadillac.

In subsequent years, a number of courts reexamined the 1982 *Rowley* standard and made clear, as the *Rowley* decision does, that *Rowley* required special education services to provide more than just a minimal or trivial educational benefit. In fact, the *Rowley* decision made clear that receiving passing grades and progress from year to year is not necessarily sufficient evidence that a child is receiving a free and appropriate public education. Indeed, *Rowley* called for an individualized assessment of each child's needs and progress in making a determination of whether the child was receiving a free appropriate public education (FAPE).

Following the *Rowley* decision, other courts translated the *Rowley* language into a somewhat more powerful standard, indicating that the child's educational program had to confer "meaningful" benefit or progress. Minimal or trivial progress was not sufficient.[2] Twenty-six years after the decision, however, parents, schools, and courts continue to struggle with the level of educational benefit that must be provided to meet the needs of children with disabilities.[3] As will be discussed below, amendments to the IDEA since 1975 have incorporated detailed new requirements to the IEP process, creating more elaborate rules for how school districts develop IEPs and adding more detailed requirements for the contents of IEPs, to ensure that children's needs are being met. Arguably, the 2004 amendments to the IDEA have gone even further in expanding the scope of the FAPE requirement and ensuring that IEPs, as well as the programming provided by the school system, are based on appropriate professional practices, provided by qualified teachers, and backed by scientific research that supports the effectiveness of the programs being proposed.[4]

In determining whether a child has received a FAPE, the IDEA specifically indicates that the fact that a child is receiving passing grades, advancing from grade to grade, or has not been retained is not by itself evidence that the child is receiving a FAPE.[5]

Although the standard for a FAPE continues to evolve, the details of the process remain enormously important. It is essential that parents, clinicians, and others understand the rules of the IEP process—and the required contents of an IEP—to participate effectively in IEP meetings and assess whether the school district is complying with proper procedures.

E=MC² Advocacy Strategies

Although the standard for free appropriate public education has in some respects been expanding, it remains clear that schools are not obligated to provide every imaginable or preferred service that parents might request for their child. As parents, clinicians and advocates interact with schools, it is critical that they focus on the programs, related services, and accommodations that are necessary for the child to make meaningful educational progress, or any educational progress, rather than on programs or services they feel would be optimal or ideal—but that are not necessarily essential for the child to make educational progress.

The IDEA requires that every child who is eligible for special education have an IEP in place at the start of the semester after the student is found to be eligible, and/or at the beginning of the school year, whichever comes first. The IEP must include a team of individuals, including special educators, at least one regular educator, the parents, and, under some circumstance, the child.[6] The IEP meeting must be convened with advance notice to the parents, informing them of the time, location of the meeting, agenda, and participants at the meeting. The parents must be given the opportunity to meet at a mutually agreeable time and place, although typically the meetings occur during the school day and at the child's school.[7]

At the IEP meeting, the team typically follows a prescribed sequence. First, based on the available evaluations, information, and data on the child, the team determines the identified needs that arise from the child's disability or disabilities. These can include both the needs that arise directly from the disability and those that are indirectly related. Once the needs are identified, the IEP team develops annual goals to address each of the areas of need. As part of the development of the annual goal, the school district is required to identify the child's present level of performance or current functioning at the time of the IEP meeting, to have an accurate baseline in determining progress. Once the current level of functioning has been determined, the team identifies objective and measurable goals that the child can reasonably be anticipated to achieve over the course of the school year. The team also identifies the evaluation methods that will be used periodically to assess the child's progress in relation to those goals.[8]

Under the 2004 IDEA, a prior requirement that every goal be accompanied by short term objectives or benchmarks was deleted. It was left to the states and school districts to decide whether to utilize short term objectives or benchmarks. (Many states and school districts have opted to continue to use them, although this is not universally true.)

Once the team develops the child's goals (and/or also utilizes short term objectives or benchmarks), the next step is for the team to determine the special education, related services, and supplementary aides and accommodations that the child needs to achieve the goals. As will be discussed in more detail, the IEP must provide considerable detail with respect to how, when, and where the various educational services, related services, accommodations, and supports will be provided. The law defines special education as specialized instruction that adapts, as necessary, the content, methodology, and mode of delivery of instruction.[9]

Only after the child's needs, present level of functioning, goals, and needed services are identified is the IEP team—with the participation of the parent—ready to make a determination as to the appropriate special education placement for the student. This recommendation must take into account the IDEA mandate that the child be served in the least restrictive environment appropriate for the child's needs. Consideration should be given, for example, to providing supplemental supports so that the child can be served in a less restrictive environment. Further, even if the child is to be served in a more restrictive environment, the IEP team must consider ways to allow the child to be mainstreamed to the maximum extent appropriate.[10]

Unfortunately, in some cases, participants see the IEP process as a necessary bureaucratic requirement that must be satisfied for compliance reasons, rather than as a process that can provide important information in developing effective plans, evaluating whether the plans are working, and adapting or modifying the plans as needed. Many school staff perceive the IEP planning process—and the documentation required as an adjunct to the IEP process—to be highly burdensome and undesirable, robbing them of time that would otherwise be available for instruction. As a consequence, IEP meetings are not always used as effective planning and review tools. Further, because the IEP process can be highly adversarial and is often seen as *pro forma,* or "make work," it sometimes contributes to alienation or even conflict between parents and educators. This is completely the opposite of the intent of Congress, which adopted the IEP process in an effort to promote a partnership between parents and educators—a collaboration in the development of appropriate programming for children with disabilities that would capitalize on the differing information, skills, interests, and priorities of the participants. The result, as Congress intended it, would be a program most likely to allow the child to achieve meaningful progress.

Three key elements of the IEP process have become focal points for conflicts. First, the IDEA requires that parents have a right to participate as "equal participants" in the IEP meeting but gives the ultimate decision as to the content of the IEP to the school staff. Parents are led to believe that they will participate equally but are often surprised when their objection to a particular element of a proposed program is ignored or denied. In fact, the IDEA allows parents to challenge decisions of the IEP team by requesting a due process hearing, rather than by exercising a simple veto at a meeting.

A second source of conflict and misunderstanding involves the process of developing annual goals and the significance of these goals. Many parents assume that the IEP goals are, in effect, a binding contract on the school system. The failure of the student to meet the goals constitutes for some parents evidence that the school district has failed to meet its obligations. There are many reasons that students may fail to meet their goals and objectives, however, and not all those reasons are based on the school district's failure to do its job. The school district's responsibility is to ensure that appropriate and reasonably achievable goals are developed, that proper services are identified to help students reach the goals, and that the services are actually implemented. Where the school fails to fulfill these obligations, it may be legally responsible either for developing an inadequate IEP or for failing to implement an appropriate IEP. However, this is very different from being automatically at fault because students did not achieve their goals. Failure to meet goals, among other things, could be due to illness, the development of other areas of disability, or the IEP team's deliberate decision to adopt especially challenging goals (with the recognition that the student might not achieve all of them). Still, because parents are seeking as much progress for their child as possible, the failure to meet goals is often a source of tension. Conversely, schools often set a low bar in relation to the goals to make it more likely that the student will achieve them, thereby giving themselves some protection against assertions that their program is inadequate.

Finally, there are frequent disputes between parents and educators over the level or nature of services to be provided, and/or the methods to be used. Schools often provide services based on the educational models and related service professionals they have available, rather than on the individual needs of a particular student. Conversely, parents often seek educational services, methods, types, or intensity of services that are not readily available in the school system. Educators sometimes argue that these issues are outside the scope of the IEP process, claiming that methodology is not even an IEP issue. The IDEA, however, makes clear that methodology is indeed an appropriate consideration in the IEP process, if the method is necessary for the student to benefit from education. Examples of methodologies that sometimes cause disputes are applied behavioral analysis for children with autism or a multisensory reading program for children with reading disabilities. In addition, the 2004 amendments explicitly require that programs be based on peer reviewed research to the extent practicable.[11] This new requirement has encouraged parents to engage in more specific discussions at IEP meetings about the nature and intensity of their child's program, rather than leave it to the discretion of the school team.

IEP team participants

According to the IDEA, participants in the IEP team must include:

1. the parent or parents of the child with the disability (for children aged 3 to whatever is the legal age of adulthood in each state); the child's legal guardian, or the child's surrogate parent;
2. at least one of the child's regular education teachers, if the child is or may be participating in regular education;
3. at least one special education teacher or other special education provider for the child;
4. a representative of the school district who is qualified to provide or supervise the instruction provided to the student, is knowledgeable about the general education curriculum, and is knowledgeable about the resources available in the school system;
5. a school representative who is qualified to interpret the "instructional implications" of any evaluation results;
6. any individual with knowledge or special expertise concerning the child who is invited by the parent or the school district.[12]

If a child is 18 years of age or older, he or she should be invited, rather than the parent, unless the parent has established legal guardianship or has been authorized by the child to act on his or her behalf, pursuant to the state's procedures for allowing such parental involvement.[13]

In addition, if the child is 16 or older and the purpose of the IEP meeting is to discuss transition planning, the school is required to invite the student, although it remains the parents' choice as to whether the child attends, unless the child is the age of majority and has not been declared incompetent by a court.[14]

Transition planning for students aged 16 and older has additional requirements. If, in order to implement some part of the transition plan, the school system is considering referring the child to another agency for services, the school must ensure that a representative from that agency is invited to the meeting.[15] In addition, if the child is transitioning from early childhood (birth to age 3) services to special education services (ages 3 to 21), the parents must be advised that, at their request, the school must invite a representative from the early childhood team to participate in the initial IEP meeting.[16]

Under the 2004 IDEA, required members of the IEP team may be excused from participation, for part or all of the meeting, if the parent and the school district agree that the person's attendance is not necessary because the topic of the meeting is not related to that individual's responsibilities.[17] The new amendments allow a team member to be excused, even if the subject of the meeting is relevant to his or her area of responsibility, if the parent and the school system agree to the excusal and the staff person, prior to the meeting, submits a written report to the parent and the team concerning the topic being discussed. On the other hand, if parents wish to have other people attend—whether they are friends, relatives, outside clinicians, advocates, or experts—the law gives parents the sole discretion to determine whether the individuals meet the requirement for having "knowledge or special expertise regarding the child."[18]

Similarly, the school may invite individuals at its discretion, but the IDEA also requires that, prior to any IEP meeting, the school district must provide the parents with written notice indicating "the purpose, time and location of the meeting and who will be in attendance." Unless or until the child reaches the age of majority, the school has the option of inviting the student, but the parent retains the discretion as to whether the student will attend. When the purpose of the IEP meeting is to discuss transition planning, the school is legally required to invite the student.[19] If parents opt to have their child excused from the meeting, the school district is required to obtain the student's input by some other means.

Historically, the U.S. Department of Education interpreted the IDEA to require that an official who has the authority to approve the funds or resources needed to implement a child's program must attend the IEP meeting. Under the 2004 IDEA, however, there is no specific requirement that an administrator with authority to approve resources be present. Instead, the law vests in the IEP team the authority to make the decisions regarding the child's special education program, placement, and services.[20]

Decisions made outside of the IEP meeting by administrators or others, without the participation of the IEP team, and particularly without the participation of the parents, would appear to violate this requirement. Thus, even though the regulations do not expressly list a person with authority to commit resources as a required participant, this is arguably necessary anyway.

In order to promote parental participation, the law requires that the school district give parents sufficient advance notice of the IEP meetings to ensure that they have an opportunity to attend and that the meetings are scheduled at a "mutually agreed on time and place." In reality, meetings are typically held at school during school hours.

The law does require, however, that the school district make a "good faith effort" to include the parents at a mutually agreeable time and place. If parents cannot attend in person, the IDEA requires that the school offer them the ability to participate by phone. If the school district has made a good faith effort to secure the parents' participation, and the parents still do not attend, the district is permitted to go forward with the IEP meeting without their presence.[21]

E=MC² Advocacy Strategies: Preparing for IEP Meetings

(1) It's advisable for parents always to make sure they know the identities of the individuals identified in the IEP meeting notice, prior to arriving at the meeting.

(2) Parents should be aware of the agenda for the meeting and try to determine, in part based on who is invited to the meeting, how the

school may be intending to modify or change their child's eligibility or placement. (For example, if the school district invites a representative of a particular program—a person who has not previously been involved with the child—it may indicate that the district is contemplating changing the child's placement to that new program.)

(3) Some school districts require advance notice if parents intend to bring additional parties to the meeting. It is questionable whether this kind of advanced notice requirement is permitted by the IDEA. However, if parents are aware of the requirement and do not have problems with it, it is generally preferable to avoid conflict around the issue.

(4) It is generally desirable for parents to avoid surprises and notify the school in advance if they are bringing people who the school district does not expect. This is particularly a concern if parents are bringing an advocate or attorney. If the parent arrives at an IEP meeting with an advocate or an attorney and the school district has not been alerted, the school may simply postpone or cancel the meeting to make sure it has legal counsel present. (However, parents and their advocates must make their decision about notification on a case by case basis.)

(5) It is generally a good idea for the parent to go to IEP meetings with a spouse, significant other, or someone who can provide support, information, advice, and a second set of ears. The support person can also take notes, allowing the parent to focus better on what's being said.

(6) If the child has been evaluated or is being treated by outside professionals who have relevant information about the child's disabilities, eligibility, needs, or current functioning, it may be useful for parents to invite them to meetings as well. Again, it is often advisable to give advance notice to the school district. It is also useful to stress the nonadvocacy roles of the professionals—as evaluators or therapists, for example—in order to preserve their credibility with the school staff.

(7) If parents want specific school staff to be at the meeting, and the staff members are not listed in the meeting invitation, it is wise to contact school—via the director of special education, a case manager,

or other officials—and request that the person attend, then confirm the request in writing.

(8) The new rules do allow particular staff members to miss IEP meetings and submit a report in lieu of appearing. However, when the topic of the meeting directly involves a school employee, the written report may be an inadequate substitute. Parents should exercise caution in excusing staff people from meetings simply in an effort to accommodate the school system, particularly if they have concerns about matters that are the staffer's responsibility. Indeed, excusing any staff member can be detrimental since even the staffers who are not involved with agenda items can provide useful information or input.

(9) When parents invite friends, relatives, or other people to attend the meeting, it is important to advise the individuals in advance about the meeting agenda, the parents' plans for the meeting, and the role the person is being asked to play. For example, a person might be asked to serve as an advocate or as the parents' primary spokesperson. However, parents should avoid bringing anyone to the meeting who does not understand the process or might get involved in ways that are unhelpful, combative, or based on misinformation. Ultimately, the parents must set the tone; people who accompany them must respect their wishes.

(10) At times, parents may prefer that certain school staff members do not attend the IEP meeting. They can raise this issue with school administrators in advance of the meeting or at the meeting, but they generally do not have the legal right to prevent a school employee from attending as long as the person was listed on the prior meeting notice and has some knowledge of the child or, in the school's opinion, has relevant knowledge or expertise.

On the other hand, if a school staff person, consultant for the school district, or school attorney arrives at the meeting and was not listed on the formal meeting notice, the parent does have the right to exclude that person. The parent should exercise this choice carefully since asking to exclude an individual may simply result in the meeting's being postponed in order for a proper notice to be issued that does list the person. Parents should be especially concerned, however, when school districts invite their attorneys without providing prior written notice. If the parents feel uncomfortable about proceeding with the IEP meeting in the presence of the school attorney, it may be important to object to the attorney's presence, even if it means the meeting has to be postponed. The postponement in this case would also allow parents a chance to bring their own attorney or advocate to the rescheduled meeting.

(11) Because it is not uncommon for school districts to set time limits on IEP meetings, it is advisable for parents—before or at the start of the meeting—to establish how much time has been allocated. That way, parents are fully prepared and aware of how much time is available to hear school input and provide their own feedback. If the amount of time provided is insufficient or if a meeting is not finished at the point when the clock runs out, parents have the right to request that the meeting be adjourned and reconvened at a later date. The school district has the right to honor or refuse this request. However, parents always have the right to request additional IEP meetings at any time, as long as the scheduling does not become excessive.

If the school district terminates an IEP meeting prior to the parents having an adequate opportunity to raise questions, share their concerns, or address any problems or issues they have, parents should document their request that the meeting be either continued or reconvened. In addition, parents should document in the IEP report itself or in a follow up letter their belief that the school district would not allow them to participate fully or express some or all of their concerns. If parents were accompanied by clinical professionals whose input was not permitted or whose input was not documented in the IEP report, it is important that this oversight be documented as well. Parents should write a letter or insert in the IEP report that the school district did not provide adequate opportunity for input from outside professionals.

Contents of the IEP

The IDEA provides a logical, sequential, and integrated procedure for developing an educational program that addresses all of the needs related to a child's disability. It establishes goals for the child to achieve during the school year; assures that the content of the program is relevant, both in assisting the child to progress in relation to the general curriculum and the child's particular needs; and lists in detail the special education, related services, accommodations, adaptations, and supports the child should receive to make meaningful educational progress.

The IDEA also specifies a decision making process in which the school must consider multiple placement options to meet the child's needs. The school must document that the option selected provides the child with appropriate education in the least restrictive environment.

The IDEA requires that the IEP document the disability category or categories under which the child is eligible to receive services.[22] This disability label is the threshold for entry into the special education system. However, it is not supposed either to predetermine or limit the needs that may be identified as a result of the child's condition, nor should it predetermine or limit the educational services that the child may require or be provided. The law requires that the IEP identify not only the disability itself but also any collateral effects of the disability that require remediation.[23] In addition, as previously noted, the definition of "adverse effect on educational performance" is more broadly construed under the 2004 IDEA to incorporate the child's academic, developmental, and functional performance.[24]

In addition to a more general statement identifying the child's disability or disabilities, both by category and based on their specific manifestations, the IDEA requires that the IEP include a statement about the child's present level of academic achievement and functional performance.[25] This statement is often referred to as "present level of performance (PLOP)." It is of special importance because it establishes a baseline, in relation to the child's current level of functioning, which allows the IEP team to determine what the annual goals should be for the child, including the amount of desired or anticipated progress the student should make during the school year.

The present level of performance in each area of need should be described in objective and quantifiable terms that allow for meaningful comparison over time. It is not enough that the present level of performance states that the child is below grade level. Rather, the statement should indicate the skill that is of specific concern and the student's actual level of functioning in that area. For example, a present level of performance might read that a student is currently able to decode words for reading at a 1.2 grade level—the level of a first grader—although the child is in fifth grade. The assessment used to establish the PLOP should also be specified, so that the child's progress can be accurately compared to their initial level of functioning.

In addition, the initial statement of current functioning should explain how the child's disability affects his or her involvement and progress in the general curriculum. For preschool children, it should state how the disability affects the child's participation in age appropriate activities. For children who, by virtue of the severity of their disability, are identified as requiring alternative assessments to the standard state wide achievement testing, the IEP should also identify a description of the benchmarks or short term objectives that will be used for that child over the course of the school year.

Once the child's present needs and levels of performance are identified, the IEP team should develop measurable annual goals to address each of the academic, developmental, or functional needs already identified. These should include goals that address the child's ability to participate in and make progress in the general curriculum and that meet the child's other educational needs. Though they are no longer legally mandated, short term objectives or benchmarks are still being used by many states and school districts. It is important for parents and clinicians to find out in advance of any IEP meeting whether their school district utilizes these tools so that they are adequately prepared to discuss them. Whether short term objectives or benchmarks are used in addition to annual goals, the law continues to require that the IEP contain a description of how the child's progress toward meeting the annual goals will be measured. It also establishes the procedure for periodic reporting on the progress the child is making. The IDEA indicates that this evaluation and reporting procedure can be provided through "quarterly or other periodic reports, concurrent with the issuance of report cards." [26]

In the development of the IEP, the law requires that the team take a number of specific factors into account. The IEP must consider the strengths of the child; the parents' concerns about enhancing the child's education; the results of both the initial and the most current evaluations concerning the child; and "the academic, developmental and functional needs of the child."[27]

The IEP should not be focused solely on the child's deficits but should also capitalize on the child's strengths. For example, if a child is an auditory learner, rather than a visual learner, the IEP might call for teaching strategies that take advantage of oral instruction while also providing remediation for the child's difficulties using visual formats.

Parents' input must be given serious consideration by the IEP team, and the IEP must address broad areas of academic, developmental, and functional needs. This language is of sufficient breadth that it would appear to include essentially all areas of the child's functioning at school. "Developmental needs" includes such things as communication, motor skills, social skills, daily living skills, and the ability to function in school in general. Functional performance is equally important, as it reflects the mandate that the IEP address how the child performs in the real world. It is not enough that the child can do well on a test of language in a clinical setting. The child should be able to use the language appropriately within the classroom, in the lunchroom, or on the playground.

$E=MC^2$ Advocacy Strategies: Writing Goals and Objectives

(1) Goals are supposed to reflect what can realistically be accomplished over the course of the school year. The goals are based on the best professional judgment of the school team, with the input (and, in the best circumstances, the agreement) of the parents. Goals are not contractually binding but are supposed to reflect a reasonable determination of what the child can achieve, given the provision and implementation of appropriate programming.

(2) Goals are supposed to address each area of identified needs for the child. In developing goals, a balance should be struck to ensure that critical areas of need are addressed but that there aren't so many goals that the child and staff are overwhelmed. There is no rule that sets a minimum or maximum number of IEP goals.

(3) If parents have previously had an IEP that listed short term objectives or benchmarks—and now have an IEP that calls for year end goals only—they should incorporate the short term objectives into the new plan. For example, if the child previously had a school year goal to improve reading—and short term objectives for decoding, reading comprehension, and fluency—the parent should try to make sure that decoding, reading comprehension, and fluency are referenced in the new goals.

(4) Where short term objectives or benchmarks are used, it may be helpful if the objectives are sequential, each building toward the accomplishment of the ultimate goal. For example, if the goal were to expand sight word vocabulary by 100 words from the child's baseline, the short term objectives might call for 25 new sight words each quarter. Alternatively, short term objectives may address different skill sets that need to be remediated in order for the child to reach the ultimate goal. If the goal is to improve social skills, there might be a short term objective addressing initiation of social contact and a second short term objective addressing listening skills or allowing a conversation partner the opportunity to talk.

(5) Goals are always supposed to be directed at what the child will accomplish. At times, schools have set goals that address what the staff or even what the parents are expected to accomplish during the year. Any activity that is expected of the school staff should be written into the IEP in the special education, related services, supplemental aids, and support section. All services should list the starting date, frequency, and duration within the IEP. The activities of the school staff are not goals for an IEP. Rather, they are expectations for job performance.

At the same time, although parents have moral and legal responsibilities for the upbringing of their children, the IEP cannot set goals for parent performance. If there are activities that the parents are asked to do or volunteer to do, these activities can be indicated in a "supplementary services" or "note section" of the IEP. There is neither a legal basis for writing parental goals nor a legal basis for holding parents accountable for completing activities that the IEP team deems desirable.

(6) Goals should not only identify the task to be completed but should also contain the criteria that will indicate that progress or mastery has occurred. For example, a goal might be that a child "will initiate an appropriate social greeting to a typically developing peer, in four out of five trials in a week."

Implicit in this statement is not only the outcome measure but also a condition affecting how the goal will be completed: to wit, a greeting to a typically developing peer. This would suggest that the child must have opportunities for interaction with typically developing peers in order for the goal even to be practiced.

Other examples of how conditions can be written into goals might state, for example, that Student A will achieve goal B "when given a teacher prompt"; or "when given grade level, age appropriate reading material"; or "when provided with reading material at child's instructional level."

By writing the goals in a manner that incorporates the strategy or circumstances that will be used, it is possible to build in more direction as to how the goals will be achieved and more precision as to how they will be evaluated.

(7) All goals must be both attainable and relevant to the child's needs. A goal that allows for mastery at too low a level is of little or no utility. Similarly, a goal that provides for a student to accomplish something that they are already capable of doing would not be appropriate. A goal that addresses an irrelevant skill is not appropriate, either. For example, it would not be appropriate to write a goal for a student to complete algebraic equations if the student is still working on basic math facts.

(8) Goals should be written with clarity, using words and terms that will be understood by anyone reading them. As a rule of thumb, people who are not members of the IEP team or do not know the student should be able to understand the goal as well as the people who participated in writing it.

(9) The outcome measure for the goal must be as objective as possible, involving concrete measurements instead of informal or subjective observations. For example, if the child currently knows multiplication tables from one through five, the present level of performance should state that accomplishment, and the goal might be for the child to master multiplication tables from six through ten. In addition, the goal could include an assessment procedure based on testing or work samples; in this case, a teacher's observations—"John did better this year in math"—would not be sufficient.

(10) In some instances, however, the nature of the goal does require subjective judgment. This is particularly true with respect to behavioral and social goals. Where more subjective goals are written, it remains important to have clear baseline data and to have a measurable goal and evaluations that can be compared to the baseline data.

For example, when a child has difficulty with social initiation, the baseline might read: "Given opportunities for social greeting with a peer, the child currently initiates a social greeting in one out of five trials."

The outcome measure for the goal might be: "Child will initiate social greetings with a peer in three out of five trials."

(11) Quantitative goals should not be set in ways that are impossible to evaluate. For example, a statement that "child will improve self esteem with 80 percent accuracy" would defy objective assessment. It is important that the goal be stated in a way that allows for assessment of measurable and meaningful outcomes.

(12) Goals should not be unrealistic or stated as absolute even if the desired outcome is 100 percent compliance. Some goals should be accompanied by direct linkage to staff responsibilities. For example, if a child is an escape risk, it may be appropriate to write a goal that "the child will refrain from leaving the classroom inappropriately or without permission 70 percent of the time." However, a notation in the supports and aids section of the IEP should call for staff supervision of the child and a safety plan to assure that, if the child does leave the classroom, he or she will be safely intercepted and redirected back to the classroom. A goal that the child will refrain from leaving the classroom 100 percent of the time is meaningless in the absence of an adult plan to ensure that the child remains in class.

In addition to these considerations, the IDEA also contains particular requirements for children with specialized needs. For children whose behavior interferes with their learning or the learning of others, the IEP team must consider the use of positive behavioral intervention strategies and supports and other strategies to improve the child's behavior.[28]

The emphasis on positive behavioral intervention strategies and supports can cover a wide variety of strategies, services, and accommodations. They could include counseling services to address the child's emotional or psychological needs, social skills training to assist the child with social deficits, a positive reinforcement system to reward or motivate the child for displaying appropriate behavior, and/or environmental modifications to remove or modify environmental or academic problems that provoke the child's inappropriate behavior.

With respect to children with limited English proficiency, the IDEA requires that the child's language be taken into account. It also requires that students who are blind or visually impaired be provided instruction in Braille (unless the team determines that the use of Braille is not appropriate for the child). For children who are deaf or hard of hearing, the team must consider the child's language and communication mode as well as opportunities for interaction with peers and professionals who utilize the child's language and communication mode. In addition, for all children with disabilities, the IDEA requires that the IEP team consider whether the child needs assistive technology devices and services.[29]

The IDEA defines *assistive technology* broadly to include both "assistive technology devices," including any device that is used to increase, maintain, or improve the child's functional capabilities and "assistive technology services," which include evaluation of the child's assistive technology needs; procuring assistive technology devices; selecting, designing, customizing, adapting, maintaining, and repairing devices; coordinating the use of assistive technology with other therapies or services; and training the child, the family, and professional staff on the use of the technology.[30]

Obviously, the breadth of evaluation and the provision of hardware, software, and services to address the assistive technology needs of children with disabilities—as well as to help their families and the staff members who work with them—offer broad opportunities for helping students.

It should be noted that assistive technology includes everything from "low tech technology" such as adaptive pencil grips and basic picture symbol systems to complex computer based systems, which help with communication, reading, writing, math, or other subjects.

IEP meeting process

The IDEA also provides detailed procedures for when and how IEP meetings are conducted. Under the 2004 IDEA, parents and school staff may now informally agree to modify an IEP without the necessity of an IEP meeting if the staff person and parent mutually agree to the change. When this occurs, the change in the IEP must be shared with the parent upon request and with the remainder of the team after the informal IEP discussion.[31]

This change will promote efficiency and reduce the need for unnecessary IEP meetings when there is genuine agreement between the parents and the school. However, it is also ripe for causing disagreements with respect to whether genuine agreement had occurred.

Parents, clinicians, and educators are strongly encouraged to ensure that any proposed informal modification of an IEP be put in writing prior to the consideration of the change and that all team members, including the parent, sign off on the proposed change before it is considered official. If there is any question about the desirability of the informally proposed change, parents should insist on convening a formal IEP meeting.

Statement of programs and services

Once the goals and, where appropriate, short term objectives or benchmarks are written, the IEP team must write a statement identifying all special education and related services to be provided to the student.[32] This statement must include any supplementary aids and services that the student may require, as well as provide details about program modifications or supports that school personnel may require to implement the IEP. In addition, the special education and related services to be provided must be "based upon peer reviewed research to the extent practicable." Further, the program developed by the IEP team must be designed to enable the child to advance appropriately toward his or her goals; to participate in and make progress in relation to the general curriculum; to participate in extracurricular and nonacademic activities; and to be educated and participate with other children as much as possible. Further, the program must include a statement about any accommodations that are needed to measure accurately the child's academic achievement and performance using state or district wide assessments or any alternative means of assessing the child if he or she is exempted from the traditional assessment process. The law also requires that the IEP provide an explanation of the extent to which the child will be educated separate from children without disabilities, either with respect to classroom activities or in relation to other school activities.[33]

The 2004 IDEA introduced for the first time the requirement that the special education program offered to the student be based on peer reviewed research to the extent practicable. Historically, school programs were sometimes based on what the school had available, without regard to whether the program had a foundation in peer reviewed research or had a track record of success.

The new requirement that the school's programs be based upon peer reviewed research to the extent practicable requires that schools examine the programs they have offered and/or are proposing. They must do so not only based on their prior experience but also based on sound educational research. In addition, the requirement suggests that a discussion about the research behind a particular proposed program is an appropriate topic for the IEP team, including the parents.

Parents may be better able to address concerns about the adequacy of a particular program if they have seen the program's peer reviewed research. If it doesn't have a peer reviewed research base, there is a stronger argument to use other programs that are based on peer reviewed research.

The IEP must also specify the starting date, frequency, duration, and location of services of all special education, related services, and supplementary aids and supports.[34] This means that the IEP should spell out in detail when, where, for how long, and in what intensity each service will be provided for the student. These details are important to the school staff to make sure they know what is to be provided but also help parents make sure their child is receiving what he or she is supposed to.

The requirement that the IEP specify the necessary supports for school personnel—which are provided to enable the child to make progress on goals—opens up the critical issue of whether the IEP team has the training, resources, time, and support necessary to implement the IEP adequately. Where a child has needs that go beyond the available time, training, or experience of the IEP team, the IEP should specify the additional supports the staff should receive to be able to implement the program effectively.

In addition to these services, the IEP must include a statement of the assistive technology and assistive technology services that the child needs to benefit from his or her education and a statement of how the child will be provided access to the general curriculum, regardless of whether the child is primarily based in regular education or special education classes.[35] The IEP must also include a statement about the placement options that were considered and rejected by the team and the reasons they were rejected, as well as the extent that the child will participate in regular, nonacademic, and extracurricular activities, even if the child is not based in regular education.[36] Along with this, the IEP must specify all modifications, supports, and aids that the child requires, including those necessary for the child to participate in regular education. It must also specify any positive behavioral intervention strategies and supports that the child requires.[37]

Timing of the IEP

For those children who are not yet in special education, the IEP must be developed within 30 days of the date that the child is determined eligible for special education and must be implemented as soon as possible following the development of the IEP. For students already in special education, the IEP must be in place no later than the beginning of the school year.[38]

Access to the IEP

At the conclusion of the IEP process, the parent must be provided with a copy of the IEP at no cost. In addition, the contents of the child's IEP must be provided to each regular and special education teacher or other service provider who is responsible for its implementation. Further, each staff person responsible for its implementation must be informed of his or her specific responsibilities related to the IEP and the specific accommodations, modifications, and supports that must be provided for the child in accordance with the IEP.[39]

E=MC² Advocacy Strategies:
General IEP Strategies

(1) Many people perceive the IEP process to be a burdensome bureaucratic exercise, without recognizing the significance of the IEP in helping to shape the breadth and depth of the child's program and the specific services the child will receive, to provide an accurate way for assessing the child's progress, and to provide accountability regarding the services being offered. Difficult as it may sometimes be, the IEP process is an essential part of ensuring that a child receives an appropriate education.

(2) Parents should maintain ongoing discussions with school staff about their child's needs and progress. When problems are occurring, regular communication between parents and school staff, in anticipation of the potential revision of the IEP, will help to ensure that the IEP meeting will be as productive as possible. In general, meetings will be more productive if there are fewer surprises.

(3) Prior to the IEP meetings, it is important for parents to have as much information about how their child is doing as possible to ensure that the program is working effectively. If the child is making insufficient progress, the parents should research ways that the program could be changed to increase the potential progress the child might make. If the child is making especially good progress, it may be appropriate for the child to be considered for less restrictive settings, less intense services, and/or a return to regular education status.

(4) If parents feel that the child is not being adequately served within the existing program, they should research other options that may be available through the school system or outside the system. Unfortunately, it should not be assumed that all options that may be appropriate for the student will necessarily be presented to the parent. If other options are available that may be more appropriate or effective, parents may need to research or locate them on their own and will be more able to secure those services if they can convey the reasons that such programs or services are necessary.

(5) If the parents have concerns regarding the child's unmet, new, or changing needs, it is important that they organize data supporting those concerns in advance of the IEP meeting and have it available for presentation at the IEP meeting. This can include clinical information from outside professionals, review of school district progress reports and IEPs, and the parents' own observations with respect to the child's functioning. This can be based on information such as a collection of the child's homework, review of the child's study patterns, or observation of academic or other behaviors that cause the parent concern.

(6) If the parent has ideas for needs, goals or, where utilized, short term objectives or benchmarks, it is sometimes useful to share these with school staff in advance of the meeting, as well as to obtain any information from the school staff as to their perceptions of the child's needs and to review draft or proposed goals that they may have concerning the child. The law precludes school districts from determining the child's goals or placement in advance of the IEP meeting. Thus, staff is sometimes fearful of sharing information with the parents in advance, even in draft form. However, as long as

information is shared by the school in draft form and is truly open to discussion and modification at the IEP meeting, the school district is not legally compromised by having developed such information in advance of the IEP meeting.

(7) Parents, prior to the IEP meeting, may wish to prepare a checklist of their concerns about their child to ensure that the concerns are addressed.

(8) If the parents have questions about any information shared at the meeting, they should ask for an explanation. They might need to know the meaning, for example, of the terminology that is used—the alphabet soup that school staff may use concerning the child. They can ask questions about the meanings of test scores, the data supporting conclusions or observations that the school staff is providing, or any other information shared or referred to by school personnel. It is better to ask questions than not to understand what is being discussed.

(9) In addition, under federal law, parents have a right to obtain copies of the student's school records. Thus, most (though not necessarily all) information discussed at the IEP meeting will ultimately be obtainable by the parent based on a request for the records, even if the records are not provided prior to the meeting.

If parents have serious concerns with respect to how the child is doing and/or feel that there is a developing conflict with the school district, they may wish to request a copy of the child's school records well in advance of the IEP meeting or can request the opportunity to review them prior to the meeting.

(10) At the conclusion of the IEP meeting, it is advisable for parents to review the IEP document carefully to ensure that it accurately reflects the discussion that occurred. This does not mean parents need to edit every typographical error or minor misstatement. But it is important to make sure that the document adequately and accurately captures the present levels of performance, goals, services, modifications, accommodations, and supports that are going to be provided, as well as any concerns, suggestions, or objections that the staff or parents raised.

(11) If parents disagree with the IEP, they have the right to submit a dissent or statement clarifying their concerns or objections. They have the right to request a due process hearing to challenge the content and conclusions of the IEP at any time. However, expressing objection to the IEP does not serve as a blanket veto of the IEP. If parents wish to block or overturn the IEP and the school is unwilling to change its position, the parents' remedy is to pursue a due process hearing.

(12) If the IEP recommends a change of placement for the child, the parents should be aware that if they request an immediate due process hearing, the school district must maintain the last agreed upon educational placement until the due process procedure is concluded.[40] The only exception to this rule is if the school district is suspending the student for fewer than ten days or transferring the student for up to 45 school days to an interim alternative educational setting due to the allegation that the student was in possession of drugs or dangerous weapons, harmed themselves or another student, or posed a serious harm to themselves or another student (as determined by a hearing officer).[41]

(13) In some instances, parents may feel that a specific methodology is required to address their child's educational needs. Some school districts take the position that methodology is not an IEP issue and refuse to discuss it at the IEP meeting. The IDEA defines special education as specialized instruction, including adapting, as necessary, the methodology for the student. Therefore, methodology is an appropriate discussion item at the IEP conference, particularly if there is evidence that the student is not making adequate educational progress with the programming that the school district has been providing or is recommending.[42] However, parents do not have the right to require a particular methodology simply based on their own preference or their dislike of a methodology the school utilizes, as long as the school's methodology is professionally accepted and supported by peer reviewed research.

(14) Parents, clinicians, and educators should utilize the IEP meetings as a collaborative process to solve problems and promote improved educational outcomes for the child. Wherever possible, parents should

set priorities and pick their battles carefully to ensure that they do not get caught up in contentious disputes with the schools over issues that are relatively insignificant in relation to the child's overall educational functioning.

Similarly, schools should attempt to work collaboratively with parents and address their concerns respectfully and seriously, even if the staff perceives that the parents may be questioning some aspects of the school's programming.

(15) When parents have concerns with respect to the competency, experience, personality, or conduct of a particular school staff person, it is often preferable that these issues be addressed with the staff person privately and/or with the staff person's supervisors or higher level administrators, rather than in the context of an IEP meeting.

Discussions of teacher performance or competence at an IEP meeting are likely to lead to defensive reactions from school staff and make it more likely that the administration will defend the staff person. However, if these concerns are not successfully resolved, it is important that parents document these concerns in writing with the school district.

E=MC² Advocacy Strategies: Supports for School Staff

(1) Under the law, school staff members can be given a wide variety of supports that help enable them to implement the IEP effectively.

(2) In the context of the IEP meeting, where possible, it is preferable that parents and outside clinicians raise suggestions about the need for staff support in a manner that conveys support for the staff and sympathy for their need for assistance, rather than criticism or skepticism about their competency. While this is not always possible, framing the suggestions in a positive way may make it more likely that suggestions will be adopted.

(3) Because the requests for more support sometimes put the direct service staff in conflict with the school administration, it is not always politically feasible for school personnel to bring up their concerns about

their ability to carry out aspects of the IEP. However, when staffers bring up the need for support at the IEP meeting—or raise concerns about their ability to accomplish certain parts of the IEP without it—their statements provide a powerful springboard for building additional staff supports into the IEP (and improving its effectiveness and success).

(4) Examples of support for the staff include in-service training with respect to the child's disability and the educational strategies necessary to assist the child. Such training may be provided to groups of teachers during school wide in-service training programs, through the use of outside consultants or master teachers to provide training to staff in relation to a particular child, or through district support for staff to participate in continuing education programs or conferences where they can obtain the necessary training. Most state departments of education also have staff that provide technical support and training to school districts and their staff.

(5) In-service training may be suggested as part of the school district's ongoing staff development plans and may include in-service training prior to the start of the school or during teacher institute or staff development days.

In addition, in-service training can be provided on an ongoing basis through the school year, through consultation or support from special educators, master teachers, related service professionals, or expert consultants.

Typically, schools provide limited in-service training on any given topic. here possible, it is desirable to build in ongoing in-service training to boost staff skills and promote the staff's ability to carry out desired tasks effectively. For example, a teacher may not have experience working with a child who is nonverbal and uses technology to communicate. Targeted training on how to use the child's communication system would be critical to the teacher's ability to work with the student effectively. Sometimes schools provide a particular methodology for the student, which requires special staff training, but do not provide the teacher the intensity of training needed to implement the method or programs successfully. An introductory overview to a program is not the same as a training program designed to prepare the teacher to implement the methodology. Parents, clinicians, and educators should all be leery of the commitment to provide a particular methodology without sufficient ongoing training, consultation, and support to ensure that the staff actually has the expertise to implement the method or intervention.

(6) In many school districts, team teaching or collaborative teaching models are being adopted in which special education and regular education teachers may co-teach a class that includes both regular and special education students.

Sometimes this model incorporates the collaborative teaching on a formal basis throughout the school year, with each teacher having specified responsibilities for different parts of the curriculum. In other models, a special education teacher may be present in the classroom to assist students one on one, while the regular education teacher remains responsible for the primary delivery of the curriculum and instruction.

(7) Often, teachers may require consultation with respect to the programming for a particular student. This can include consultation on curriculum modification, behavioral management, use of assistive technology, provision of particular remedial teaching strategies, and the like.

(8) When, by virtue of the complexity or intensity of the children's needs, the involvement with one or more children with disabilities requires extra time for the staff, the IEP can specifically incorporate plans that give teachers extra preparation time. This provides them with greater opportunity to spend the time needed for planning or carrying out services for the children with disabilities, while also managing responsibilities for other students. The IEP can also specify that the teacher receive assistance from a curricular consultant or get other help so that he or she can meet the needs of the specific students and the rest of the class as well.

(9) With respect to children with behavioral challenges, the IEP team may identify the need for behavior intervention specialists to assist in the development, monitoring, implementation, and modification of behavior intervention strategies in the classroom. Many schools are adopting school wide positive behavioral intervention and support

models. These are often helpful but not necessarily sufficient for the needs of particular children with behavioral challenges.

Many teachers, moreover, do not have experience in conducting functional behavioral analyses or in developing and implementing behavior intervention plans for individual children. Behavior specialists are important in assisting staff in these types of situations.

(10) Under some circumstances, the nature or severity of a child's disability may require the provision of a classroom or one to one paraprofessional or aide to assist the teacher. The teacher must always retain supervisory and direct responsibility for the child's instruction, but specific tasks can be delegated to the paraprofessional.

The provision of a one to one aide may be based on the child's need for medical or health management; the need to assist the student with the use of technology; the need to help the student carry out basic academic tasks (such as a student who is severely dysgraphic and cannot write or type); or the need to provide adult supervision for a student who is extremely hyperactive or aggressive and needs help to remain on task or maintain appropriate behavioral control.

Some schools have policies that limit the provision of one to one paraprofessional support for particular categories of disability. Such policies are inherently suspect and contrary to the IDEA. They also violate Section 504, which prohibits discrimination based on the nature or severity of disability. The entitlement to a classroom or one to one aide should be based on the child's individual needs, not based on the category of disability or a school policy.

(11) While one to one and classroom aides are often useful, it is important that the IEP build in protections to ensure that teachers remain actively and directly engaged in the child's instruction and in supervising the aide.

(12) Often, schools will articulate concerns that the child will become "aide dependent." This is a real concern, which should be addressed by appropriately defining the duties and responsibilities of the aide,

appropriately supervising and training the aide, and appropriately regulating how the aide conducts his or her activities. Even when a child needs a one to one aide, it is important to ensure that the aide strikes an appropriate balance between providing assistance to the student and promoting the student's ability to complete tasks independently as much as possible.

E=MC² Advocacy Strategies: IEP Communication and Accountability Strategies

(1) Although the IEP should be written in a manner that builds in basic monitoring, assessment, and reporting procedures—including the requirement that progress be reported to parents on a periodic (typically quarterly) basis—there is often a need for more frequent communication between the school and the parents. At times, this may be based on a genuine need for collaboration and coordination. At other times, parents may desire more frequent communication because they feel the school has not been fully implementing the IEP and/or is not providing accurate information about the child's functioning. Where these concerns are present, there are a wide variety of communication mechanisms that can be incorporated into the IEP. It's important to note that, as with any other desired services, accommodations, or supports, the parents may request the strategies, but the school is not obligated to accept them automatically.

(2) Frequently, schools utilize a daily or weekly notebook that travels between school and home. With this method, a designated teacher and/or all of the service providers record the activities conducted with the student during the day and note positive accomplishments and/or specific problems. Similarly, the parents provide notes back to the school indicating what the student worked on while at home and detailing problems at home that may be relevant or of concern to the school staff in order to allow them to work more effectively with the student.

(3) In lieu of daily notebooks, it is also common for schools to utilize a daily or weekly summary report of the child's activities. This report

may be completed by the case manager, the lead teacher, or by all of the school staff. At times, it can be as simple as a form with activities listed that can be checked off, a brief rating scale and a section for notes or comments.

(4) When children have a behavior intervention plan, a plan for specific accommodations or supports, or specific academic or related service interventions, the school can send home copies of daily or weekly charts that show the student's activities and performance.

(5) In addition to, or instead of, these types of notebooks, weekly reports, or charts, it is sometimes possible for parents to communicate with school staff by email or to arrange for periodic or even weekly phone calls from a designated staff person to keep them up to date. This is sometimes done informally or, with agreement of the IEP team, can be written into the IEP.

(6) When a student needs to have medication provided at school, it is often useful to have a copy of the medication log sent to the parent on a weekly or monthly basis to ensure that the child is receiving the appropriate medication at the right times on a regular basis.

As indicated previously, research indicates there are sometimes errors in the administration of medication at school. Whether the medication is necessary for basic physical health (for example, in the case of seizure disorders, epilepsy, or severe allergies) or the medication is necessary to treat psychiatric conditions such as attention deficit hyperactivity disorder (AD/HD) or bipolar disorder, the failure to provide medication on a timely basis can have profound consequences on the child's health or performance at school. It is important for parents to be confident that the medication is being provided as needed.

(7) When a child receives related services (such as occupational therapy, physical therapy, or speech therapy), it is often useful to have the logs of those therapy sessions provided on a weekly or monthly basis so that the parents can reinforce the activities at home.

This is especially useful when parents are also providing private therapy services at their own expense; reviewing the logs can ensure that the efforts of the school therapist and private therapist are coordinated and mutually supportive.

(8) When a child's needs are particularly complex or when there have been significant problems with respect to communication and trust, it is sometimes helpful to establish quarterly, monthly, or even weekly informal meetings between parents and the teacher or IEP team. Parents who ask for more frequent meetings are likely to face more resistance from schools. On the other hand, for children with complex needs, regular meetings between the parents and school can frequently assist all parties in promoting the child's functioning at the highest possible level. This can reduce the potential for confusion, conflict, and breakdown of trust between the parents and school staff.

(9) Although the IDEA requires that the IEP be reviewed at least annually, it is not uncommon for the parents and school to agree that they will have a mid year IEP meeting to review the child's progress or, if the child is in a new placement or a placement that may be subject to change, to schedule an IEP meeting 30–60 days after the initiation of the placement. This allows the team to review the child's progress, make adjustments in the program as needed, or even to assess whether the placement is appropriate.

(10) Parents should try to observe the student in the school program on a periodic basis. Parents should be careful not to visit school with such frequency that they are perceived to be overly intrusive or disruptive. However, it is generally desirable for parents to observe the student at school, particularly where there are concerns, at least twice a year. If there are significant concerns with how the child is functioning at school, it may be desirable for parents to arrange for outside clinical professionals, with expertise in the areas of concern, to observe the student. School district policies vary in this matter, but parents have a right to request copies of the school observation policy. Although there are no rules in the IDEA that guarantee the right of parents or outside consultants to conduct observations in schools, parents and other individuals involved with children who have IEPs enjoy the same rights under the school policy as anyone else. In situations where there are conflicts between the parents and school, observation can be

> arranged through mediation or, if necessary, by requesting the right to observe from an impartial due process hearing officer, if a due process proceeding is already pending.

In addition to the specific services and requirements outlined in this chapter, the IDEA also requires that the IEP identify whether children require extended school year services and identify the degree to which children require support for participation in nonacademic school activities and services.[43]

Extended school year

The eligibility for extended school year services (ESY) or special education summer school is determined by the IEP team on an annual basis. ESY is different from regular summer school for several reasons. First, it is based on the child's needs as determined by the IEP team, whereas regular summer school is usually elective (and may not even be available in some school districts). Second, if a student is eligible for ESY, it must be provided at no cost to the parent, whereas schools typically charge tuition for regular summer school.

Often, the decision about the need for ESY services is made in the spring, for services that will begin in the coming summer. To determine eligibility for ESY, many school districts use what is known as the "regression/recoupment standard." Under this standard, the school district looks for evidence of whether children have significantly regressed during periods when they were out of school—such as summer vacation, winter break, and spring break—requiring excessive time to catch up or "recoup" after the break to warrant continuing services over the summer. This is intended to allow children to return to school in the fall without having to spend a lot of time relearning material previously covered.

Although the regression/recoupment standard is widely utilized, a number of courts have determined that the standard is overly limiting. The more appropriate standard, these courts have held, is one provided by the IDEA, which uses broader criteria for eligibility—incorporating both regression/recoupment data and also professional judgments. The IDEA regulations specify that ESY services shall be provided "as necessary to provide free appropriate public education . . . as determined on an individual basis."[44]

The regulations also provide that school districts may neither limit ESY services to a particular category or categories of disability nor "unilaterally limit the type, amount or duration of those services."[45] This suggests that school districts are not allowed to have a blanket policy that predetermines which categories of disability are eligible for ESY services or that predetermines the nature, amount, or duration of ESY services for a particular child.

Extended school year services are particularly important for children who have complex and intense needs, for children who require repetition and consistency to maintain educational gains, and for children who experience significant regression when educational services are disrupted. In particular, there is research supporting the need for virtually year round services for many children with autism, who require constant and consistent reinforcement of the skills they are learning to maintain educational progress.[46]

Non-academic services

The IEP must also contain specific provisions promoting the involvement of children with disabilities in nonacademic and extracurricular activities to allow children equal access to those services. When necessary, the IEP should include supplementary aids and services that are determined by the IEP team to be necessary to facilitate the child's participation in nonacademic and extracurricular activities. This could include providing an aide or peer mentor, altering the nature of the participation, or providing support to other students on how to interact with the student.[47]

The IDEA regulations include a long list of these activities, which include counseling services, athletics, transportation, health services, recreational activities, special interest groups or clubs sponsored by the school, and referrals to or involvement with agencies that provide assistance to people with disabilities.[48] The list of activities that is specified in the regulation is not intended to limit the activities that are covered but are instead provided as examples of the many services and activities that may warrant support through the IEP process. Although the regulations do not specifically indicate them, a child may also require assistance in nonacademic activities such as eating lunch, playing on the playground during recess, and participating in school wide activities, such as school plays, assemblies, and the like.

CHAPTER 5

Special Education and Related Services

U nder the Individuals with Disabilities Education Act (IDEA), a free appropriate public education is defined as special education and related services that are provided at public expense, under public direction, and without charge and that meet the standards of the state and include appropriate preschool, elementary, or secondary school education. The services must be provided in conformity with an individualized education program (IEP) that is consistent with the requirements of the law.[1]

As previously indicated, special education is often assumed to mean educational services that are provided by a special education teacher in a special education classroom. Contrary to this popular perception, the IDEA defines special education very differently.

Under the IDEA, special education is a service rather than a place of instruction. The IDEA regulations define special education as "specially designed instruction at no cost to the parents to meet the needs of the child with a disability, including instruction conducted in the classroom, in the home, in hospitals and institutions, and in other settings and instruction in physical education."[2]

The regulations further provide that special education includes speech and language pathology services or any other related service defined by state law as an educational service rather than a related service. It can also include physical education, travel training, and vocational training.[3]

As defined by the regulations, specially designed instruction means adapting—as appropriate to the unique needs of an eligible child—the content, methodology or mode of delivery of instruction, while also ensuring that the child has access to the general curriculum, enabling the child to "meet the educational standards" that apply to all children within the jurisdiction of the school district.[4] The requirement of specially designed instruction conveys that the child's education must be individually adapted to meet the child's needs, whether in regular education, in a special education program or classroom, or both. Special education means instruction that is specially designed for the student, rather than instruction that is provided in a special education class or exclusively by a special education teacher.

In addition, the regulation's proviso that special education services can be offered in classrooms, homes, institutions, or other settings conveys the requirement that the school district have available a continuum of instructional services that can meet the needs of the individual student in a variety of settings, including based in the regular classroom. Special education in the regular classroom, including by a regular education teacher, can occur in a wide variety of ways. It may include additional assistance from the regular educator in working on the particular skill that is in need of remediation; it can include modifying the content of the curriculum, the format of the material or how it is presented to the student. It can include adjusting the volume of work, the ways or timelines for completing the work, or the criteria for grading the work. It can also include techniques involving direct or indirect support from a special education teacher, paraprofessional, or related service providers, either in the regular class or elsewhere.

Chapter 6 will discuss the requirements for services in a least restrictive environment in greater detail. However, the IDEA clearly intends that children be served in regular education where it is possible to do so, with the provision of supplemental aids and supports when appropriate.

The IDEA requires that children who are eligible for special education receive not only specialized instruction but also that they receive any "related services" that are necessary in order for them to benefit from their education.

The statute and regulations contain a lengthy list of these related services, including "transportation and such developmental, corrective and other supportive services as are required to assist a child with a disability to benefit from special education."[5] The specific examples of related services on the list include speech/language pathology and audiology services; interpreting services; psychological services; physical and occupational services; recreation, including therapeutic recreation; early identification and assessment of disabilities; counseling services, including rehabilitation counseling; orientation and mobility services; and medical services for diagnostic or evaluation purposes.[6] It should be noted that 2006 amendments to the IDEA regulations also added interpreter services as an explicit service covered under the related services category.[7]

The definition of related services also specifies that related services include school health services, school nurse services, social work services in school and parent counseling and training as well.[8]

While the 2006 amendments provided some additional related services, they excluded some services as well. The new amendments declared that related services do not include medical devices that are surgically implanted, such as cochlear implants, and do not include repairs, maintenance, optimization, or replacement of such devices.[9] However, the regulations state that this restriction does not limit the right of the IEP team to provide related services necessary for the child to receive an appropriate education. In addition, the restriction does not limit the responsibility of the school system to monitor appropriately and maintain any medical device that is needed to maintain the health and safety of the child, including devices related to breathing, nutrition, or other bodily functions. The regulations also allow for the routine checking of an external component of a medical device to make sure it is functioning properly.[10]

With respect to health services, the law requires schools to provide medical services, defined as services that can be provided only by a physician, solely for the purpose of diagnosis or evaluation for the purpose of determining the child's eligibility for special education or educational needs. The IDEA, meanwhile, does not restrict the provision of quasi-medical services, such as nursing services, catheterization, and other services that can be provided by either a nurse or a lay person even if those services might also be provided by a doctor.[11] In fact, the IDEA regulations specifically define school health services as "services that may be provided either by a qualified school nurse or other qualified person."[12]

Several related services that get little attention provide potentially more expansive services than schools typically offer or acknowledge. Orientation and mobility services can include services that enable children to orient themselves and move safely within their environments in school, at home, and in the community. These include teaching children spatial and environmental concepts and how to use sensory information to help them navigate. These services also include the use of canes, service animals, or other tools, and the use of other aids, concepts, and techniques.[13] Orientation and mobility services may be of use to students with a variety of disabilities, though they are most often considered for students who are blind or have mobility impairments. For example, a child with severe attention deficit hyperactivity disorder (AD/HD) may require assistance in learning to cross streets safely, or a child with severe spatial orientation problems may need help in learning directionality.

The IDEA also includes broad provisions for mental health services for the student and even for the parent. The IDEA incorporates psychological services for purposes of assessment, consulting with staff concerning school programming, planning and managing psychological services for the child and parents, and assisting in developing positive behavioral intervention strategies.[14] It also covers counseling services, which can include services provided by qualified school social workers, psychologists, guidance counselors, or other qualified personnel.[15] Social work services are perhaps the most expansive mental health service and are defined to include:

> [p]reparing social developmental histories concerning a child, providing group and individual counseling with the child and family, working in partnership with the parents and others on problems in the child's living situation, including home, school and community that affect the child's adjustment in school, mobilizing school and community resources to enable the child to learn as effectively as possible, and assisting in the development of positive behavioral intervention strategies.[6]

This language covers a wide array of services that go beyond what may be addressed in school and are geared to deal with the child's mental health and address a variety of problems in an integrated way.

In addition, though rarely discussed or provided, the IDEA allows for parent counseling and training, defined to include "assisting parents in understanding the special needs of their child, providing parents with information about child development, and helping parents to acquire the necessary skills that will allow them to support the implementation of the child's program."[17]

The IDEA also defines occupational therapy in a manner far more expansive than the definition typically utilized by school districts. Under the IDEA regulations, occupational therapy is defined to include "improving, developing, or restoring functions impaired or lost through illness, injury or deprivation; improving ability to perform tasks for independent functioning, if functions are impaired or lost; and preventing, through early intervention, initial or further impairment or loss of function."[18] It is significant that this definition includes the requirement for preventing, developing, improving, or restoring function. Most often, school districts focus only on remediating deficits rather than on preventing, developing, or improving functioning.

Speech and language services also incorporate a wide range of services, including some that the typical IEP team might not consider. Under the regulations, for example, speech and language pathology services include

> the identification of children with speech or language impairments, the diagnosis and appraisal of specific impairments, referral for medical or professional attention to provide habilitation of speech and language impairments, provision of speech and language services for the habilitation or prevention of communication impairments, and counseling and guidance of parents, children and teachers regarding speech and language impairments.[19]

The provision for speech and language pathology services requires remediation and also evaluation, assessment, habilitation, and prevention. This is a substantially wider scope of services than is typically considered within the realm of school related service providers.

Some school districts and/or service professionals limit eligibility for related services by using narrower eligibility standards than the ones contained in the IDEA. The most troubling of these common limitations is the practice of precluding the provision of a related service such as speech, physical therapy, or occupational therapy, if the child's speech or motor performance is not below his or her "developmental level." For example, a child who is diagnosed with mental retardation and functions at a level four years below grade level may, using this inappropriate standard, be determined ineligible for speech and language services if his speech and language are commensurate with his overall developmental level.

Further, because motor, language, and other skills addressed through related services also have an impact on the child's ability to learn and perform as measured by IQ tests and developmental functioning assessments, the refusal to provide these services makes it more likely that the child will continue to perform at a lower level on the IQ tests or global assessments. This then creates a self fulfilling prophecy in which the child's overall development is suppressed. The child is deprived of appropriate related services and, because of the lack of interventions, is less able to make progress in his or her overall development.

There are other common reasons that school districts refuse related services. A school system or a particular provider, for example, may make an internal decision to use a very limited threshold for eligibility for services in general or for a related service in particular. For instance, some children may be refused physical therapy services if they are able to navigate the halls and stairs of a school safely, even if physical therapy services would be critical to their ability to participate in physical education, engage in recreational activities, or even maintain appropriate physical posture and stability during the course of the school day while sitting at their desk.

Similarly, some occupational therapists may limit eligibility for occupational therapy based on an assessment of the child's handwriting, without regard to whether the child has other fine motor deficits that impact her ability to participate in academic activities or her ability to successfully complete other important life skills, such as brushing her teeth, tying her shoes, buttoning her pants, or organizing her school materials.

An additional point of dispute with regard to occupational therapy services centers around the potential need for the student to receive occupational therapy to address sensory integration or sensory regulation issues. Many private occupational therapists and school occupational therapists recognize that some children with regulatory and/or motor deficits benefit from strategies, typically supervised and/or implemented by occupational therapists, which assist the child in developing improved sensory integration or sensory regulation. Examples of this include children who are hypersensitive to noise, touch, light, or smell, or who may need sensory breaks or the use of calming techniques to maintain greater composure and attention within the instructional environment.

Many occupational therapists have a wide array of strategies for addressing sensory integration and sensory regulation needs. However, these sensory integration and regulation techniques remain controversial, with some school districts readily accepting them as legitimate educational services, while others challenge the validity of the underlying disorder and/ or the intervention strategies to address them. Some schools, moreover, dismiss them as irrelevant or challenge their validity as educationally related issues. Even when schools accept the legitimacy of the sensory integration or regulation deficits, their therapists may not have the training or equipment necessary to address the concerns. However, some sensory integration strategies are very simple and involve little training or expense. These include giving the child periodic breaks or quiet time or giving the child a small squeeze ball as a way for the child to discharge excess energy or to provide some sensory input. Again, across the board policies that limit access to services, rather than making individualized determinations about the need for those services, are arguably inconsistent with the law.

E=MC² Advocacy Strategies: Obtaining Appropriate Related Services

(1) When a school district has a cap or rigid formula for the assignment of the number of minutes of a particular related service, such formulas or caps are contrary to the requirement that the IEP be based on the child's individual needs and may violate the prohibition against discrimination on the basis of the nature or severity of a person's disability. The determination of how much service a child is entitled to must be based on the child's unique needs.

(2) It is important to note that the list of related services contained in the statute and regulations is quite broad. The law requires that the school provide any nonmedical related service that is necessary for the child to benefit from education.

(3) While there is no clinical formula for the nature or intensity of related services that should be provided in response to a given disability, professionals, through the IEP team and with input from the parents and any private clinicians, must make a professional judgment as to the nature and intensity of services to be provided. A parent's desire for more related services is not by itself sufficient to justify more services. Rather, if a child is not making meaningful progress in the area being

addressed by the related service, that information would suggest a need for more intensive services, different intervention strategies to deliver the service, or both.

(4) Unfortunately, the strategies used by related service providers are sometimes provided one on one, without sufficient attention paid to whether the strategies are shared with school staff and the parents and reinforced throughout the school day and at home. The goal should include generalization of the skill in the classroom, home, and community, as well as in the therapy session, and reinforcement of the skill in the classroom, as well as in the therapy session.

(5) To accomplish this, it is important for the IEP to include a mechanism for the other members of the IEP team to be informed of the things the related service providers are working on. It is similarly important that team members be updated regularly on the child's progress and on the strategies being used to promote that progress, so that the efforts can be supported by all individuals working with the child. This will maximize the child's ability to make progress in the various areas of difficulty.

(6) Even if the IEP does not include these mechanisms, if the parent has arranged for private therapies for the student, it is advisable for the private therapists, with appropriate release of information forms from the parent, to reach out periodically to the school therapists in order to coordinate their experiences with the student, their strategies, and their progress.

(7) Because related service providers often have heavy case loads, it is useful to build into the IEP some mechanism for documenting each session of related service; it can be useful, for example, for the individual provider to keep a log that is regularly shared with parents. This helps to confirm that the services are being delivered, as well as to assist the parent in keeping track of the child's progress.

(8) A very confusing aspect of the description of related services in the IEP process involves the question of where or how the service is provided.

Direct service is service provided by the related service professional to the student; consultative service is provided by the related service provider to the school staff members, to train them or apprise them of the related service activity so they can support that activity or so that they can use the strategy or intervention in their own work with the student.

(9) Generally, it is desirable to have the IEP specifically identify the number of minutes of direct service and consultative service in order to be clear that the child is getting the number of minutes that the team agreed to and/or that the parent and their clinical professionals believe are necessary for the student within the school setting. If the IEP merges direct and consultative minutes, there is no way to hold the school accountable with respect to the number of direct service minutes the student is actually provided.

(10) In addition to specifying the direct and consultative minutes, it is important to specify whether the particular service will be provided to the student one to one or in a group setting. Schools often omit reference to whether the service will be provided individually or in a group. Obviously, there are significant differences in the delivery and intensity of the services, depending on which option is provided.

Under some circumstances, provision of a particular service in a group may be desirable. For example, there may be some situations where it is advisable for a student with speech and language needs or mental health needs to participate in a speech and language group, a social skills group, or some form of group therapy with other students. Conversely, the student may also need individual direct services on a one to one basis. If the IEP does not specify individual versus group, therapists have discretion as to how they provide the service, even if the parent may feel that a different form of service was necessary.

(11) Finally, it is important for the IEP to identify whether the service will be provided on a pull-out or push-in basis. Pull-out services are those that involve the student's being removed from the classroom environment and provided the service directly by the related service

provider in a separate setting. Push-in services involve the related service provider's going into the classroom environment to provide the service.

Again, there may be circumstances where each strategy may be desirable for the student. However, if the IEP does not specify how the service is going to be delivered and in what setting, the therapists may feel that they have discretion to provide the service in the setting they prefer.

(12) When a parent desires a related service that the school is not offering and particularly when they desire one that is not contained in the list of related services in the statute and regulations, it is generally useful, if not essential, that the parent obtain outside clinical evaluation documenting the need for that particular related service.

It may also be important for the parent, in conjunction with the outside clinical professionals, to provide professional, peer reviewed research that identifies the related service as necessary for the child to benefit from special education services.

6

Least Restrictive Environment

Along with the right to a free appropriate public education, the Individuals with Disabilities Education Act (IDEA) requires that children eligible for special education be educated in the least restrictive environment to the maximum extent appropriate. While the phrase *free appropriate public education* has been the source of the greatest controversy in special education litigation, the phrase *least restrictive environment to the maximum extent appropriate* has also been the source of considerable conflict.

When the IDEA was first enacted in 1975, large numbers of children with disabilities were either excluded from public education altogether or were entirely segregated in self-contained classrooms or self-contained schools. As indicated above, one of the central outcomes of the class action lawsuits that gave rise to the passage of the special education law in 1975 was the right to be educated in the least restrictive environment. When the law was passed, the initial focus was on bringing those children with disabilities who had been totally excluded from public education into the school system and ensuring that all children with disabilities had access to education. Subsequently, as most children with disabilities were successfully enrolled in the public educational system, increasing attention was paid to where and how they were being educated in relation to their typically developing peers. The statutory requirements for least restrictive environment considerations have remained relatively consistent since 1975, as will be described shortly. However, the educational philosophy, funding priorities, interpretation of the law, and community support for inclusion of children with disabilities in the least restrictive environment have evolved and changed dramatically in the last 30 years.

As indicated, in the late 1970s and early 1980s, the emphasis of the federal government and school systems was primarily focused on bringing children into the school systems and in developing the special education bureaucracy to provide for educational services for children with disabilities. In 1986, an initiative spearheaded by Madeleine Will, then assistant secretary of the U.S. Department of Education, gave rise to what was called "the regular education initiative." The regular education initiative (REI) for the first time provided philosophical and educational encouragement for the participation of children with disabilities in regular education classrooms. However, the initiative was focused on children with disabilities who had sufficient skills to be accommodated in regular classrooms with minimal accommodation, modification, or extra support.

Subsequent to the REI, in the mid to late 1980s, schools increasingly began to focus on greater opportunities for "mainstreaming" or "integration" of children with disabilities in regular classes. The concept of mainstreaming focused on children with disabilities whose individualized education programs (IEP) called for them to be educated predominantly in self contained classrooms or special education settings but provided for them to be mainstreamed or educated in regular education classes to the extent possible. Going hand in hand with the mainstreaming effort was the effort to promote "integration" of children with disabilities into settings with typically developing students. Integration activities included efforts to have children with disabilities participate in the school lunchroom, school assemblies, and extracurricular activities. It also promoted opportunities for children with disabilities to interact with typically developing peers through a variety of unstructured and structured social opportunities. Typically developing peers were utilized, for example, to provide tutoring to students with disabilities, in peer-buddy systems, and in get-togethers over lunch or "lunch bunches."

The effort to promote mainstreaming was focused on creating opportunities for children in special education classrooms to participate in regular classes on a selective basis to the extent that the children's ability level allowed them to do so. Often, this meant that students with disabilities might be included in subjects such as art, music, physical education, and other electives. Under some circumstances, it also could involve these children's participating in selected regular education academic classes. Mainstreaming was often based on children "earning" their way into regular education by demonstrating the ability to perform at or near grade level. This contrasted with the notion that the child's participation could be beneficial even if he or she were not at grade level, especially if given supplementary aides and support.

The effort at mainstreaming and integration also incorporated the idea of "reverse integration," in which typically developing children were mixed into the special education classes to provide tutorial and/or social opportunities for the children with disabilities. The assumption behind these mainstreaming and integration efforts was that children with disabilities would participate in regular classes if and only to the extent that they had the ability to participate reasonably successfully and at the curriculum level of the class, without substantial modification of the curriculum or support of the student.

In the mid to late 1980s, in concert with a number of landmark lawsuits seeking to secure the placement of children with more severe disabilities into age and grade appropriate classrooms, an educational philosophy called *inclusion* gained momentum. Although there are different variations on the inclusion theme, the fundamental premise of inclusion is that children with disabilities, regardless of the severity of their disability, have a legal right to be educated in the least restrictive environment based in the regular school classes they would have attended if they did not have a disability. Although educational researchers and philosophers have interpreted the concept in a variety of different ways, the presumption is that inclusion is both a civil right and a more effective way to meet the educational, social, and other needs of children with disabilities. Some adherents of inclusive education believe that children with disabilities should be served in regular education virtually full time, while others stress that children should be based in their neighborhood school and grade level regular education class and that various environments of the school and community should be utilized, as appropriate, to meet the students' needs with less rigid focus on the regular classroom itself. Thus, the proponents of inclusion have expressed a range of views but have shared a common belief that the child should be seen as a member of the regular education class and the school they would otherwise attend, allowing these children to be integrated or involved fully in the key activities of the classroom and school.

However, the term *inclusion* is not mentioned in the IDEA. Rather, the term arose from the research and writings of experts in the special education field who promoted the concept of inclusion as the moral and educational fulfillment of the IDEA requirement that children be educated in the least restrictive environment to the maximum extent feasible. Since the advent of the "inclusion movement" and in the wake of a number of landmark court decisions requiring that children with severe disabilities be included in or primarily based in regular education classrooms, the inclusion movement gained momentum from the late 1980s through the 1990s. However, its implementation across the United States has been highly inconsistent.

Data from the U.S. Department of Education indicate that many children with disabilities are still educated for the majority or all of their day in self contained classrooms or specialized schools. The placement of children in more restrictive settings varies enormously from state to state. Further, for those students with more severe disabilities who are included in regular education, the success of the educational experience is highly variable.

Some schools do an excellent job of providing appropriate curriculum modification, teacher training and support, adaptation of materials, and additional assistance to the staff, to children with disabilities, and to classrooms as a whole to promote the child's ability to participate successfully in regular education along with his or her typically developing peers. By contrast, in other schools where children with severe disabilities are included in regular education, these children may be physically present but are neither actively included in the activities in the classroom nor provided effective curriculum modification, adequate mechanisms for communication and participation in classroom activities, and/or sufficient teacher and staff support to participate fully and meaningfully. Thus, even for those students who are "included" on paper, the educational experience is highly variable depending on the nature and effectiveness of the inclusive practices utilized by the particular school system or classroom. In fact, in some places, there is a backlash against inclusive education, based on a perception that children with disabilities are being dumped in regular education without adequate support, depriving them of the services they need to make adequate progress, while creating excessive burdens for the teacher and unfairly detracting from the educational experiences of the other students. Much of the hostility toward inclusive education arises not from the inherent shortcomings of inclusive education but rather from the failure of school systems to train their teachers adequately, provide sufficient support and resources, and allow for sufficient flexibility to meet the needs of students within regular classrooms.

The controversy over inclusion is aggravated by the ambiguity in the language of the IDEA itself. The IDEA provides that:

> to the maximum extent appropriate, children with disabilities, including children in public or private institutions or other care facilities are educated with children who are not disabled, and special classes, separate schooling, or other removal of children with disabilities from the regular educational environment occurs only when the nature or severity of the disability of a child is such that education in regular classes with the use of supplementary aids and services cannot be achieved satisfactorily.[1]

This language could be read as a powerful mandate in favor of the participation of children with disabilities in regular education based on the language "to the maximum extent . . ." and the language that the child shall be removed "only when the nature or severity of the disability . . . is such that education in regular classes with the use of supplementary aids and services cannot be achieved satisfactorily." Taken together, these words imply a strong mandate in favor of the education of children with disabilities in regular education. However, the least restrictive environment language cited above contains the key modifier *appropriate*, which substantially dilutes what would otherwise appear to be an absolute requirement for services in the least restrictive environment. Given the subjective nature of the word *appropriate*, the IEP team makes judgments based on the individual student's needs and other factors as well. In addition, the phrase "only when the nature or severity of the disability . . . is such that education in regular classes with the use of supplementary aids and services cannot be achieved satisfactorily" also gives rise to subjective judgment by the IEP team about the child's placement.

The regulations implementing IDEA make clear that school systems must have available a variety of educational options, including a continuum of educational placements, in order to meet the needs of children with disabilities. The regulations provide that "each (school) must ensure that a continuum of alternative placements is available to meet the needs of children with disabilities for special education and related services."[2] These alternative placements can include a variety of different settings and services, including "instruction in regular classes, special classes, special schools, home instruction and instruction in hospitals and institutions." In order to promote the feasibility of serving the child in a regular setting, the law also requires the IEP team to consider provision of "supplementary services such as resource or itinerant instruction to be provided in conjunction with the regular class placement." This means that the school should consider services to support the child's successful participation in regular classes through the use of extra tutoring, extra support, or limited instruction outside of the regular class to supplement the regular instruction. Inherent in the requirement for a continuum of alternative placements is the requirement that schools be able to serve children with disabilities in other settings as needed.

The regulations make clear that the commitment to services in the least restrictive environment is not only a goal but is also a decision making process, requiring that a number of factors be taken into account when determining which placement is the least restrictive appropriate placement for a particular student. It is notable that the regulations require that the placement decision is made in conformity with the least restrictive environment provisions and is made by a group of people, including the parents and others who are knowledgeable about the child, the meaning of the evaluation data, and the school's placement options.[3] The team should generally include at least one regular education teacher.[4]

Least restrictive environment

The federal regulations also list the factors to be considered in determining the appropriate environment for the particular child. The regulations require that "the child's placement is determined at least annually, is based on the child's IEP, and is as close as possible to the child's homes."[5] In addition, the regulations contain requirements that are at once sensible and confusing. The regulations provide that "unless the IEP of a child with a disability requires some other arrangement, the child is educated in the school that he or she would attend if not disabled."[6] As with the requirement that the children be educated in the least restrictive environment to the maximum extent appropriate, this provision states a strong rule coupled with an equally strong exception. It appears to require the child to be educated in the school that he or she would attend if not disabled—unless the IEP requires otherwise. Again, the ambiguous language gives IEP teams the ability to make a determination that children's needs cannot be met at the school they would otherwise attend and instead to place them in some alternative setting. Because of the conflict between the rule and the exception, which is often misunderstood or unnoticed by parents, conflict often arises between the parent and the school.

The regulations go further in delineating the considerations for deciding the least restrictive environment appropriate for the child, stating the following:

> In selecting the least restrictive environment, consideration is given to any potential harmful effect on the child or on the quality of services that he or she needs and that a child with a disability is not removed from education in age appropriate regular classrooms solely because of needed modifications in the general education curriculum.[7]

As the regulation requires the consideration of potential harmful effects on the quality of services that the child needs, this provision should be linked with the 2004 IDEA requirement that the child's IEP be "based on peer reviewed research to the extent practicable."[8] In other words, whether the educational placement being proposed is based on the peer reviewed research should be one of the "harmful effects" considered in deciding which placement is least restrictive and appropriate.[9] The law also now provides that the child should not be removed from education in age appropriate classes solely because of needed modifications in the general education curriculum.[10] This expands the obligation of the schools to consider curriculum modification to allow a child to participate successfully in regular education classes. Previously, this may have been a significant element in a school's decision to recommend that a child be placed in a more restrictive setting due to the need for modifications in the general curriculum. Again, however, this language is qualified, in this instance, by the term *solely*. Many schools may identify additional factors, whether real or fabricated, other than the need for modification of the general curriculum, as grounds for a child to be educated in a more restrictive setting.

The IDEA requires not only that the least restrictive environment mandate be applied to the child's participation in classroom settings but also be applied to non-academic settings, extracurricular services, and activities, such as meals and recess periods. In addition, the mandate extends to such things as athletics, recreational clubs, special interest groups, and employment activities. According to the regulations:

> each public agency must ensure that each child with a disability participates with non-disabled children in their extracurricular services and activities to the maximum extent appropriate to the needs of that child. The public agency must ensure that each child with a disability has the supplementary aids and services determined by the child's IEP team to be appropriate and necessary for the child to participate in non-academic settings.[11]

Clearly, the IDEA requires schools to promote the involvement of children with disabilities in regular activities at the school. At the same time, the IEP team has discretion to make individualized decisions about what is appropriate in relation to the child's involvement in non-academic activities as well.

The process by which the participation of children with disabilities in regular education should be decided is also designed to facilitate consideration of less restrictive placement options. First, the IDEA explicitly requires the participation of a regular education teacher in the IEP team in any situation where the child is being educated in regular education to any degree or where regular education is being considered. They also require that the regular education teacher "must to the extent appropriate, participate in the development of the IEP of the child."[12] The regular education teacher must also help determine "appropriate positive behavioral interventions and supports and other strategies for the child," as well as "supplementary aids and services, program modifications, and support for school personnel" consistent with the law.[13]

Indeed, owing to the least restrictive environment requirements—and the fact that participation in regular education should always be a topic of discussion—it would appear that a regular educator should be involved in all IEP placement decisions.

The IDEA also requires that children with disabilities be involved in, and to the extent possible make progress in, the general curriculum.[14] Although involvement with the general education curriculum does not itself mandate participation in regular education classrooms, the ability to have access to and make progress in the general curriculum is inextricably linked to the child's ability to participate effectively in regular education as much as possible. If a child placed in a more restrictive setting is not given access to the curriculum that is being taught to that child's typically developing peers, it is that much more difficult for the child to participate successfully in regular classes when given the opportunity to do so. It also precludes that child from the opportunity to learn the age appropriate skills that are deemed necessary for all children.

In addition, the regulations require that the IEP team be familiar with and consider "placement options."[15] This has been interpreted to suggest that public schools must consider a range of placement options, rather than only considering one option. In addition, the IDEA requires that the placement decision include the parents.[16] Finally, the process requires that the IEP team document and provide "an explanation of the extent, if any, to which the child will not participate with non-disabled children in the regular class and in the activities described."[17] This is intended to encourage more thoughtful consideration of regular education options and discourage more restrictive placements that are not justified.

As noted, the IDEA contains a strong preference for children with disabilities to be served in the least restrictive environment. At the same time, this preference is not an absolute mandate. The law outlines a decision making process and a number of factors that the IEP team must consider in determining whether the child can be served fully in regular education, predominantly in regular education with support and/or some limited involvement in other settings, or requires instruction based in a more restrictive setting with opportunity for participation with typical peers as much as possible. Because there are widely divergent views on this issue and because the ability of children with disabilities to succeed in a regular education environment may be heavily dependent on the nature and effectiveness of supports provided by the school, the placement decisions involving least restrictive environment can become highly controversial and conflicting.

Legal decisions regarding least restrictive environment

Jonathan was a first grader diagnosed with Down Syndrome. He had mild mental retardation and some speech, language, and behavioral issues. However, he was highly social and had demonstrated the ability to complete various academic readiness tasks and skills. Jonathan's neighborhood school recommended that he be placed in a self contained special education classroom in a different school. The school system had a policy of grouping children with more severe disabilities in self contained classrooms.

After unsuccessfully attempting to mediate their disagreement with the school system regarding Jonathan's placement, his parents successfully pursued a special education due process hearing that led to an order that Jonathan be educated in his neighborhood school in a regular classroom. With the provision of appropriate supplementary aides and services, Jonathan was able to participate successfully with his peers in the regular education program and progress from grade to grade through elementary school.

Kinzie was a ninth grader with multiple severe disabilities. She was nonverbal and sometimes had difficulty controlling her physical movements. Kinzie was successfully included in regular education programs based in her neighborhood schools throughout elementary and junior high school. When Kinzie moved to high school in a new school district, the high school initially sought to place her in a self contained special education program. When the parents objected, the school relented and agreed that Kinzie could participate in a regular education based program with the involvement of one to one aides for her freshman year.

Kinzie successfully participated in her regular education program for most of her freshman year, but, toward the end of her freshman year, she engaged in head-butting, a behavior related to her disability. On two occasions, this resulted in injuries to school staff. As a consequence of these injuries, the school district determined that Kinzie should be moved to a more restrictive educational setting, although evidence suggested that the injuries may have been avoided if the staff involved had followed the appropriate protocol in relation to how they physically positioned themselves when working with Kinzie.

After protracted litigation, the parents and school entered a settlement allowing Kinzie to remain in regular education on a part time basis with a program that was supposed to be supervised by outside consultants. During the first few months that she was back in school, Kinzie did very well and worked well with the teacher and aide, with whom she developed a very positive rapport. The staff reported that she was making progress on most of her goals and objectives and was able to participate, with some modification, in grade level curriculum and classes.

When Kinzie returned to school the next year, however, the school staff who had been working with her had been replaced with new staff that were unfamiliar with her and had received virtually no training in the techniques necessary to assist her. Kinzie's performance (and behavior) deteriorated quickly, aggravated by health problems. Within two months after her return, the school district initiated a renewed recommendation that Kinzie be served in a self contained program for children with severe disabilities "anywhere other than in her home school." Ultimately, after lengthy litigation, the courts ruled that Kinzie's behavior was sufficiently problematic to require placement in a specialized setting capable of meeting her behavioral needs.

In the 1980s and early 1990s, courts were asked to interpret the least restrictive environment provisions of the IDEA. These cases led to several different standards for the determination of whether a child with a disability should properly be educated in the least restrictive environment or in a more restrictive setting. Several of the cases used multifactor tests for considering the appropriateness of the regular education environment as opposed to a more restrictive setting. The factors included the potential benefits for the child of the regular and more restrictive setting; the extent to which supplemental support and modification would be needed for the child in the regular educational setting; the potential nonacademic benefits for the child in each of the settings; the potential harmful effects on the student of either placement; the impact of the child's placement on the ability of the teacher to fulfill his or her obligations to the rest of the students; and the impact on the classroom environment.

A second set of cases adopted a different standard, which required that the child be placed in the regular education environment if there was any practical way the supports of the more restrictive setting could be offered in the regular setting to allow the child to be educated effectively in that environment. A third set of cases primarily focused on whether the schools had appropriately considered all the factors in reaching the decision as to the appropriate environment for the student, including whether they had already tried or given serious consideration to providing the supplementary aids and services in regular education that would allow the child to be successful. These cases essentially held that schools could not move children to more restrictive settings unless less restrictive options, with support, had been tried and failed or at least had been given serious consideration. The general trend, with some exceptions, was in favor of children being served in the least restrictive environment.

More recently, however, some court decisions have supported more restrictive placements for children with disabilities. Courts have been especially sympathetic to more restrictive settings when one of four factors was present.

First, the courts have been supportive of more restrictive placements where the child has had a period of participation in regular education with supplementary aids and supports that have, from the court's perspective, not proven to be successful.

Second, the courts have been more likely to rule in favor of a more restrictive placement when the child is older, particularly in high school, and the gap between the child's educational functioning and that of his or her age peers is substantial, requiring greater modification of curriculum and (allegedly) limiting the extent to which the child can participate in a meaningful way in the academic activities of his or her peers.

Third, the courts have been more likely to support restrictive environments where the child has severe behavioral challenges involving either dangerous or disruptive behavior. In instances such as the case study involving Kinzie, there may be disputes as to whether the school's academic and/or behavioral interventions were appropriately developed or implemented, but the courts have been more willing to order more restrictive placements in these circumstances, even where the efficacy of the support for the student has been in dispute.

Finally, the courts have been quite consistent in ruling that a child may be moved to a school other than his or her neighborhood school, if that school offers opportunity for participation in regular education where the neighborhood school does not. The courts have fairly consistently held that, despite the fact that parents might prefer their child to attend a neighborhood school, the neighborhood school is not obligated to duplicate all the necessary supportive services for a child if such services are available at another school in the area. In many of the court cases, the extent or effectiveness of the school's support for the student in regular education was contested, but the courts accepted the school's conclusions with respect to the need for the more restrictive setting and gave credit to the school's efforts, even if more could potentially have been done to support the student.

Furthermore, while effective inclusive practices are the norm in some states and in some school districts, these practices have not been universally adopted. While some schools have programs that effectively support students in the regular education environment, there is also a paradoxical phenomenon in which schools adopt a policy that all children should be served in the least restrictive environment, thereby limiting the availability of alternative educational placements. Schools that adopt this position sometimes end up compromising children's needs. There are children, for example, who may be unable to get an appropriate education in regular school settings, even when supports are provided or because appropriate supports are not provided. In these cases, alternative placements may be appropriate, but are not provided due to the district's failure to offer a range of placement options.

E=MC² Advocacy Strategies: Promoting Inclusion

(1) In seeking more inclusive opportunities for a child with disabilities, it's important for parents and their consultants to show the various ways that the child will benefit from participation in regular education. This can include information about the child's academic progress; the child's need for academic, social, behavioral, and communication role models; improvement in the child's behavior when involved with typical peers (compared to his or her behavior when with other children with disabilities in more restrictive settings); and any evidence that the child benefited from past involvement in regular school settings. IDEA 2004 requires that the school's proposed program be based on peer reviewed scientific research to the extent possible. Parents should investigate whether research supports the proposed placement as this is an important new consideration for the IEP team.

(2) As with any situation where there may be a dispute between parents and educators, school records and anecdotal information about the child's prior functioning can be useful. If the child has been in a less restrictive setting, it's important to document the ways that the setting has provided benefit and the child has made progress. Conversely, if the child has been in a more restrictive setting, different evidence may be necessary. If the child has made substantial progress in the more restrictive setting, it may be useful to gather data indicating that the child has made so much progress that the child no longer requires or benefits from the setting. Alternately, if the child is making minimal progress, it may be important to highlight shortcomings of the restrictive setting. These might include insufficient stimulation, or insufficient exposure to appropriate curriculum, or access to peer models for behavior, social interaction, or communication. Environmental variables that disrupt the child's progress should also be highlighted. These could include the presence of children with disruptive or aggressive behaviors that interfere with the child's functioning or performance; the absence of children with whom the child can have meaningful interaction; the absence of age appropriate curriculum or materials; or the presence

of significant distractions (such as noise or frequent rotation of children and professionals in and out of the classroom).

(3) Whenever parents are seeking a change in placement, whether to a less or more restrictive setting, it is desirable for the parents to observe the child in the current setting, as well as to observe the desired setting. In many instances, it is also helpful for the parent to ask outside clinicians who have experience working with the child to observe the child in the current setting and the desired setting. Such observation is also desirable when the parents wish to have the child continue in the current placement and the school is recommending a change.

(4) When school placement is at issue, parents should obtain as much academic, behavioral, and anecdotal material from the school as possible. They should also review the child's IEPs, progress reports, and report cards. This data should be compared from year to year to look for patterns or trends in the child's performance, as well as to identify variables that might affect the child's experience, negatively or positively, within the current or desired setting.

(5) It is also useful to correlate the child's performance with any health or other factors that may have influenced the child's performance in one setting as opposed to the other. For example, if the child has recently had behavioral problems leading to a proposal for a more restrictive setting—but the child's behavioral problems were accompanied by a health issue, a family crisis, or other outside variables—this information would be important in considering whether a different setting is appropriate under the circumstances.

(6) If a child is being considered for a more restrictive setting, it should first be determined whether the school has conducted a functional behavioral analysis, developed and implemented an appropriate behavior intervention plan, considered and provided appropriate supplementary aids and services to give additional support to the child within the less restrictive setting, provided appropriate modifications to the curriculum, and provided appropriate support to the staff.

(7) If the parents are seeking a less restrictive setting, it would be important to learn whether the more restrictive school that the

child currently attends has been using appropriate instructional methodologies, providing meaningful individualized instruction, modifying the curriculum to meet the student's individual needs, and providing opportunities for the student to interact with typical peers in regular education.

(8) It is not uncommon for a student to spend part of the day in a regular classroom and the remainder of the day in a special education classroom. Data indicating how the child performs in the different settings are often useful in highlighting that the student may be more successful in one setting rather than the other. Again, obtaining this sort of data from the school district is very important in helping to shape the decisions regarding the child's appropriate placement.

(9) Sometimes, the IEP team may not have experience with the proposed setting or the type of disability being served in that setting. If school personnel have not had such experience, it may be helpful for parents to find successful programs the school staff could visit, to obtain information about how the programs work.

(10) It is also helpful if parents review the child's schedule, period by period, to determine where the child has success and where he or she has more difficulty. This helps to identify ways to meet the child's needs and gives important information about what settings or classes are most successful.

(11) When a child has been in regular education and a more restrictive setting is being contemplated, the parents may need to document either the absence of appropriate supports within the IEP and/or the failure of the school to implement the supports called for in the IEP. If the child is being recommended for a more restrictive placement but appropriate supports have not been provided, it would be reasonable to seek the implementation of those supports before considering whether to transfer the child to a more restrictive setting.

(12) One area where schools often are reluctant to consider support is in relation to the provision of one to one aides. This is a controversial service because, although aides can sometimes be very helpful in allowing a child to function successfully in a regular education

classroom, at other times they may serve to isolate the child from the instruction provided by the teacher and from the other students. Where one to one aides are being considered or used, care should be taken in defining the role of the aide to ensure that the teacher retains responsibility for the child's actions and that the aide plays a support role rather than completing work for the student.

(13) Depending on whether the parents are seeking a more or a less restrictive placement, consideration should be given as to how the goals for their child are drafted. For example, if parents are seeking a less restrictive setting and the desire is to promote the child's social interaction with typically developing peers, a goal could state that "given the opportunity for reciprocal interaction throughout the school day with a typical age appropriate peer, the child will initiate social greetings and will maintain a reciprocal communication in x out of y trials." Conversely, if the parents are seeking a more restrictive setting, goals might be written in a manner that says "given the provision of individualized instruction in a small group setting, the child will display skill x with y accuracy or in x out of y trials." The school may resist writing goals in this manner precisely because of the desire to avoid slanting the plan in the direction of the parents' preferred setting. But, for parents, it is helpful to prepare goals that are more likely to be achieved in the desired setting than in the nonpreferred setting.

The IDEA requirement that schools provide a continuum of services, from regular education to and including specialized schools, goes hand in hand with the law's overall philosophy that children be served in the least restrictive environment to the extent feasible. It is clear that many children with disabilities can be successfully educated in regular education, either with limited or substantial support. This is true not only for children with mild disabilities but also for children with more severe disabilities. It is also clear that the success of inclusive or less restrictive placements is heavily influenced by the school staff's training, commitment, and willingness to individualize programs for the student. Participation in regular education can be highly successful, if implemented appropriately. Conversely, physical presence in a classroom without meaningful participation does not constitute an appropriate program or placement in the least restrictive environment.

Physical presence is the starting point, but meaningful participation is the measure of success.

Unfortunately, some children with disabilities fail to have a successful education experience because schools fail to provide appropriate or adequate supports. Where this occurs, parents must make a difficult choice. They can push the school to improve the quality and appropriateness of supports in the regular education environment. Alternatively, they may decide to seek or accept placement in some more restrictive setting, not because the nature of the child's disability requires it but rather because the parents cannot obtain sufficient compliance from the school in providing the services required.

At the same time, there are some children whose disabilities require that they receive services outside of the regular education environment or who have sufficiently unusual and severe disabilities that a more restrictive setting may be the only realistic option. Even where this may be the case, the decision to place the child in a more restrictive setting should not be viewed as a solution. Instead, it should be seen as a part of the process of determining and ensuring that the child receives the appropriate instructional services, related services, and other supports that he or she needs to make appropriate progress. In other words, while there may be children for whom a more restrictive setting may seem desirable, it remains equally important to ensure that appropriate education and supports are provided even within that more restrictive education environment. Efforts should be continuously made to allow children to participate with typically developing peers, preferably in the school and community where they live.

7

Private Placement

Tom was a regular education sophomore in a public high school. During Tom's freshman year, his grades began to decline, he began missing class and school, and he showed signs of depression. At one point, the school social worker met with Tom and became concerned that he might be suicidal. The social worker contacted Tom's parents and recommended that they seek private therapy for him.

In Tom's sophomore year, his behavior continued to deteriorate. Soon after the start of second quarter, after receiving a number of Fs in his regular classes during first quarter, Tom was found with marijuana in the school bathroom. The school district sought to have Tom expelled. His parents obtained a psychiatric evaluation that concluded that Tom had attention deficit/hyperactivity disorder (AD/HD) and depression and needed placement in a therapeutic residential school, due to the severity of his psychological problems. Tom's parents placed him in a private therapeutic residential school. A due process hearing officer ordered the school district to pay for Tom's placement in the private therapeutic school because the school had failed to respond to Tom's deteriorating behavior, his failing grades, and his evident emotional distress, while also failing to respond to a number of requests from Tom's parents that Tom be evaluated or provided with additional assistance.

Jimmy was a fourth grader in a public school where he received special education services due to his identified learning disability and speech and language disorder. During the time Jimmy was in the public school, he made little educational progress but was increasingly subjected to harassment and bullying by other students, which led him to become increasingly isolated and resistant to attending school. While in the public school, Jimmy's special education teachers used traditional worksheets and practice methods to teach him reading skills. The school did not use any research based methodologies designed to remediate the reading deficits that had been identified. Although the school district had previously refused to consider providing specialized methods to remediate Jimmy's learning disabilities or to consider a change of placement, the school did ultimately agree to pay for Jimmy to attend a private, specialized school for children with learning disabilities that offered research based methodologies for remediating his reading disorders.

Sally attended a private regular parochial school in her community. At her parents' request, the public school evaluated Sally and determined that she had mild learning disabilities and a speech and language disorder. Because Sally attended a private parochial school and the parents did not wish to enroll her in the public school, the school district offered to provide her with speech services for 30 minutes a week. The district indicated, however, that it would not provide any services specifically designed to address her learning disability. The parents objected to the school's refusal to provide tutoring for Sally at the private school regarding the learning disability. However, the public school ultimately refused to do so.

Under the Individuals with Disabilities Education Act (IDEA), there are different rules regarding the rights of children in private school placements, depending on how the decision is made to place the children and the circumstances of their placement.

The IDEA requires public schools to have a continuum of placement options for children with disabilities, ranging from placement in regular education to placement in publicly operated special education schools, including private day schools and residential schools if such programming is determined necessary for the child to make educational progress.[1]

Public school funding of private placements

When an individualized education program (IEP) team determines that a child cannot be effectively educated within the public school or within any of the alternative options that are available through the public school system, the IEP team may consider and authorize placement of the student in a private, special education day school or in a therapeutic residential treatment center. If the IEP team makes the decision that this placement is necessary for educational reasons, the public school system is legally obligated to pay the costs of this placement, including tuition, transportation, and, when the child is placed in a residential program, the room and board expenses associated with the placement. If other state agencies have funding that can be used to support some of the cost of this placement and the child qualifies for such funding, the schools may work out arrangements in which the public school pays for the educational expense, while the other agency pays for the residential or other expenses associated with the placement. However, even in the absence of contribution from other state agencies, if the IEP team determines that the private placement is necessary for educational reasons, the public school must assume the financial responsibility for the cost of the placement. Typically, when the public school does decide to place the child in an approved private day or residential school, the state Department of Education may reimburse the school system for some of the cost.

The extent to which schools utilize private day or residential programs varies from district to district and state to state. This variation is based to some extent on the availability of appropriate programming to meet the needs of children through the public schools, as well as on the way that different states reimburse some of the costs of these expensive private services. Although state funding is supposed to be placement neutral, this is not true in all states. As a general rule, schools are unlikely to recommend and fund programs in private day or residential schools for children with disabilities unless the school has exhausted all other available options.

In rare circumstances, such as when a child experiences a severe crisis, the school may recommend a private day or residential program before less restrictive options have been exhausted, to provide sophisticated or intensive programming that is only available in a specialized private program. Under some circumstances, if the student displays highly disruptive or dangerous behavior or has highly unusual medical or other needs, schools may sometimes recommend private day or residential schools because it is easier or less disruptive for them to pay for the tuition of a private facility.

Even where a child is "tuitioned out" to a private day or residential facility, the public school remains responsible for ensuring that the child's IEP is appropriately implemented and for monitoring the child's progress to ensure that the child returns to less restrictive options as soon as possible. Further, even while in the private facility, the public school should seek opportunities for the student to be mainstreamed as much as possible while in that setting. Generally, a school district will only consider placement in a private day or residential program that has been approved by the state Department of Education and/or other appropriate state credentialing agencies. Apart from the presumed quality control attendant to state licensure, school districts are more likely to place students in state approved facilities, as state approval may be a requirement for partial reimbursement from their state Department of Education.

Unilateral placement by parents in private specialized schools due to public school failure to provide a free appropriate public education (FAPE)

Under some circumstances, parents conclude that their child's needs are not or cannot be met within the programs that have been offered by or could be offered by the public school. Presented with this situation, some parents identify private day or residential programs that they believe can meet their child's educational needs. When parents have the resources to do so, the law allows them to place the child in the private facility at their own expense.[2] This is called a unilateral placement. If the parents believe that the child required placement in the private facility because the public school failed to provide the student with a FAPE, the parents may seek reimbursement from the public school. The public school is not obligated to agree to reimbursement, but the parents may request a due process hearing to demonstrate that the public school has failed to provide a FAPE and that the program that they obtained unilaterally did provide the child with a free appropriate public education. When the parents are able to demonstrate this to a hearing officer, the public school may be ordered to assume financial responsibility for the cost of the private placement.[3]

When a parent wishes to obtain reimbursement from the public school for a unilateral placement, the public school may seek to have the reimbursement reduced or denied under three circumstances: (1) if the parents failed to give notice of their intention to make the unilateral placement at least ten business days prior to removing the child from the public school or the parents failed to give notice of their intention at the most recent IEP meeting prior to removal; (2) if the parents provided such notice, the school sought to have the child evaluated prior to the unilateral placement, but the parents refused; or (3) if a court determines that the actions taken by the parent were unreasonable under the circumstances.[4]

On the other hand, reimbursement to the parent may not be reduced if: (1) the school prevented the parents from providing the notice; (2) the parents had not been informed of the obligation to provide prior notice by the school; (3) compliance with the prior notice section would likely result in physical harm to the child; (4) the parents are not literate; or (5) compliance with the notice requirement would likely result in serious emotional harm to the child.[5] In other words, if parents have the ability to provide the school with advanced written notice either ten business days prior to the placement or at an IEP meeting prior to the placement—and fail to provide that notice—the reimbursement they might have been entitled to can be reduced or denied. On the other hand, if parents are unable to provide the notice because they aren't informed of the obligation to do so by the school, because there was a serious emergency necessitating immediate placement or because the parents lacked the literacy skills to understand the notice requirements— the hearing officer or judge may order reimbursement despite the failure to provide the notice.

The unilateral placement provision gives parents the option of making a placement on their own, without a prior determination by the IEP team that such placement is necessary. When parents make placements of this sort, they retain the right to seek reimbursement from the school after the fact. However, they do so at their own financial risk, as there is no certainty that they will ultimately prevail in obtaining reimbursement from the school. As most families do not have the financial means to pay for expensive private day or residential programs without funding from the school system or the state, the unilateral placement provision typically is of use only to a small minority of wealthy families whose children require special education. Several Supreme Court decisions (including *Burlington School Committee v. Commonwealth of Massachusetts*[6] and *Carter v. Florence County School District*[7]) have made clear that parents may make a unilateral placement at their own risk, but may obtain reimbursement from the school if they can demonstrate that the school has failed to provide a FAPE and that the private program does provide that education. The *Carter* decision holds, for example, that parents can receive reimbursement if they show that the public school had failed to provide a FAPE and the private school did provide it, even if it did not meet the technical or licensure requirements of the state. This means that, under some circumstances, parents with financial means may have access to a wider array of programs, obtained unilaterally, than parents of more modest means may have through the public school system.

E=MC² Advocacy Strategies: Documenting the Need for Private Placement

(1) In theory, public schools have the obligation to provide children with a FAPE in the least restrictive environment. However, unless the public school has at its own initiative raised the need to place a child in a private day or residential school, it is likely that the burden will fall on the parent to demonstrate that private placement is necessary.

The first step in doing so is to document the inappropriateness or ineffectiveness of the public school's current or proposed placement. A key element in documenting the inappropriateness of the current or proposed program is to show that the child has not been making meaningful progress, whether academically, behaviorally, or otherwise, or is actually regressing in relation to key skills.

(2) Documentation of lack of progress or regression can be obtained by comparing the individualized achievement tests the child has periodically taken as part of his or her special education evaluation and reevaluation for special education eligibility. Parents should also compare the test scores obtained from the school or statewide achievement tests that are given to all students. If these results show

little progress or regression, it may be evidence of an inappropriate program.

Another source of information to document a student's relative lack of or decline in progress is to compare the student's report cards from year to year. Generally, a decline in grades in a short period of time is insufficient to show that a program is not working, particularly if the school has not yet had an opportunity to provide additional services to address the decline. If, however, the student has shown a pattern of decline or continuing failure over several years or a dramatic decline in a short period, the report cards can provide useful information that the program is not working. In addition, report cards typically have ratings and/or anecdotal comments about the child's functioning, with respect to timeliness, participation, behavior, and other nonacademic variables. This information can be useful in documenting that the child is having continuing or accelerating difficulties.

(3) The IEP itself is a source of information to document the child's lack of progress. A number of different aspects of the child's IEP can be compared to establish a lack of progress. These include the reports of the child's current level of functioning, the areas of identified need, the present levels of performance used to develop goal statements, the goals themselves, and the reports on progress in relation to mastery of the goals.

(4) If the child has not been making progress, one would expect the IEP to include more intensive services and/or different approaches to address the lack of progress. If the plan for the child remains relatively constant or even documents reduction of service at the same time that the child is showing a lack of meaningful progress, this is further evidence of the inappropriateness of the child's program.

(5) For children having behavioral difficulties, it is important to review the formal behavioral records, including disciplinary notices, incident reports, documentation of behavioral issues in the IEP, and, if possible, anecdotal school data that demonstrate how the child's behavior is deteriorating over time. Another source of useful information regarding the child's behavior is often found in the informal communications

between the school and the parent, including notebooks exchanged between the school and parent on the child's daily activities, emails expressing concerns about the child's behavior, written communications, or phone calls between the school and the parent raising concerns about the child. In addition to tracking the child's behavior over time, it is useful to track the school strategies or interventions being used to address the behavior, to show that they were insufficient, inappropriate in their design, insufficient in their intensity, inconsistently or incompletely implemented, or otherwise inadequate.

(6) Even when there is a lengthy history of lack of progress, it is often useful to have independent evaluators examine the child to determine if the child is making appropriate or expected progress and, if not, to make recommendations for how the child's needs can be effectively addressed. After determining the child's lack of progress, evaluators may recommend a more intensive program, through the public school, or through a specialized private program. Although independent evaluators may be reluctant to recommend a particular program, it can be very useful if they recommend the components of a program that are necessary for the child to make appropriate progress educationally and otherwise. Recommendations, for example, might address the child's need for smaller classes or smaller teacher to student ratios, the use of particular technology, a small school setting with fewer transitions between classrooms, or the presence of staff with training and expertise in relation to the child's particular disability. Evaluators might also suggest particular methodologies for addressing the child's education or behavioral needs, particularly peer reviewed research based methodologies that may not be available in the public school, more intensive related services, or other new interventions.

It may also be useful for the independent evaluator to identify components of the child's educational program that should be avoided or that are contraindicated. For example, the child may require placement in a setting with minimal transitions or few distractions. The child may not be successful in an environment with a large number of students or a large physical plant. The child may require placement in a setting with peers who have particular characteristics that will promote the child's progress. Conversely, the independent evaluator may highlight the child's vulnerability and the need to avoid programs or classrooms that put the child at risk in relation to distraction, disruption, or abuse by other students.

When a child has been doing adequately for a period of time and the need for private placement arises as a result of some rapid deterioration or acute crisis, clinical assessment and recommendations become especially important. In the absence of a history of academic or behavioral failure, clinical judgment about the need for a specialized private program is critical to justify the leap over the possible less restrictive options that may not yet have been tried by the public school.

Where possible, it is very important for independent evaluators to have the opportunity to review the child's school records. It is generally helpful for independent evaluators also to obtain direct input from the school staff as to how the child is functioning. This can occur through direct communications with the school staff or by the school staff's complete various rating scales concerning the child. Although observation is not always possible, it is essential that the independent evaluator incorporate as much information from the school staff about the child's functioning as possible. Such information is very useful in addition to the reports of the parents or the evaluator's own impressions of the student.

In addition to demonstrating that the child is not making appropriate progress in the public school setting, it is necessary for the parent to demonstrate that the desired private placement is appropriate for the student. Again, an independent evaluator's knowledge of a private program can be helpful in demonstrating its appropriateness. If the independent evaluator lacks that knowledge, it would be useful for parents to share the information they have about the program, so that the evaluator can have some confidence that the program does have the desired components.

(7) Apart from information shared with the independent evaluator, the parents should thoroughly evaluate the private program to ensure that it has the essential elements for the student to be educated effectively. Information should be obtained from the school's literature and from

its Web site and by determining the school's accreditation with the state Department of Education and/or with private accreditation agencies. Obviously, if possible, the parents should visit the program before enrolling their child. It is important to ascertain that the private program employs teachers who are trained and experienced in working with children with the identified disability and, preferably, have appropriate special education credentials from the state in which the facility is located. In addition, it is desirable that the facility have some form of individualized plan, comparable to an IEP, that will drive the child's program and be used to evaluate the child's progress.

(8) In addition to documenting that the child cannot be appropriately served in the public school setting and requires private placement, it is very important that the parents establish that the child can or has been admitted to the private school and that the private school has space to enroll the student. Unfortunately, parents sometimes pursue private placement based upon things they have heard about the private facility or out of desperation to find something different from the public school, without verifying that the private school is appropriate, will accept the student, and has an actual space available. It is a tragic waste of the parents' time, effort, and resources to push for a private school placement only to discover that the facility is not appropriate, will not accept the student, or would accept the student but does not have space. In addition, because the process of securing public school funding for private placement can sometimes be very time consuming, it is important for parents to verify the ongoing availability of the private school slot to ensure that, when or if funding is obtained, the child can still be accommodated.

(9) If the parent has already enrolled the student in the private school, it is very important to obtain as much data as possible about the private school's admission/evaluation procedures, the private school's plan for the student, and the private school's documentation of the child's services and progress. Obviously, this information is needed to compare and contrast the child's functioning in the private school with his or her lack of progress in the public school.

(10) If the dispute concerning funding for a private school reaches the stage of a due process hearing or a court procedure, it is generally

important to have appropriate staff members of the private school testify about the program they offer and demonstrate the ways in which that program can or is meeting the needs of the child. Conversely, it is generally unwise to use the private school staff to criticize the public school program, as the private school staff may be perceived as having a vested interest in the child's placement. Private staff are better used to assess the child's needs and the ways that their program is meeting those needs.

Services for children voluntarily placed in a private school for reasons unrelated to a denial of a free appropriate public education

Many parents choose to place their child in a regular or a parochial private school for reasons unrelated to a concern that the child is not receiving a FAPE, but rather because the parents prefer the private or parochial school for other reasons. As a general matter, the IDEA does not require public schools to provide the same level of services to children with disabilities who are voluntarily placed by their parents in private schools for reasons unrelated to their special education needs. When a student attends a private school based on a voluntary decision by a parent and it is suspected that the child has a disability, the public school district in which the private school is located is required under "the child find" requirements of the IDEA to evaluate the child and determine whether the child has a disability, pursuant to the evaluation requirements of the IDEA.[8]

However, once the required parental consent has been obtained and the child enrolled in private school is evaluated, the child's entitlement to services is different from that of children who are identified as eligible for special education services and who attend public schools. In fact, under the IDEA, children voluntarily placed by their parents in private schools do *not* have a right to receive the special education and related services that they would receive if they were enrolled in public school. There is no individual right to special education and related services for parentally placed private school students.[9] Instead, the IDEA provides that the school district, after consultation with private schools located in the school system and representatives of the parents of private school students in those schools, shall provide equitable services based on a proportionate share of the federal funds available to serve children with disabilities in the school district. The proportionate share is based on a calculation of the number of children with disabilities voluntarily placed in private schools in proportion to the total number of children with disabilities residing in the district.

Thus, the school district must expend a fraction of its IDEA funding equivalent to the fractional number of children enrolled in private schools by their parents relative to the total number of children with disabilities identified as residing in the district. Once the school system consults with the private schools and interested parents of children in those private schools, the school district may decide how it will allocate the "equitable share" funds to most effectively meet the needs of the private school students. When private school students do receive services as a result of the public school's determination, the public school must develop a "service plan" that describes how the services will be provided.[10]

These service plans must be developed, reviewed, and revised in consultation with a representative of the school that the child attends. In addition, the service plan must indicate whether the services will be provided, at the discretion of the public school, on the premises of the private school or on the premises of the public school, with transportation provided by the school system.[11] The parent has no right to use a due process hearing to challenge the decision regarding whether a child will receive services or what nature of services are to be provided.[12]

However, a private school official may submit a complaint to the state Department of Education that the public school has not properly followed procedures in the development of the plan for provision of equitable services to students with disabilities enrolled in private schools.[13] In providing equitable services to children voluntarily placed in private schools by the parents, the public school may use public school personnel to provide these services, including at the site of the private school, but may not use IDEA funds to finance services that are already provided by the private school or to otherwise benefit the private school.[14]

The bottom line is that children who are voluntarily placed in private schools by the parents may be eligible to receive limited services from the public school but are not entitled to receive the same degree of special education services as would be required if the student were enrolled in a public school. In addition, parents who disagree with the decisions of the public school with respect to the provision of services to children in private schools do not have an individual right to challenge the public school's decision through the due process procedures that would be available to them if the students were enrolled in public school.

CHAPTER 8

Behavior Management
and Discipline

From the outset, special education law has recognized that children with disabilities are likely to have more frequent behavior problems than may be typical of children without disabilities, stemming from their difficulties in understanding rules and learning appropriate behavior, problems with controlling their behavior, and vulnerability to the inappropriate behavior of others. The special education law defines emotional disturbance to include emotional disabilities that are internally focused, such as depression, obsessive compulsive disorder, social skills deficits, phobias, manic depression, schizophrenia, anxiety disorders, and other disorders that may impact on children's functioning at school but have less impact on the environment.

The Individuals with Disabilities Education Act (IDEA) defines emotional disturbance also to include externalized behaviors—in other words, those that are directed toward or more overtly have an impact on others, including disruptive or aggressive behaviors. The IDEA recognizes that emotional and behavioral disorders can be disabling and can have a substantial adverse effect on the ability of the child to function successfully at school. The IDEA also recognizes that, by virtue of the nature of the child's behavioral problems, he or she may be more likely to engage in behavior that is contrary to the school's rules or code of conduct. As such, the law anticipated that the application of regular discipline to students with disabilities, without special accommodation to take into account those disabilities, could lead to improper exclusion of the student and/or to punishments for behavior that actually require remedial assistance. In this era of perceived increased violence and criminal conduct by students, many schools have adopted harsher disciplinary policies, including zero tolerance policies for drugs, weapons, and activities associated with gang involvement. Similarly, in the face of some of the tragic shootings in public schools, many schools have taken a very strong stance in response to students who display any behaviors involving a perceived threat of violence. As a consequence, in the last ten years, the law has shifted dramatically. The IDEA 1997 Amendments provided considerable protections for children with disabilities that have emotional and behavioral issues. The 2004 Amendments continue to provide children with emotional disorders with specialized services, but schools have greater discretion to transfer the children to more restrictive settings and/or to use regular education disciplinary procedures to respond to their misconduct.

> *Bart was a student with attention deficit/hyperactivity disorder (AD/HD) and learning disabilities who was in a public high school. Bart brought a pocket knife to school, which he claimed he had been using before going to school and had inadvertently placed with his notebook in his backpack. While on the school bus, another student saw Bart with the pocket knife. She grabbed the knife from Bart, who snatched it back and returned it to his backpack. Several days later, the student reported to school authorities that Bart had a knife in his backpack, and the authorities searched Bart's backpack and locker. The knife was not there. Despite this, Bart was suspended from school and was recommended for expulsion. In order to avoid long-term exclusion from school, Bart's parents worked out an arrangement with the school system that allowed Bart to attend an alternative school for the remainder of the academic term, rather than being expelled from school altogether.*

> *Sarah was having difficulties in school and was having particular conflict with a school counselor. Sarah and a friend wrote graffiti on a bulletin board making negative references to the teacher and wrote a note on the notepad on the teacher's door that contained vaguely threatening language concerning the teacher but no explicit threat. Sarah was suspended and recommended for expulsion. After negotiation with the school*

> *system and obtaining outside evaluations from mental health professionals indicating that Sarah was not a danger to herself or others, Sarah was allowed to return to the public school but was required to participate in a more restrictive program for children with behavioral disorders.*

At the outset, when children are initially evaluated for eligibility for special education and when they are reevaluated either at the three year reevaluation point (or when a reevaluation is specifically requested), the evaluation must assess the child in all areas related to the child's suspected disability, including the child's social and emotional status.[1] In determining whether a child has emotional, behavioral, social, or other related needs, the school's obligation in evaluating the student and developing a program for him or her should address the student's primary suspected disability as well as assessment of all areas of difficulty that may be related to the suspected disability and any other areas of suspected disability, as well. In addition, the evaluation process must address the child's developmental needs and must address what the child knows and can do academically, developmentally, and functionally.[2]

Evaluating the child's needs in areas other than academics is particularly important in ensuring that children with behavioral challenges are being adequately assessed to identify the cause, nature, and extent of those emotional and behavioral needs in order to develop appropriate interventions. Although the special education category of emotional disturbance focuses explicitly on a child's behavioral functioning at school, a variety of other disability categories may also carry with them symptoms or characteristics that result in problematic behavior. For example, children eligible for special education under the "other health impaired" category due to AD/HD or Tourette Syndrome may engage in disability related behaviors that are contrary to classroom or school rules, such as talking out of turn or inappropriate language. Similarly, some children with autism may display a variety of behaviors that violate the school conduct code, including tantrums, self abusive behaviors, or physical contact with others—behaviors that appear to be due to an emotional disorder but actually are directly related to the children's autism. On the other end of the autism spectrum, children with Asperger Syndrome may have problems with social perception, difficulty understanding nonverbal communication, and difficulty in interpreting humor or body language, which may cause them to misinterpret other children's words or actions and react inappropriately.

Even children who have disability labels that do not seem to have an overt behavioral component may well experience behavioral difficulties as a consequence of their disorder. For example, a child with mental retardation may have difficulty understanding school rules, understanding directions being given by school staff, and interpreting the behavior or communications of other students, resulting in actions that are either perceived to be noncompliant or that cause the student to get upset in reaction to the behavior of those interacting with him or her. Students with a learning disability may experience depression or other emotional consequences of their disability, which may ultimately lead to either internalized or externalized behaviors that adversely affect their functioning at school and/or get them into disciplinary troubles.

E=MC² Advocacy Strategies: Appropriate Labeling

(1) As indicated in the eligibility section (Chapter 2), labels often take on exaggerated significance in the school system. It is important that children be accurately labeled, although it is equally or more important that they obtain appropriate services, regardless of their label. However, in the arena of behavioral management and discipline, it is important to recognize that the "emotionally disturbed" (ED) label is not a prerequisite to a school's development of positive behavioral strategies to address a child's behavioral needs. In addition, the ED label is not the only basis for concluding that a child's behavior is related to his or her disability.

(2) In the disciplinary context, there are now more limited grounds than prior to 2004 for determining that a child's behavior is related to his or her disability. As a result, it is especially important that parents and clinicians work with educators in the individualized education program (IEP) process to describe fully the emotional and behavioral issues that children may be experiencing that could adversely affect their functioning at school, even if they are not currently having severe behavioral difficulties. Identifying the child's potential emotional and

behavioral concerns in advance makes it possible to develop a broader range of positive interventions to assist the child in managing and/or preventing these emotional or behavioral problems. At the same time, the early identification of these problems makes it easier to connect subsequent behavioral difficulties to the child's disability if the child displays a behavior that leads to disciplinary action.

The IDEA expressly requires that the IEP team consider and identify the emotional and behavioral needs of children with disabilities and consider appropriate strategies for assisting the student in dealing with those needs. The regulations require that "the IEP team must in the case of a child whose behavior impedes the child's learning or that of others, consider the use of positive behavioral interventions and supports and other strategies to address that behavior."[3] Significantly, this language is not restricted to a child whose behavior is disruptive of others but also includes behavior that impedes the child's own learning. This could include failing to come to class on time, difficulty in completing assignments on time, completing assignments but failing to turn them in, speaking in class without being called on, taking excessive breaks or needing to move around in class inappropriately, and having difficulty participating in groups due to social skills problems. Some schools assume that positive behavioral interventions and supports are only appropriate for children who are displaying behaviors that are dangerous or disruptive to others. The IDEA clearly requires the use of positive behavioral intervention and supports not only for these behaviors but also for behaviors that adversely affect the child's own learning.

As noted earlier, the IDEA also now requires that the IEP team include a regular education teacher who can assist in "the determination of appropriate positive behavioral interventions and supports and other strategies for the child and supplementary aids and services, program modifications and supports for school personnel."[4] Thus, the IDEA clearly conveys that positive behavioral intervention and supports are intended to be used by special education staff and in special education classrooms or programs, but also within the regular education classroom under the supervision of regular education teachers, as well.

E=MC² Advocacy Strategies: Development of Proactive Behavioral Strategies and Supports for Children with Behavioral Challenges

(1) When children are at risk for inappropriate behaviors or display emotional problems that have an impact on their functioning at school, it is important that the IEP identify the student's emotional and behavioral needs. Once those emotional and behavioral needs are identified, the IEP should include goals to address those needs, whether they involve externalized or internalized behavior, including behavior that affects the child's academic functioning and the child's social participation in the school. For example, if a child is disorganized or has trouble getting to class on time or has difficulty being on task in class, it would be appropriate for goals to address these behaviors. Similarly, if a child is socially awkward and has difficulty understanding appropriate social behavior with his or her peers—resulting in limited social involvement at school and/or difficulty participating in group activities—this would also be an appropriate topic for an IEP goal.

(2) The IEP should specify the behavioral supports that are needed by the student, including related services. Students with emotional, behavioral, and social difficulties may require social work, psychological, and/or counseling services. In some instances, it may even be appropriate to include a parent training or counseling component to assist the parents in reinforcing the appropriate behaviors or skills that the school is working on.

(3) In addition to related services, the IEP should identify whether the child may need individualized assistance, up to and including the provision of a one to one aide for part or all of the school day in order to assist the student in functioning within the regular education environment or even when functioning in a more restrictive setting. The need for a one to one classroom aide should be expressly stated in the IEP. Beyond the provision of additional personnel, the IEP should spell out the behavioral strategies that may be used with the student, such as the use of a positive reinforcement system; the opportunity to take a

time-out to allow the student to cool down; or the provision of specific behavioral techniques to allow the student to deescalate. The IEP can also specify strategies that should be avoided because they are not successful with the student, such as avoiding the use of confrontation or physical prompting for students who are not likely to respond well to these techniques.

For students with identified behavioral needs, it may be appropriate to seek the completion of a functional behavioral analysis (FBA) to determine the triggers for the child's behavioral difficulties and to use that data to formulate a behavior intervention plan that provides effective strategies for the staff and the student. An FBA is a structured method for gathering data about the circumstances and consequences of the child's behavior to identify patterns or causes of the behavior. This information can then be used to develop more effective strategies for helping the student to behave appropriately. Generally, an FBA should involve observation of the student in the environments or situations where he or she is having the behavioral problems. Data should be gathered about the behavior, but also about the events surrounding or preceding the behavior (antecedents) and the effects or result of the behavior (consequences). This data can help to determine why the behavior is occurring and whether the reactions to the behavior from the staff and others are helping to improve the child's behavior or making it worse. For example, a child may display aggressive or disruptive behaviors but only in noisy or unstructured environments. This information could lead to changes in the child's environment, greater structure, or teaching the child more appropriate strategies to cope with his or her discomfort in these environments.

Similarly, it might be discovered that a student was consistently acting out during activities involving reading. The consequence of this disruption was that the student was removed from the reading activity, which allowed the student to avoid an undesirable activity. This data might indicate the need for a reading evaluation, assistance with reading and behavioral strategies other than removal from reading to address the behavior.

183

(4) In addition to using related services personnel to provide specific remedial and intervention services to assist the student, it may also be useful to identify within the IEP adults whom the student trusts and/or can seek assistance from in the event that he or she is encountering difficulties. When a student is experiencing problems at school and feels isolated or unable to obtain support from key adults, behavioral problems may escalate and lead to more serious disciplinary difficulties. Friendly teachers, administrators, or others who can serve as mentors, informal advocates, or otherwise provide support to the student can be useful in showing the student ways to address problems as they come up so that they can be resolved early on, helping the student to return to the appropriate activities of the classroom.

(5) As part of the IEP and/or the behavioral intervention plan, it is sometimes appropriate to identify classroom or school rules that will be modified or waived for the student. For example, a child who talks out of turn by virtue of his or her disability might be exempt from rules resulting in discipline for that type of behavior. A student who is in a classroom with a demerit system based on tardiness, late completion of work, or getting out of her seat without permission, might be exempt from these rules if these behaviors are resulting from a disability. Instead, it might be appropriate to establish a positive reinforcement system for this student to earn rewards based on compliance with the rules, while exempting the student from disciplinary consequences of violating the rules.

(6) When schools are conducting a functional behavioral analysis, it is important that this analysis be based on direct observation of the students in the environments in which they appear to be having the greatest difficulty. Sometimes, a school conducts what purports to be a functional analysis using teachers' recollections of a child's pattern of behavior, rather than direct observation. This is far less accurate in identifying what the actual triggers to the child's behavioral or emotional problems may be. Under some circumstances, the school's disciplinary response to the child's behavioral problem may serve to reinforce the inappropriate behavior, rather than help to reduce it.

(7) When behavioral strategies are developed, goals should be set for incremental progress, rather than for the child to display perfect behavior at the outset. Expecting too much improvement too quickly may be a setup for failure for the student and doom the plan before it's implemented. Rewards should be relatively immediate, concrete, and meaningful for the student. As the plan is implemented, its effectiveness should be regularly reviewed. If the student is making progress, it may be appropriate either to increase the expectation for the child's behavioral performance or move to other targeted behaviors that need to be addressed. Conversely, if the child is not making appropriate progress, it would be appropriate to assess why the child is not making progress and determine whether additional or different strategies or supports are needed.

(8) In developing behavioral intervention strategies, it is critical to recognize that many students may lack the emotional, behavioral, or social skill that is necessary to display the desired behavior. The student may require training or assistance in developing the skill, whether through provision of specified skills training, counseling, modeling of behavior, participation in groups with other students to role play or practice the behavior, and/or ongoing constructive feedback and support from staff.

(9) In any behavioral intervention system, it is critical that the child and the parents provide input, in order to ensure that the child understands the behavioral interventions, that the child perceives that the strategies will be useful, and that any expectations, rewards, and consequences are meaningful to the student and to the parents. Further, it is important that the parents "buy in" to the behavioral strategies, so that they can reinforce the strategies at home. If the parents and the school disagree as to the behavioral approaches to be used for the student, it is far less likely that the behavioral systems that are employed will be successful.

Special disciplinary procedures for children with disabilities

Under the IDEA, children with disabilities have a number of protections in the application of school discipline procedures that are dramatically different than those who do not have disabilities. Although the protections available to students with disabilities were more extensive prior to the amendments to the IDEA in 2004, they still provide substantial protections beyond those available in regular education.

In general, children who are eligible for special education can be suspended for up to ten school days cumulatively during the course of the school year without triggering special protections. However, if a student with a disability is suspended in excess of ten school days either cumulatively or consecutively during a school year, special rules apply with respect to how the school must address the child's behavior and to the application of disciplinary procedures.[5]

If the child has been suspended one or more times that in total exceed ten school days during the school year or is recommended for expulsion, the student will generally still be entitled to receive special education and related services that allow him to make progress on his goals and objectives, to have access to the general curriculum, and to receive assistance with the behavior that led to his disciplinary exclusion.[6] This is sometimes called the "no cessation of services" rule. If the student has accumulated ten days or more of suspensions over the course of a school year, but none of the suspensions individually exceeded ten days, the school IEP team may evaluate whether those suspensions are connected and reflect a pattern, in order to determine whether the cumulative suspensions constitute a change of placement.[7] If the team determines that these behaviors do reflect a pattern or if the child is being considered for suspension in excess of ten school days or for long term exclusion (expulsion), the school must convene an IEP meeting to determine if the behavior is related to the disability. This meeting is generally called a *manifestation determination meeting* and must include the IEP team members, the parents, and other individuals with special expertise relating to the child's behavioral issues.[8] If the IEP team, through the manifestation determination process, determines that the child's behavior is not related to the child's disability, the school may go forward with disciplinary exclusion in excess of ten school days.[9] Even if this determination is made, the child remains eligible for some special education services as a consequence of the "no cessation of service" rule.[10] If the team decides that the behavior is related to the child's disability, the school cannot go forward with the long term suspension or expulsion, but instead must maintain the child in the current placement and adjust the IEP to the extent that the team determines it is necessary.[11] The team may recommend a change of placement for the child, but parents can challenge that change by requesting a due process hearing. If this occurs, the child may be excluded from their prior placement for the period of the ten day suspension or 45 day interim placement period if they have been placed in an Interim Alternative Educational Setting (see below for details). In either situation, he may return to his prior placement at the end of the suspension or alternative placement period or on order from a hearing officer, whichever comes first.[12] However, the school may seek an order from a hearing officer or judge that the child should remain in the excluded status.

The manifestation review meeting must be convened within ten days of the behavior that has triggered the recommendation for suspension or expulsion. In making the decision as to whether the behavior was related to the disability, the team must first consider if the behavior was a direct result of the failure of the school to implement the IEP properly.[13] If it is determined that the IEP had not been appropriately implemented, the team must determine that the behavior was related to the disability and cannot go forward with long term disciplinary exclusion. However, if the team determines that the IEP was appropriately implemented, the team must then determine whether the behavior was caused by or had a direct or substantial relationship to the disability.[14]

If it is determined that the behavior was not directly caused by the disability, the school may impose a long term suspension or expulsion, subject to the right to receive continuing services based on the no cessation of services rule. If it is determined that the behavior was a manifestation of the child's disability, the IEP team must both conduct a functional behavioral assessment and implement a behavioral intervention plan or, if a behavioral intervention plan has already been developed, review the plan and modify it as necessary to address the child's behavior.[15]

If the parents object to the determination of the IEP team or to the recommendation for long term suspension or expulsion, the parents may request an expedited due process hearing to challenge the decision.[16] However, under the IDEA 2004 amendments, the child may be excluded from school while the due process procedure is pending until the period of exclusion expires or if the hearing officer orders the child returned to the last agreed upon placement, whichever comes first.[17] Prior to the 2004 amendments, the student would be entitled to remain in school while the due process proceedings were pending. This is a significant change in the application of the "stay put" placement rule, and it gives schools far more ability to exclude the child in reaction to disciplinary infractions.

E=MC² Advocacy Strategies: Addressing Recommendations for Suspensions and Expulsions at the Manifestation Conference

(1) The easing of disciplinary rules relating to the exclusion of children with disabilities makes it more important that parent and clinicians anticipate the potential for a child to be subject to disciplinary exclusion. They should build into the IEP, as much as possible, information about ways that the child's disability may interfere with his or her ability to understand or control his or her behavior—especially if that behavior may violate school rules or trigger disciplinary exclusion. By building into the IEP a clear statement of the ways the child's disability may impede his ability to conform to school rules, it will be more likely that the team will determine that there is a connection between the actual behavior and the disability at the manifestation determination meeting. Similarly, the parents and clinicians should seek to have the IEP include goals, services, and positive behavioral interventions and strategies that address some of these behaviors to reduce the likelihood that disciplinary exclusion will become an issue. These interventions should provide the school with steps it must implement to fulfill its obligation to address the child's behavioral needs prior to considering disciplinary exclusion.

(2) In the context of manifestation determinations, it is often useful for the parents to secure professional consultation from outside mental health professionals to address the question of whether the child's behavior was related to the disability. In addition, such outside consultations may

address the nature or scope of response from the school that will be most likely to assist the child in managing or developing appropriate behavior in the future.

(3) Parents may also benefit from obtaining information from school staff, whether through a review of school records or through seeking direct input from particular staff members, indicating how or why the behavior may be related to the disability and/or why the disciplinary exclusion will be undesirable or inappropriate for the student.

(4) If the IEP team determines that the behavior is not related to the disability or recommends long-term suspension or expulsion and the parents disagree, the parents may request a due process hearing, which must be convened on an expedited basis within 20 school days of the date that the request for the hearing is filed. A decision is required within ten school days after the hearing is completed.[18]

Emergency placements in interim alternative educational settings

Since 1997, the IDEA has allowed schools unilaterally to place children with disabilities in "interim alternative educational settings" (IAES) for especially serious behavior. Under the 2004 IDEA, there are more circumstances where a child can be unilaterally transferred to an interim alternative educational setting for up to 45 school days. This can occur if a child is found to be in possession of illegal drugs or dangerous weapons at school or at a school function or has caused a serious injury to another student or staff.[19] In addition, if children have not yet caused injury to themselves or others but the school believes they are substantially likely to harm themselves or others, the school may request an expedited due process hearing to obtain an order from a hearing officer allowing them to transfer the student to an interim alternative educational setting.[20] If the school determines that any child should be transferred to an interim alternative educational setting, the decision as to where the child is placed should be made by the child's IEP team.[21]

Although the IEP team is authorized to make the decision as to where the child will be placed, the decision that the child will be placed in an interim alternative educational setting is assigned to the school administration, rather than the IEP team, unless the school is seeking an order from a hearing officer based on risk of serious harm.

The decision by the IEP team as to where the child should be transferred is supposed to be made within ten days of the decision to place the child in an interim alternative setting. The parents, as members of the IEP team, have a right to participate in making this decision. If the parent objects either to the decision to place the child in the interim alternative setting or to the chosen placement, the parent retains the right to request an expedited due process hearing. However, the child will remain in the interim alternative setting until a hearing officer rules the child should return or until the period of exclusion ends, whichever comes first. When a child is being considered for suspension beyond ten days or an expulsion or has been transferred to an interim alternative educational setting, parents are strongly encouraged to seek the involvement of outside mental health professionals in determining the child's emotional and behavioral status and needs. They are also advised to seek consultation from a knowledgeable special education advocate or an attorney to advise them as to whether there is a basis to challenge the school's decisions and to assist them in participating effectively in the decision making process regarding the child's potential discipline.

Procedural safeguards for children suspected of having disabilities who are not yet in special education

In general, the special education procedural safeguards regarding disciplinary actions do not apply to children in regular education, even if those children may have unidentified disabilities. However, the special education safeguards do apply to children in regular education if the school is deemed to have knowledge that the child has a disability.[22] According to the regulations, a school will be deemed to have knowledge that a child has a disability:

> if before the behavior that precipitated the disciplinary action occurred, (1) the parent of the child expressed concern in writing to supervisory of administrative personnel of the (school) or a teacher of the child, that the

child is in need of special education and related services;
(2) the parent of the child requested an evaluation of the
child . . . ; or (3) the teacher of the child or other personnel
of the (school) expressed specific concerns about a
pattern of behavior demonstrated by the child directly to
the Director of Special Education of the (school) or other
supervisory personnel of the (school).[23],

However, the school will not be deemed to have knowledge if the parent has
refused a requested evaluation of the child, the parent has refused services
proposed for the child, or the child has been evaluated by the school and
determined not to have a disability.[24]

If a child in regular education is being recommended for suspension or
expulsion or has been suspended or expelled, the parent retains the right to
request an evaluation of the child to determine if their son or daughter has a
disability, which must be completed in an expedited manner.[25] However, the
child will remain in the excluded status while the evaluation is completed.
The child will be entitled to receive services if, upon completion of the
evaluation, it is determined that the child does have a disability.[26]

If the parent suspects that the child has a disability and the child is
being subjected to regular education suspension or expulsion, it is advisable
for the parent to request an expedited evaluation for consideration of
special education eligibility. Such a request should be made in writing,
with the parents retaining copies of the request and preferably obtaining
documentation that the school has received the request. The school retains
the ability either to agree to conduct the evaluation or to deny the request
for evaluation. However, if the school decides not to conduct the evaluation,
it must provide the parents with a "Notice of the Decision to Refuse the
Evaluation," give the reasons for the refusal, and inform the parents about
the right to a due process hearing.

CHAPTER 9

Special Issues Concerning Transition and Graduation

The Individuals with Disabilities Education Act (IDEA) was enacted to promote the ability of children with disabilities to be as productive and successful as possible upon leaving the public schools. As the opening language of the 2004 law puts it,

> Almost 30 years of research and experience has demonstrated that the education of children with disabilities can be made more effective by having high expectations for such children and ensuring their access to the general education curriculum and the regular classroom to the maximum extent possible, in order to meet developmental goals and to the maximum extent possible, the challenging expectations that have been established for all children; and to be prepared to lead productive and independent adult lives, to the maximum extent possible.[1]

In order to accomplish this goal more effectively, the 2004 IDEA and its accompanying regulations placed increased emphasis upon the importance of transition planning for children with disabilities, expanding the scope of transition evaluation, planning, and services beyond that which the law had encompassed in the past.

Under the 2004 law, schools must now have a transition service plan in place no later than the first individualized education program (IEP) in effect when the child turns 16 or earlier if the IEP team determines that is appropriate.[2] The IDEA regulations define transition services in a manner that encompasses a wide array of services including three broad elements. First, the plan must focus on desired outcomes for the student after he or she leaves school. It requires activities designed to promote a results oriented process, that is, focusing on improving the academic and functional achievement of the child with the disability to facilitate the child's movement from school to post school activities. This includes postsecondary education, vocational education, integrated employment (including supported employment), continuing and adult education, adult services, independent living, or community participation. Second, the plan should be based on a holistic approach to the child, "based on the individual child's needs, taking into account the child's strengths, preferences and interests." Third, in order to address those needs, the plan must include "instruction, related services, community experiences, the development of employment and other post school adult living objectives, and if appropriate, acquisition of daily living skills and provision of a functional vocational evaluation."[3]

As is evident from the language of the regulation, transition services may be directed to a wide array of post school activities, including preparation for college, vocational education, employment, independent living skills, and community participation, such as involvement in community, social, or recreational activities. The transition program should be centered on the individual student and promote his/her ability to develop postsecondary skills that are relevant to his/her abilities, interests, and needs. Further, the transition services should include special education and related services, as well as community based experiences and the development of daily living skills to the extent needed. The requirement of a "functional vocational evaluation as appropriate" is intended to assist the IEP team, the child, and the family in determining the appropriate postsecondary goals and service needs for the student.

In developing the transition plan, the school must invite the student with the disability to attend the transition planning meetings.[4] It should be noted, however, that until the child turns 18, parents can decide whether the child attends the IEP meeting. If the child does not attend the IEP meeting, the school "must take other steps to ensure that the child's preferences and interests are considered."[5] This generally means that the school staff interviews the student separate from the IEP/transition meeting.

If there's a possibility that the transition planning process will result in the provision of services by agencies other than the school system, the school—with the consent of the parent or the child if the child is over 18—must invite representatives of the other agencies that may be responsible for providing or paying for the services.[6] At the initial IEP meeting for the purpose of developing the transition plan and annually thereafter, "The IEP must include (1) appropriate measurable postsecondary goals based upon age appropriate transition assessments related to training, education, employment and, where appropriate, independent living skills and (2) the transition services, including courses of study needed to assist the child in reaching those goals."[7]

This requirement is significant in a number of important respects. First, it requires that all "age appropriate transition assessments" address the child's training, education, employment, and independent living skills. This assessment process goes beyond academic or vocational assessments and includes all the key areas of the child's potential needs upon graduation, such as life skills, social skills, and time management skills. These assessments can provide critical information and identify a wide variety of the student's needs, some of which may not have been identified in the regular special education evaluation process, as those evaluations may not have been adequately focused on post high school functioning.

Equally important, the requirement that "appropriate postsecondary goals" be developed creates a dramatic shift in the planning process compared to the typical IEP meeting. The IEP process for a child under age 16, for example, would normally be driven by the child's needs at the start of the school year and would lead to the development of incremental goals that could be accomplished during the school year, without regard to the ultimate level of functioning that the school hopes to attain for the student upon graduation. By comparison, the transition planning process requires the development of "appropriate measurable postsecondary goals" that require the school to look beyond annual goals. The process sets goals beyond the student's high school graduation or beyond turning 21, for students who may be entitled to services past their senior year. As such, the process of setting transition goals requires a longer term plan than the typical IEP. Given this more far reaching requirement, it becomes necessary to assess whether the annual goals that are being developed for the student are sufficient to allow the child to achieve the appropriate and measurable postsecondary goals that have been developed for him or her. In other words, the short term approach of the general IEP process may need to be modified to address the longer term goals that result from the transition plan.

In addition, because the transition planning process focuses on academic, vocational, *and* independent living skills, the IEP may require goals and services that are substantially broader than the identified needs and goals reflected in the IEP for the student prior to age 16. Thus, the transition planning process may lead to a significant expansion in the breadth of services that the student is provided from age 16 on while they remain in public education.

Under the IDEA, students are eligible to receive special education services until they graduate from high school with a regular education diploma. They may also receive services through the age of 21 (or longer, if state law provides a longer period) if they have not received a regular education diploma, if they received a special education diploma after their senior year, or have not received a diploma at all.[8] It should be noted that a student may have received passing grades or sufficient credits for graduation but may still be eligible for services beyond 12th grade. The regulations provide that "a free appropriate public education is available to any individual child with a disability who needs special education and related services, even though the child has not failed or been retained in a course or grade and is advancing from grade to grade."[9] This suggests that the accumulation of credits sufficient for graduation does not by itself mean that a student has received a free appropriate public education (FAPE) or no longer requires special education or related services. However, the decision as to whether children are entitled to receive services beyond 12th grade is made by the IEP team on an individual basis.[10]

One year prior to the age at which the student reaches the age of majority (legal adulthood) under the state's law, the IEP must include a statement documenting that the child has been informed of his or her rights to assume responsibility for educational decision making upon reaching the age of majority.[11] This provision allows for the transfer of legal rights to the student, unless the parents have obtained legal guardianship of the student through a court proceeding. In addition, under the new IDEA, the state must have a procedure to allow the student to appoint the parents to be his or her representative. The specific mechanisms that states use for allowing parents to act on behalf of their children after they have reached the age of majority vary from state to state. Students, parents, and clinicians in these circumstances should consult state law to determine what procedure has been established by the state to allow for the continuing participation of a parent who has not obtained legal guardianship.

As noted, the IEP must identify the transition services, including courses of study, that the student needs to reach transition goals.[12] Further, the requirement that courses of study be identified is intended to ensure that the child's educational program be developed in a manner that will allow the student to take the necessary range and sequence of courses to progress toward the accomplishment of the identified postsecondary goal. For example, if the student's postsecondary goal is to attend college, the transition plan should identify—on an annual basis—the courses that are necessary for a student to fulfill the requirements necessary for graduation with a regular diploma, as well as the courses that would be necessary to have a realistic chance of meeting the course requirements necessary for admission to college. Similarly, if a specific vocational program is identified as part of the student's transition plan, the course of study should incorporate classes that are necessary for the student to meet the prerequisites for participation in the vocational program after graduation.

In addition to these explicit plans to ensure that the student completes the requisite courses necessary to have a realistic opportunity of achieving appropriate postsecondary goals, the courses of study may also include special education and related services designed to address the child's developmental and functional needs related to developing the necessary independent living skills. For example, students may have difficulties with organizational skills, money management, social skills, time management, or independent mobility. Although the students may be capable of achieving their identified postsecondary goals in other respects, if these skills are also required, the IEP and transition plan should address instructional activities or other strategies for helping students develop them. In addition, under some circumstances, the student may be capable of achieving a particular postsecondary goal but requires remedial assistance in a particular academic subject to be able to accomplish the appropriate postsecondary goal. For example, a student may have average intelligence and the general ability to succeed in college but has significant deficits in a particular academic area, such as reading or math, which require additional remediation. Again, the transition plan of the IEP should address the instructional or supportive services that are necessary to help students achieve their postsecondary goals.

If the transition plan potentially involves services from other agencies—and the other agencies fail to provide the necessary services described in the IEP—the school must reconvene the IEP team to identify alternative strategies to meet the student's transition goals.[13] Any services listed in the IEP must include the starting date, frequency, duration, and location of services to be provided.[14]

> ## $E=MC^2$ Advocacy Strategies: Ensuring Involvement of Other Agencies in a Timely Manner
>
> (1) In order to ensure that other agencies deliver the services sought through the transition planning process, it is advisable to build into the IEP a specific time frame for the school staff or case manager to verify that the other agency has, in fact, accepted the student as a client and/or has a plan in place or is delivering the identified service.
>
> (2) Unfortunately, in the absence of these specific time frames in the IEP, schools sometimes wait months or even a year without verifying that the other agencies from which services are being sought are indeed providing those services. To avoid the delays, specific mechanisms in the IEP should spell out that when outside agencies fall through, the team will swiftly reconvene to develop alternative strategies for the provision of services.

Graduation or aging out

When a child has met all the requirements for a regular education diploma and the IEP team determines that the child is eligible for graduation, the decision to graduate the student involves a change of placement under the IDEA. If the student is 18 or older, notice of the decision for the student to graduate and the proposal that services will be terminated are provided to the student, unless the parent has legal guardianship or the student has used the state's procedure to appoint the parents to act on the student's behalf.[15] As with

THE HAZARDS
OF TRANSITION PLANNING
ARE PAR FOR THE COURSE.

other changes of placement, if the parent (or the student who has reached the age of majority) objects to the decision to change the placement due to graduation, the parent or the student may request a due process hearing to challenge the graduation decision.[16] As with other situations where a due process hearing is requested in response to a proposed change in placement, if the hearing request is timely filed—in other words, before the termination actually occurs—the student is entitled to continue to receive services and to remain enrolled while the due process proceeding is pending.[17] However, if the student graduates with a regular education diploma, he or she has no entitlement to services after graduation.[18] By contrast, if the student graduates with other than a regular education diploma, the student may be entitled to receive services after graduation until his or her 21st birthday.[19] Under the IDEA, a student must be evaluated prior to the termination of special education services if such services are proposed to be terminated prior to graduation. However, if services are being terminated because the student is graduating or aging out, the school is not required to conduct a reevaluation.[20]

Prior to a student's graduating or aging out upon turning 21, the school district is required to provide a "summary of performance" for the purposes of summarizing the child's progress and continuing needs. The regulation provides that: "For a child whose eligibility terminates (due to graduation or exceeding the age eligibility provisions) a public agency must provide the child with a summary of the child's academic achievement and functional performance, which shall include recommendations on how to assist the child in meeting the child's postsecondary goals."[21] This document can be of great use to the family and the student to identify needed services for the transition to the adult service system. Under some circumstances, the summary of performance may also identify areas of need and services that the school should have provided but did not. Where the family and the student believe that the student has failed to receive a FAPE prior to graduation or aging out of eligibility, there is precedent for the student to seek what are called "compensatory educational services," to make up for services that the school should have, but failed to, provide. Typically, however, school systems do not readily agree to provide compensatory services. Instead, they may require the parent or student to pursue a special education due process hearing to prove that there was a denial of a FAPE that substantially interfered with the child's ability to make meaningful educational progress.

In addition, the 2004 IDEA establishes a statute of limitations of two years for filing a due process request, unless state law provides a different limitation period. The statute of limitations sets out the time period within which the request for a hearing must be filed from the point when the parents knew or should have known that their child had been denied an appropriate education or that some other violation of the IDEA had occurred.[22] These statutes limit the ability of the student or the parent to obtain relief more than two years beyond the point when the parent learned of the violation. As such, if the student or parent believe that compensatory services are warranted, they are encouraged to obtain consultation from a knowledgeable special education attorney as soon as possible and to initiate their request for a due process hearing as quickly as they can, in order to ensure that they are not barred from relief by the statute of limitations.

E=MC² Advocacy Strategies: Transition Services

(1) A transition plan must begin by the time the student turns 16 but may begin earlier at the discretion of the IEP team or as provided by state law. The cornerstone of transition planning is to identify the student's goals, desires, abilities, and needs after high school.

Transition assessment addresses what a student and his or her family want or need for the student to do after graduation from high school. This includes consideration of whether the student wishes to and is likely to go to college, vocational, or other post high school education. It also should be based on the student's vocational interests and abilities and whether he or she is likely to pursue employment immediately after graduation, rather than further schooling. With respect to educational and vocational plans after high school, the transition assessment should address the student's academic abilities, particularly those relevant to his or her personal plans. Does the student have the needed academic skills and life skills, with or without accommodation or remediation, to go to college? What skills does the student need help with if the plan is focused on obtaining a job? For example, does the student have a realistic career goal, appropriate training relevant to that goal, the ability to find and obtain a job, including to complete a job application and read and understand material related to the job, and the social and life skills to function in a job environment? It also is based on the student's (and family's) plans with respect to where the student will live after leaving high school—at home, independently, or somewhere other than home but with some degree of adult support, as well as whether it is likely the student will continue to live in his or her current community. It should also take into account the student's social and recreational interests.

Importantly, it should also address the student's daily living skills and ability to function independently in the many different activities of life. These range from the ability to maintain appropriate personal hygiene, to plan menus, shop, cook, clean, and manage money, including budgeting and maintaining a checking account; to plan and manage time effectively; to plan and carry out tasks independently as opposed to with assistance; and to get around the community with or without assistance.

The plan should also address the student's communication skills. To what extent is the student able to communicate effectively, orally and/or in writing, including expressing his or her wants and needs, seeking help, and engaging in appropriate routine communication with the people around them? It should also assess the student's social skills. These include the student's ability to initiate and maintain social relationships, to seek out social and recreational activities, and to maintain appropriate behavior in individual and group situations.

(2) As part of the process of assessing the student's postsecondary interests, plans, and goals, the transition planning process should also include formal assessment in those areas where needs are identified, to determine accurately the student's current level of functioning and what training, supports, and assistance the student will likely need to be able to accomplish his or her postsecondary goals to the extent possible.

Transition assessment should include not only interviews with the student and family but also a variety of formal evaluation components, which will vary based on the student's goals, abilities, and needs. Formal transition evaluations can include interests inventories, designed to help to identify general activities, skills, and/or specific jobs or career paths that are of interest to the student. It may include cognitive and academic testing to determine the student's intellectual and academic skills and challenges, to assess the student's capabilities and functional abilities, including reading, writing, math, and the ability to understand the materials involved in the activities the student wishes to pursue. It can include formal vocational evaluations, which measure the student's skills in a broad variety of areas relevant to the skills needed to find and obtain a job, skills relevant to perform in any job situation (such as following directions, being safe, and on time), and the skills that may be needed for specific vocational areas or jobs.

For those students with difficulties with life skills, the assessment process should also evaluate the student's abilities in the areas where the student has or is likely to have difficulty, such as self-help skills, basic hygiene, safety, communication, self-advocacy, social skills, organizational skills, and the ability to function independently. Formal tests or rating scales are available to assess most, if not all, of these areas.

(3) Once the student's goals, abilities, and needs are identified, an interactive process involving the IEP team, including the parents and the student, must be ongoing, to develop realistic and measurable postsecondary goals for the student, as well as to identify the services that will be needed to potentially be able to accomplish the goals. Making these decisions involves a difficult process of determining realistic postsecondary goals that take into account the student's desires, abilities, and needs. They should also take into account the student's ability to progress toward these goals given appropriate transition services during the time the student remains eligible for special education services, that is, until he or she graduates or turns 21 (or later, if provided for under state law).

In some instances, the student's interests, abilities, and needs will lead everyone to an obvious and mutually agreed plan for the student after leaving school, as well as to a clear transition plan and program to achieve the postsecondary goals that have been set. At other times, however, there may be disagreement as to whether the student's goals are appropriate or realistic and the extent to which they are attainable. Disputes may also arise from disagreement between the family and the school as to the nature, intensity, and duration of transition services the student needs or is entitled to in order to meet his or her postsecondary goals. For example, the parents may feel that a goal for the student to attend college is realistic but requires that the student receive additional academic remediation, which the school believes is either not likely to be effective or beyond its legal obligation to provide a FAPE. The student may need assistance in a variety of life skills areas that the school feels go beyond its obligation or ability to provide. Some students may have sufficient credits to graduate at the end of the senior year, but there is disagreement as to whether they need additional years of special education services to have a more realistic chance to meet their postsecondary goals.

All these issues can also create disagreement as to what the postsecondary goals should be, as more ambitious goals may require more intensive services. School officials may resist these goals and push for more limited goals, because they think the proposed goals are unrealistic or they don't want to be responsible for the additional services that might be needed to make the more ambitious goals potentially feasible. It should be noted that, because the transition planning process requires that the current plan, tied to the IEP, be based on the student's appropriate and measurable postsecondary goals, the IEP goals themselves should take into account these longer term postsecondary goals. It may be argued that the smaller, more incremental measures of progress that are often contained in annual goals for younger students may need to be beefed up to make it more possible to achieve the broader long term goals identified in the transition plan.

Ultimately, though, it is up to the student and the parents, guardian, or person delegated authority by the student to identify what the student wants to do after leaving school. Whether the school agrees with those goals or is willing to provide transition services sufficient to assist the student to meet the goals is a separate matter and may be subject to dispute.

(4) Although the transition process begins at age 16, the plan written at that time is not static. It should be reviewed annually along with the IEP. It should be adjusted as needed. The student's interests may change. He or she may be making more or less progress than anticipated toward the postsecondary goals. This may suggest the need for more or different services or strategies. In addition, in many instances, a transition plan may include services that may be available from agencies outside the school, such as the state vocational services department, mental health agencies, or agencies that provide housing for persons with disabilities. Where the team believes that the student requires services from outside providers, representatives of those agencies must be invited to the IEP/transition planning meeting. However, if the outside agencies fail to

attend the meeting or fail to provide the desired service identified in the transition plan, the IEP team must reconvene to consider other strategies for addressing that need. It is generally advisable to have the transition plan include some mechanism for assuring that the school is verifying whether the identified service is or will be provided in a timely way and a plan for reconvening as soon as possible after it is learned that the outside agency is not or will not provide the desired service.

(5) Because the IDEA 2004 strengthened the requirements for transition planning and services, many schools are still in the process of developing the evaluation procedures and programs necessary to meet their new responsibilities. As with other aspects of special education, the quality and availability of appropriate transition assessment, planning, and services will likely vary widely from school to school and state to state. This is compounded further because of the wide range in quality of services for adults with disabilities from state to state. Parents and advocates should research the school's evaluation procedures and programs, as well as the evaluations and programs that are available from other state agencies and private providers in the area.

It may be necessary to "think outside the box" to address some of the student's transition needs, particularly where the school or community does not have an appropriate program already in place. Some schools offer transition programs that are based within the public high school. In some instances, schools are developing off campus sites that are designed to replicate the home or work environment in order to create more realistic environments for students to learn needed skills. In many instances, schools have cooperative arrangements with vocational programs operated by state or private agencies, community colleges, or local employers to allow for transition services to be delivered in more relevant environments. Community based vocational instruction is an important component of transition plans for students with needs in these areas.

(6) Many students and families strongly desire to participate in the school graduation ceremony at the end of the senior year, even if the student is not graduating. Some states have adopted legislation allowing students with disabilities to participate in the graduation

exercise even if they are not receiving a diploma at that time. Even where state law does not provide for this circumstance, it may be possible to arrange for attendance with the specific school district.

(7) However, graduation with a regular education diploma results in termination of the student's eligibility for special education services. This is a decision that is supposed to be made by the IEP team prior to graduation. It should be based not only on a determination of whether the student has sufficient credits to graduate but also whether the student has met his or her goals and objectives and whether he or she has additional transition needs that have not been met even if he or she has met his or her goals and objectives. If the school recommends graduation, but the student or the parents (if they are the guardian or have been authorized to act on the student's behalf) does not feel that the student is ready to graduate and requires additional special education services beyond the student's senior year, they may request a due process hearing to challenge this decision. If the hearing request is timely filed after the recommendation for graduation and before the student actually receives his or her diploma, the student should, according to the stay put placement rule described in the due process section (Chapter 10), be allowed to continue to receive services while the due process procedure is pending.

10

Procedural Safeguards, Mediation, and Due Process

Children with disabilities and their parents have a wide array of protections under the Individuals with Disabilities Education Act (IDEA) and Section 504 that are not available within the regular education system. Under the IDEA, these include the right to be involved in the key meetings to determine eligibility and to develop and revise the child's individualized education program (IEP); the right to revoke consent to special education; the right to consent to individual testing concerning the child and to consent to a child's being determined eligible for special education; the right to have notice of proposed meetings concerning the child, including information about the agenda, the participants, and the time and place of the meeting; the right to be informed of any proposal to change or terminate the child's programming or eligibility; and the right to challenge the school district's decisions by means of mediation or through a due process hearing. In addition to these procedures, both the IDEA and Section 504 give parents the right to file complaints against their school district alleging violation of these laws with the state Department of Education regarding special education violations and with the Office for Civil Rights regarding Section 504 violations. This chapter will provide an overview of some of the key procedural rights of parents under these laws.

It is very important that parents be aware of their procedural rights. It is equally important that parents be aware of the ability to seek mediation, to request a due process hearing, or to file an administrative complaint for violations of these laws because the right to file complaints is the ultimate recourse available to parents if they·are unable to otherwise resolve their disputes with the public schools. At the same time, these procedural safeguards are very technical and are often implemented by school districts with less than full adherence to the law's strict requirements. Moreover, when parents raise concerns with respect to the school's failure to follow all of the technical requirements of the law, it is not uncommon for school officials to become defensive and even less willing to work out solutions that are consistent with the legal requirements of the law and with the child's needs. Similarly, while parents have the ability to file administrative complaints with the state Department of Education or the Office for Civil Rights and request due process hearings, the resulting proceedings are often complicated and time consuming and often are weighted in favor of schools.

Many parents find it intimidating to become involved in an adversarial process with schools, particularly given that schools have greater access to legal counsel, to professional experts, and to more information about the child's functioning at school, and the requirements of these laws. As such, the more the parents know about how these procedural safeguards work, the more effective they will be in advocating for their children. At the same time, parents must exercise judgment as to which battles are worth fighting and seek consultation from knowledgeable professionals when they are hitting brick walls with the school district, in order to assess accurately the basis for their complaints and have the greatest assistance possible in counteracting any educational or legal arguments the school district may make. Parents may also benefit from such consultation in helping them to determine whether the particular complaint is worth fighting over, whether there are grounds for compromise, or whether it makes sense to pursue the complaint at all. As a general matter, adversarial proceedings between parents and schools tend to be a lose-lose situation for the child, regardless of who prevails and the outcome of the complaint or hearing process.

This is not to say that parents should never avail themselves of the complaint and due process procedures. There are a variety of circumstances where parents have attempted to resolve matters with a school and have not been successful, but the consequences for the child are sufficiently serious that filing a complaint or a due process request may be the only available option. Again, consultation with knowledgeable special education advocates or attorneys is advisable under these circumstances. At times, when a parent files an administrative complaint or due process request, the school district may be motivated to avoid the conflict. This may lead the school district to negotiate or concede what the parents are seeking, where it would have otherwise been unwilling to do so. Thus, while administrative complaints and due process hearings are generally to be avoided, there may be circumstances where taking aggressive action can result in a solution without having to take the complaint or the due process procedure to its conclusion. Whenever possible, parents are encouraged to negotiate solutions with the school district, whether informally or formally, to avoid the necessity of a formal legal process.

Procedural safeguards

The IDEA provides parents with a wide range of safeguards that give them the ability to participate more fully and with greater knowledge than parents of children in regular education. As is true of all children in public education, parents of children with disabilities have a right to have access to their child's educational records. However, in addition to their general right to access such records, parents of children with disabilities have a specific right to receive access to and a copy of their child's evaluations and IEP, as well as to receive periodic written updates on their child's progress regarding the IEP.[1] The IDEA provides parents with an opportunity to receive advance written notice of all meetings for the purpose of considering the child's need for evaluation, eligibility, and placement, including the agenda for such meetings, the time and place of such meetings, and the participants in those meetings.[2] Parents may seek to have the meetings changed to a time that is mutually convenient for the parents and the school.[3] They may also participate in those meetings by phone, if they are unable to participate in person.[4] Parents must be provided with detailed explanations of all actions the school district proposes to take or refuses to take regarding the child.[5] This includes decisions relating to testing or refusing to test, developing or modifying the child's IEP, changing the child's placement, and determining that the child no longer requires special education services.[6] Parents also have the right to have all procedural safeguards provided to them in writing at least annually, as well as when there is a referral or request for an evaluation, when a complaint or due process request is filed, or when the child's placement is being changed for disciplinary reasons.[7] In addition, parents have the right to be accompanied to meetings by any person who they believe has special knowledge or expertise concerning the child, including a special education advocate or lawyer.[8]

As previously indicated, parents also have the right to share any information they consider relevant about the child with the school and to have the school consider that information as part of the planning process.[9] Further, they have the right to request that the child be reevaluated if they believe such reevaluation is necessary.[10] If they request an evaluation or reevaluation, the school must either agree to conduct the evaluation or provide the parents with a written explanation of its decision to refuse the evaluation, the reasons for the refusal of the evaluation, and notice of the parents' right to request a due process hearing to challenge that refusal.[11]

In addition, as discussed in Chapter 3, "The Evaluation and Reevaluation Process," the parents have the right to have independent evaluations at their own expense, which they may share with the school district and which must be considered by the school district as part of the assessment and planning regarding the child.[12] If the parents disagree with an evaluation conducted by the school district, they have the right to request an independent evaluation at the school district's expense.[13]

Parents have an absolute right to refuse consent to special education when a child is first determined by the school to be eligible for special education.[14] If the parents make this choice, the IDEA provides that the school is not responsible for the child's lack of progress as a consequence of the parents' decision to decline special education services.[15] Parents also have the right to refuse the school district's request for evaluation or reevaluation, although the school may seek a due process hearing or an order overruling the parents' refusal of consent for evaluation if the school believes strongly that the child does require evaluation.[16] Recently, the U.S. Department of Education changed the IDEA regulations to allow parents to withdraw consent for special education even after their child is receiving special education. Under the new rule, the school system is required to honor the parents' request and remove all special education services. However, the school is immune from liability for failing to provide special education services if the parent makes this choice. See the OSEP website at www.ed.gov/about/offices/list/osers/osep/index.html for information on the new regulation. If the parent revokes consent for special education, both the parent and the school retain the right to request evaluation for special education eligibility at a later date. Parent revocation of consent for eligibility for special education does not change the child's potential eligibility for Section 504 protections and services.

Generally, one of the most important procedural protections for the parent is the right to participate in the IEP meeting. Although the right to participate does not give the parent the ability to exercise an absolute veto over the school's proposals and schools are not required to do whatever the parents wish, schools are required to allow parents to have a full and meaningful opportunity to participate in the IEP process.[17] In order for parents to be able to do so, the law requires that they have access to the student's records, to be provided a copy of the child's IEP, and to receive periodic reports on the child's progress on their goals.[18]

When parents disagree with the outcome of the IEP meeting, they have several options. First, they can attempt to resolve informally whatever disputes they have with the school district, either through the staff immediately involved with the child, the case manager, the special education director or principal, or higher level administrators. If these efforts are unsuccessful, the parents have the right to file an administrative complaint with the state Department of Education, to request that the state appoint a mediator to help resolve the dispute, and/or to request a special education due process hearing. Under the new regulation just adopted, parents also may revoke consent for special education services if they are unable to otherwise resolve matters with the school district.

As previously discussed, if the school district is proposing to change the child's placement and the parent immediately requests a due process hearing, the IDEA provides that the child must remain in the last agreed upon placement until the hearing process has been concluded.[19] These hearings can sometimes take months or longer, during which time the school remains obligated to educate the child in the setting and with the program previously agreed upon. As discussed in Chapter 8, "Behavior Management and Discipline," the only exception to this rule is in situations where the child's placement is changed unilaterally by the school district by virtue of a decision that the student will be suspended, expelled, or placed in an interim alternative educational setting.[20] The requirement that the school maintain the child's placement while due process proceedings are pending is sometimes called the "frozen placement" or the "stay put placement" provision.[21]

Mediation

When parents and schools are in a dispute concerning the child's special education program, either the parent or the school district may suggest participation in mediation for the purpose of seeking a voluntary resolution of the dispute.[22] Mediation is a voluntary and mutual process; both the parents and the school must agree to it in order for it to proceed. If the parties agree, an impartial outside mediator (typically hired by the state Department of Education) will be appointed for the purpose of meeting with the parties in an effort to identify the issues in dispute and determine whether there is a mutually acceptable means of resolving matters.[23]

The mediation process is confidential: any information shared by either party during the course of the mediation discussions may not be subsequently used as evidence in a due process hearing or in court.[24] The underlying purpose of this confidentiality rule is to make it easier for the parties to speak openly and to resolve disputes based on frank discussions, without the concern that anything said might be used against them later on.

Generally, participation in a mediation session is limited to parents, their advocate or attorney, one or two school representatives with the authority to make decisions on behalf of the school district, and any legal representative that the school officials might bring. Although the specific rules of mediation vary from state to state, both parties have the right to bring attorneys if they wish to do so; in most states, they may bring a special education advocate if they choose. In most states, the school district may have representation by an attorney, even if the parents do not have legal representation. The New IDEA regulations issued December 1, 2008, leave it to each state to determine whether non-lawyers may represent either party in a due process hearing.[25]

Unlike a due process hearing, in which formal decisions are rendered by the hearing officers, in mediation, the mediators have no power or authority to make a decision of their own—nor is that their purpose. Rather, the mediators are there to serve as facilitators between the parties for the purpose of identifying common ground and helping to develop solutions that may address the concerns of both parties. If mediation is unsuccessful, the parties retain the right to go forward with administrative complaints or with a special education due process hearing. If mediation is successful, the mediation agreement should be written down and signed by both parties.

Once the mediation agreement has been agreed to in writing by the parties, it is enforceable in state or federal court.[26]

The mediation process is intended to be informal. It is not designed for the purpose of establishing that one party is right and the other is wrong, nor is it set up for the purpose of presenting evidence or laying out in detail both parties' arguments or factual support. Instead, it is intended as a forum for sharing general concerns and each side's ideas to help the dispute to be resolved. Typically, the mediator opens the mediation session with a brief explanation of the rules of the mediation process, as well as with some explanation of the mediator's philosophy or plan for conducting the meeting. In many instances, the mediator has not been provided with any information concerning the dispute prior to the mediation session. Generally, mediators come to the mediation with a "clean slate." Typically, the mediator has the party who is requesting the hearing or their representative provide a brief statement outlining the nature of their concerns or complaints and describing the solution or solutions that they are seeking to resolve the dispute. The other side is then generally given an opportunity to ask questions or seek clarification about statements made by the opening party. After this occurs, the second party is given an opportunity to provide a brief response, which is also subject to questions or comments from the party who made the initial statement. Typically, mediators strongly discourage either party from interrupting the other party or from getting into arguments with the other party, particularly at the outset of these discussions.

If the parties are having a sufficiently productive discussion during this initial phase, the mediator may allow the discussion to continue and serve as a facilitator or referee of the discussion to zero in on points of agreement or areas where compromise or resolution can be achieved. At times, these open discussions can result in a full resolution of the issues in dispute. If this occurs, it then becomes necessary to put the verbal agreement into written form and obtain the signatures of the parties.

At other times, after the initial presentations and discussions, it may be necessary for one or both parties to have a private caucus for the purpose of considering the information provided by the other side before responding further. At times, the parties may be physically separated. When this occurs, mediators may sit in with the parties, if the parties wish for them to do so, or may simply act as go betweens as the parties either seek information or offer new ideas or proposals. Mediators are supposed to share information from one party with the other party only with the initial party's permission. This is to encourage the ability of the parties to talk openly with the mediator without fear that information that they discuss will be shared without their permission.

Mediators vary in their personality and approach to the process. Some mediators take a very neutral and passive position, acting solely as a conduit for what the parties wish to have communicated to the other side. Other mediators take a more aggressive role and stress to one or both parties the risks of failing to achieve a compromise solution. For example, a mediator may highlight to either party the cost of going forward with a due process hearing, the consequences of losing a due process hearing, and the potential expense involved if it is necessary to go through with a hearing. Some mediators may even provide a party with his or her own assessment of the viability of particular arguments that the party is making or the reasonableness of the offers for settlement that the parties are proposing. This feedback may be helpful to the parties as a reality check regarding their position but is not binding.

If it becomes clear that the parties are unable to reach an agreement, either party may opt to end the mediation at any time. Alternatively, if the mediator believes the parties are at an impasse, the mediator may choose to terminate the mediation even if the parties have not requested to do so. When the parties reach an impasse, they then have the option of proceeding to a due process hearing or the party requesting the hearing may choose to withdraw the request. This sometimes occurs because the party requesting the hearing concludes that they are not likely to be successful at the hearing, that the cost of a hearing outweighs the benefits, or simply that they do not wish to pursue the conflict for financial or other reasons.

During the course of mediation, the parties may change what they are willing to offer, either by adding demands, withdrawing demands, or coming up with alternative solutions. Generally though, the expectation is that the parties will try to move toward a middle ground. Thus, it is usually unproductive to add demands during the course of the mediation. In some instances, a solution may be offered that does not resolve the ultimate dispute but does create a process by which the ultimate dispute may be more easily resolved. For example, it is common for mediation to result in an agreement for the school district to conduct additional evaluations of the student and/ or to agree to pay for an independent evaluation of the student in areas of concern. When this occurs, the mediation agreement may not produce an ultimate resolution for the parties, but it may lead to additional information that allows the parties to reach an agreement once that information is obtained.

In addition, because the mediation agreement is generally not intended to take the place of an IEP, it sometimes provides for the reconvening of an IEP conference for the purpose of considering and/or developing changes in the IEP that are intended to address concerns raised by the parties at the mediation. If the mediation is taking place after a due process hearing has been requested, it is generally advisable that the parents make the agreement contingent not just on the completion of the independent evaluation or IEP but also on an assurance that the outcome of the evaluation or IEP meeting satisfactorily resolves the dispute. In other words, if the mediation agreement does not resolve the dispute that the parent has with the school but only calls for steps to be implemented that may resolve the dispute at a later date, the parents may want to preserve their right to go forward with the hearing if the evaluation or reconvened IEP meeting does not lead to a satisfactory resolution of the dispute. However, the school may be less willing to enter an agreement under these circumstances.

Under the IDEA, parents and schools may request mediation at any time without having requested a due process hearing. If either party has requested a due process hearing, the parties may still engage in mediation, though the IDEA technically requires that the mediation (or resolution session) be completed within 30 days of the receipt of the hearing request.[27] However, it is often the case that the parties agree to extend this 30 day period to allow for more time in which to conduct the mediation process or resolution meeting. Once a written agreement is agreed upon and signed by the parties, it is enforceable in court.[28]

$E=MC^2$ Mediation Strategies

(1) All parties should approach mediation with a positive attitude and with a sincere commitment to try to resolve the dispute. If the parties are unable to resolve disputes through informal or formal negotiation, the consequences of adversarial proceedings will undoubtedly result in substantial cost to all concerned and, most importantly, to the child. While there may be winners and losers on paper, when a due process

hearing or court battle occurs, it is almost assured that everyone will pay a high price, whether emotionally, financially, in shattered trust, and in delaying resolution and provision of what the child needs.

(2) Before participating in mediation, parents should learn as much as possible about the options available within their school or in their general community that may allow for a creative solution of the dispute.

(3) Parents should come to the mediation session with a wish list that has the best case scenario for what they hope to obtain from the school system. At the same time, parents should have a "bottom line" list (which is not shared with the school, unless necessary as the negotiation progresses) that prioritizes the elements of their wish list they feel are most important and/or are most attainable, so they are more able to assess whether proposed compromises are satisfactory. Sometimes, minor items are easily attainable but are not sufficient to address the major concerns that the parents have leading to the dispute. Alternatively, parents may be able to obtain the key solutions that they seek, even though they are not able to get all that they wanted. They should be prepared to sacrifice some elements of their wish list if doing so will result in winning the key changes necessary for their child's needs to be addressed appropriately. It is important that the "best case" wish list be reasonable. If the parents start out demanding placement at Harvard and a luxury Cadillac, it may doom the negotiation when it has hardly gotten under way.

(4) Parents should view mediation as a process where general concerns and specific solutions are outlined—not as a forum in which to present their due process case or to provide a history of grievances dating back to the beginning of creation. While parents have many legitimate grounds for anger, frustration, or outrage regarding what their child has experienced or how they themselves have been treated by the school, it is important to focus as much as possible on constructive solutions at the mediation session. This does not mean that parents cannot share the grounds for their discontent, but it is generally unproductive to have the mediation process become a "blame game" or a forum for each side to exchange accusations or insults about the other. In particular,

it is generally better to avoid attacks on the competence, honesty, or motivation of individuals involved in the process. The mediator should intercede if these comments come up from either side. In any event, mediation is more likely to be successful when the focus is on how to solve the problem, rather than on who is at greater fault.

(5) At the same time, some of these emotional issues may need to be brought to the surface to convey the level of difficulty that the parties are experiencing with each other and to try to develop mechanisms by which appropriate communication, collaboration, and planning can be conducted in the future. If the parties achieve a positive solution on paper but do not address underlying issues of trust, communication, or cooperation, the agreement may be doomed before it is implemented because of the lingering bad feelings between the parents and the staff.

(6) It is critical that the mediation agreement be written in such a fashion that everyone has a clear understanding as to what has been accomplished, what will be implemented, and what was and was not agreed to. At the same time, it may be dangerous to demand an agreement with such specificity that every remote detail becomes a point of negotiation, ultimately sabotaging the process. Thus, the parties must attempt to strike a balance between providing sufficient specificity so that there is a clear meeting of the minds, while avoiding being bogged down in such detail that reaching an agreement becomes impossible.

(7) It is often important to build into the mediation agreement procedures for reviewing the program on some periodic basis after the agreement is implemented, in order to assure that the agreement is being properly implemented and is working. It is also useful to build into the agreement communication or feedback loops to the parents that verify that their concerns are being addressed and in a timely way.

(8) Under some circumstances, the child may need programming or services that are not available through the public school, either due to insufficient staff or because the staff lacks the necessary training. When this is the case, it may be important for the mediation agreement

to include procedures for providing sufficient staff, sufficient training, or some mechanism for ongoing outside professional training, development, and consultation to ensure that the substance of the agreement can and will be appropriately implemented.

(9) As a result of the United States Supreme Court decision in *Buckhannon Bd. and Care Home, Inc. v. West Virginia Dept. of Health and Human Resources*, 532 U.S. 598 (2001), schools generally take the position that attorneys' fees are not recoverable by parents as a result of mediation agreements. The *Buckhannon* decision technically provided that attorneys' fees are legally recoverable only if the parents achieve a significant change in position with the school district as a result of the mediation agreement or settlement and that the agreement or settlement is formally adopted and enforceable through the order of an administrative hearing officer or judge. As a consequence, many school districts refuse to consider attorneys' fees as part of the negotiation or may require parents to waive their right to attorneys' fees as part of an agreement. Proposals are being developed to amend the IDEA to reverse this decision. In particularly egregious cases, parents may be able to obtain attorneys' fees, not withstanding the Supreme Court decision, if the school is highly motivated to resolve the case without a legal proceeding. The Congress will be considering legislation in 2009 which may override the *Buckhannon* decision, as well as the *Arlington* Supreme Court decision, precluding the recovery of expert witness fees for parents that prevail in due process hearings. Readers should check on the status of this proposed legislation if they are involved in mediation or a due process hearing.

(10) Parents are advised to consult with knowledgeable legal counsel about the legal propriety of such waiver provisions and whether the requirement of waiver of attorneys' fees is acceptable or constitutes a sufficient problem that they do not wish to enter into the mediation agreement. In any event, this decision should be made with consultation with a knowledgeable special education attorney.

(11) Parents should also exercise caution with respect to any mediation or settlement agreement that calls for them to waive their due process rights, including their right to stay put placement, particularly when

those waivers regard past or future claims. It is not uncommon for schools to ask parents to waive all claims that they have with respect to any allegations of past wrongdoing. This is a typical part of any settlement process. Parents should be aware that if they sign such a waiver, it precludes them from bringing up such claims against the school district in the future. Even if parents agree to such a waiver, they should be sure the agreement preserves their right to pursue legal recourse if the school fails to implement the mediation or settlement agreement or engages in new violations of the child's special education rights. Again, consultation with knowledgeable legal counsel is advisable in these situations.

(12) Remember that, even if formal mediation is unsuccessful, the parties have the opportunity to negotiate settlements at any time, up to and including immediately prior to or during a due process or court proceeding. However, also remember that agreements are not enforceable unless they are written down and approved by both parties.

Resolution meetings

In 2004, the Congress added a new alternative for resolving disputes prior to due process hearings. This new procedure is called a *resolution session*. The participants in the resolution session include the parents and relevant school members of the IEP team with knowledge of the facts alleged in the due process complaint and must include a school representative who has decision making authority. The parents and the school are supposed to determine together the relevant members of the IEP team who will attend the meeting.[29] The purpose of the meeting is to address the concerns raised by the request for a due process hearing, with the intention of trying to resolve the dispute prior to a hearing. In contrast to a mediation meeting, the resolution session does not provide for the involvement of a neutral third party mediator. Rather, the resolution session is somewhat like an IEP meeting but with less certainty as to whether the rules of the IEP process fully apply. The state's special education regulations should be reviewed to ascertain whether there are state specific rules regarding the resolution process. Unlike in a mediation meeting, in a resolution session, the school may be represented by an attorney *if and only if* the parents are represented by an attorney. If the parents do not bring an attorney to the meeting, the school may not bring an attorney on its behalf.[30] If the parent refuses mediation, the school is required to convene a resolution session within 15 days of receiving the request for a due process hearing.[31] The parties may also mutually agree to convene a resolution session, either in lieu of a mediation session or as a step prior to a mediation session. In addition, the parties may mutually agree to waive both mediation and a resolution session.[32] In the event that a resolution session is scheduled, the resolution session must be completed within 30 days after the school district receives the request for a due process hearing.[33] If the resolution session leads to an agreement, it must be memorialized in an IEP. However, even if an agreement is reached between the parties at a resolution session, either may rescind their agreement within three days after the resolution session is over.[34]

As previously indicated, discussions that occurred during mediation sessions are confidential and may not be introduced in a due process hearing or a court proceeding. By contrast, there is some controversy as to whether the discussions that occur during a resolution session are confidential. To date, there has not been a clear determination from the courts as to whether the discussions and written reporting of resolution sessions are confidential. The rationale for adding a resolution session was to ensure that school districts had some opportunity to try to resolve disputes with parents even when the parents were unwilling to participate in voluntary mediation. This was designed to increase the chances that disputes could be resolved without having to go through with formal, time consuming, and expensive due process hearings. Unfortunately, because the statute gives the school district the option of declining voluntary mediation but requires a resolution session, it gives the school district some advantage in terms of conducting a quasi-mediation process with the parent without the benefit of a truly neutral facilitator such as a mediator. Under the 2004 IDEA, if the parent refuses to participate in a resolution session, the hearing request from the parent may be dismissed.[35]

E=MC² Resolution Strategies

(1) Resolution sessions may be useful in assisting parents and schools in resolving minor disputes concerning a child's program. Questions

about the details of goals and objectives, requests for minor changes in accommodations, or modest requests for alteration in the provision or intensity of related services may be effectively addressed during resolution meetings.

(2) By contrast, it is less likely that a resolutions session will be effective in addressing major disputes between parents and schools. Because the resolution meeting does not involve a neutral party, it raises questions as to whether the school district is really interested in negotiating claims that it may see as creating substantial demands upon it, whether operationally, financially, or otherwise.

(3) Parents should seek knowledgeable consultation from qualified special education advocates or attorneys with respect to whether it is advisable to seek mediation rather than a resolution session, if the district is open to either. If the district is insistent on going forward with a resolution session, the parent should also seek consultation as to whether it is desirable to have a knowledgeable advocate or attorney present with them at the resolution meeting.

(4) In any event, if parents participate in a resolution meeting, particularly without representation, they should seek consultation from advocates, attorneys, and others knowledgeable in the special education field immediately after the conclusion of the resolution session, in order to determine whether they wish to accept what was proposed at the resolution session or exercise their right to withdraw their agreement to the resolution decision within the three days allowed by the IDEA.

(5) In my experience, the resolution session sometimes simply assists the school district in gathering more information about the nature of the parents' complaints and/or for the purpose of developing a more defensible position regarding a pending due process hearing. Despite this, because the law requires parents to cooperate with the resolution process, it is necessary for parents to go forward with the process if the school district is unwilling to participate in mediation and insists on a resolution session instead.

Impartial due process hearing

If parents are unable to resolve their dispute with the school district through the IEP process, informal discussions, formal mediation, or a resolution session, they have the option of proceeding with an impartial due process hearing. The IDEA provides for an impartial due process hearing to be initiated by either the parent or the school to resolve disputes.[36] The IDEA provides that the individual conducting the due process hearing must be impartial, which means they cannot be employed by or related to the school district or have a conflict of interest in relation to the dispute.[37] An impartial due process hearing was originally intended to be a somewhat informal process designed to give a neutral third party the opportunity to hear evidence from the parents and school district concerning the dispute about the child in order to allow that person to make a formal decision to resolve the dispute. Since the inception of the special education law, the rules governing due process hearings have become more complex, and the proceedings have become increasingly more formal and trial like.

The special education law provides that the due process hearing must be conducted within a specific time period. IDEA 2004 now allows the party against whom the due process hearing was requested to seek dismissal of the hearing request based on the insufficiency of the request.[38] At the same time, where a hearing is requested, the opposing party must file a written response to the issues raised by the hearing request.[39]

It allows parties to submit written evidence and oral testimony and gives parties the opportunity to cross examine opposing witnesses. It also requires that parties share any written evidence and evaluation and resulting recommendations they intend to rely upon and that such evidence be shared at least five business days prior to the due process hearing.[40] In addition, the law provides that the parties may be represented by third parties, although there remains controversy as to whether parents may be represented by non-lawyer advocates. Many states recognize the right of parents to have the assistance of non-lawyer advocates in a due process hearing, but this right is not universally recognized.[41] In addition, the law requires that a written or electronic transcript of the due process hearing be completed and be available to the parents at no cost.[42] Further, the law requires that, at the conclusion of the due process hearing, the parties are entitled to a written decision from the hearing officer providing findings of fact and conclusions of law.[43] Parents may also determine whether they want the due process hearing to be open or closed to the public.[44] When a due process hearing is pending, or at any other time, schools are obligated to provide parents with a list of low-cost or no-cost legal service providers who can assist them with respect to any pending hearing.[45] It should be noted that some of the details with respect to how hearing officers are selected or appointed and how due process hearings are conducted vary from state to state. Therefore, it is essential that parents who are considering requesting a due process hearing be familiar with the rules governing special education due process hearings in their state.

Once the hearing officer issues a written decision, either party has the right to appeal the decision in state or federal court.[46] Unless the state law contains a specific statute of limitations governing these procedures, the IDEA requires that the decision be appealed within 90 days.[47]

The states vary as to the form of the request for a due process hearing and to whom the request for such a hearing should be addressed. Once the hearing officer is appointed, he or she typically contacts the parties for the purpose of determining the issues in the hearing and the dates when it will be convened. Generally, unless the parties agree otherwise, the hearing must be concluded within 45 days after the 30 day period in which the parties may either engage in mediation or hold a resolution session. However, in many states, a due process hearing is often not held within 75 days of the receipt of the request for that hearing because it is often difficult to schedule the due process hearing dates within the prescribed limitation periods, when the schedules of the hearing officer, the attorneys, the parties, and witnesses are all taken into account. Once the written decision is issued, if either party elects to appeal the decision, the transcript of the proceeding and the written evidence submitted as part of the proceeding must be filed with the court. The rules for how this is accomplished vary from state to state and court to court.

While initiating a due process hearing is sometimes a necessary evil, these hearings are emotionally and financially costly, time consuming, and difficult to win. Parents should seek consultation with knowledgeable special education advocates and/or attorneys if they are considering requesting a special education due process hearing. Parents are more likely to be successful if they are represented by knowledgeable special education attorneys.

As the decision to initiate a due process hearing carries with it great consequences—and outcomes that vary widely, depending on the individual case, the child's needs, the school district's position, and even the parents' resources—it is not possible to provide a simple formula for when it is advisable for parents to pursue a due process hearing. Similarly, the strategies for preparing for and litigating these hearings are sufficiently complex to warrant a book in and of themselves.

$E=MC^2$ Advocacy Strategies: Some Due Process Basics

(1) While due process hearings give parents a unique opportunity to seek an independent review of actions (or inaction) by the school that they disagree with, it is a difficult, time consuming and costly process. Generally, schools have greater access to information, expertise, and legal resources. The quality, training, and objectivity of hearing officers vary by person and by state, as do the procedures used to conduct the hearings. While due process hearings are sometimes the only means by which a dispute can be resolved and, in some instances, can lead to a clear and positive outcome for the child, they often are bruising and emotionally and financially costly for the parents and the school district. Each side risks losing the decision because so much is at stake for both parties. At times, the decision doesn't even fully resolve the issues at hand, leaving questions unanswered or subject to conflicting interpretation. If all other efforts to resolve a dispute have failed or if there is an issue of sufficient urgency and magnitude that due process is necessary to address the situation, then a due process hearing may be necessary. However, given the many costs and shortcomings of the due process procedure, parents and schools are well advised to resolve their disputes through informal or formal means, including use of state sponsored mediation or resolution sessions, wherever possible.

At the same time, be aware that the IDEA provides for a statute of limitations that requires that any complaints be brought within a specified time from when the parent knew or should have known of the violation or issue that is the basis for the request for a hearing. The IDEA provides for a two year statute of limitations, unless the state's law provides a different limitations period. Many states have shorter statute of limitations periods, so it is very important to check state law as to the time period within which you are permitted to bring a complaint after learning of the problem. For example, if you learn that the school did not provide any social work services to your child during fifth grade, even though the IEP provided for weekly social work service, the statute of limitations would require you to file a request for hearing complaining about the failure to provide those services within two years—or the time provided in state law—from when you learned or should have known that they had not been provided.

(2) There are many things about the special education process that are complicated. The law itself is lengthy and detailed and has many aspects that are confusing or subject to interpretation. In fact, court interpretations of the law are also used in due process hearings to help to give meaning to what the law says. The process of evaluating children with disabilities and accurately identifying their disabilities, level of functioning, and educational needs is also complex and requires special expertise. There are a wide array of programs, strategies, related services, interventions, and technology that may be appropriate for a particular child, as well as research demonstrating the effectiveness or ineffectiveness of these interventions. Finally, due process hearings are legal proceedings involving the need to prove "the case" based on providing evidence and relevant law to demonstrate that the parents' position is correct. Given all these factors, it is highly advisable for parents to obtain knowledgeable consultation and, if possible, representation from an experienced special education attorney or, if one is unavailable, from others who are knowledgeable about special education, such as from the federally funded Parent Training and Information Centers. If a parent cannot obtain a knowledgeable special education attorney, in most states they may seek the help of other persons, such as special education advocates, who may have special knowledge or training with respect to the special education system.

(3) Pick your battles and your relief. As described above, due process is generally a last resort. It is important to use it where necessary but avoid it where possible. Though not always possible, it is desirable to develop and maintain positive and collaborative working relationships with the school staff. Even where this is unsuccessful, it is still wise to avoid legal conflicts with the school if the problem can be resolved through other means. It is also very important to have a clear idea of

your priorities for your child and to pursue conflicts only when the issue is of sufficient magnitude that you feel the conflict is necessary. There are many actions by the staff or the school that seem unprofessional, unfair, contrary to your child's interests, or to violate the regulations. Though these are wrong, they are not always of sufficient seriousness to warrant getting into a battle with the school.

In addition, if there is a major conflict, it is important to consider what is needed to solve the problem. If a realistic solution is available, that may make pursuing the conflict more appropriate. If a realistic solution cannot be identified or seems impractical, the conflict may not make sense. It doesn't make sense to win the battle and lose the war, by proving that a wrong was committed but not obtaining a good solution. At the same time, schools also go through a cost-benefit analysis in deciding whether to fight a due process hearing. At times, parents may get substantial services or other changes they seek by filing a hearing request, without having to go through with the hearing itself, because the school perceives its position to be weak, or the cost of the process to be greater than the cost of the settlement.

(4) Prepare a careful due process letter. Check your state's special education regulations for the procedures for filing a due process request and for finding out to whom the request must be sent. Generally, the request must identify the child's name, address, school, identification number if any, the issues that you are complaining about, available facts supporting your allegations, and the relief or solution you are seeking. It is advisable to include language indicating that the allegations, facts, and relief are based on information available to the parent at the time and that you wish to reserve the right to add information or amend the request at a later date if needed. Be aware that the decision to allow you to amend the request is up to the hearing officer. If you are allowed to amend the letter, it may also give the school another opportunity to seek to have the request dismissed as insufficient and/or may restart the clock for when the mediation/resolution and hearing process must be completed based on the date of the new letter. You can be barred from raising issues at the hearing if they were not raised in your due process request. Determine to whom your state requires that requests for hearing be sent. Your state may require that the letter be directed

to the school superintendent, the state superintendent, or some other official. Make sure that the request is sent by certified mail, return receipt requested, or delivered in person and a receipt obtained. Keep a copy of the request. If you are interested in mediation, that can be included in the letter requesting the hearing.

(5) Some states allow for a party to request a change in hearing officers. Check your state's procedures to determine if this is an option and the time frame in which you are allowed to do so. If it is an option, make sure you accept or reject the appointed impartial hearing officer (IHO) within the prescribed time frame, based on learning what you can from advocacy groups and others with experience as to whether a change in hearing officer would be desirable.

(6) Determine which party has the burden of proof. Unless your state law provides otherwise, the party requesting the hearing has the burden of proof, which means the level of information that you need to prove in order to demonstrate your case. If the party with the burden of proof fails to meet its burden, that party will lose. However, even if you initially meet your burden of proof, the opposing party may introduce evidence that contradicts your position and causes the hearing officer to conclude that the evidence in total does not support your position.

(7) Identify the evidence, including written documentation and oral testimony, needed to prove your case. If you need testimony from an individual that is not willing to testify voluntarily, you must seek subpoenas to be issued by the hearing officer where needed. Determine, based on state regulation and/or the IHO's prehearing orders, how information is to be submitted. Verify in advance of the hearing what school witnesses will be testifying. If you need testimony from a school witness, make sure there is agreement that he or she will testify or, if necessary, the witness will need to be subpoenaed to testify. Make sure that all written evidence is organized logically, whether by chronology or subject matter or both. All documents must be numbered and copies must be submitted to the other side (and generally the IHO) five business days in advance of the hearing. You will need to prepare at least four copies of the records being submitted, for the IHO, for the school, for witnesses to use, and for you to use. Make sure that

the numbering is sequential and well marked and that all of the sets of records you are introducing are the same.

(8) Seek complete school records (a) before requesting the hearing and (b) before submitting your written evidence. Requests for school records should generally include requests for the student's permanent and temporary records; grade reports; evaluations; written correspondence; disciplinary and behavioral records; standardized testing; internal communications concerning the student, including email, communication between the school and the parent, teachers' reports, and other materials; all IEPs and other formal records or reports; and any other written records concerning the child. There are some limited exceptions to what must be provided. Consult the federal and state school records acts (and/or a knowledgeable attorney or others with special knowledge in this area) if there is a dispute over whether a particular record must be provided. Include your requests for records in the information submitted to the hearing officer. Each side has the right to bar evidence from being considered that was not disclosed by the other side at least five business days prior to the start of the hearing.

(9) If you have outside professionals involved, determine what testimony they can provide. If you do not have outside professionals, such as evaluators or therapists, already involved or they are not appropriate as witnesses, determine if an outside evaluation or evaluations are needed as part of the testimony. Obtain an independent education evaluation (IEE) on your own or seek an IHO order allowing you to obtain an IEE. You may always obtain outside evaluations at your own expense, but it is up to the IHO to decide if an evaluation will be ordered at school expense. Any professional evaluations or recommendations based on those evaluations that you intend to use at the hearing must be disclosed to the school and the IHO at least five business days before the hearing.

(10) Identify procedural violations and show how they adversely affected the child's ability to receive free appropriate public education or "caused a deprivation of educational benefit" or significantly impeded the parents' ability to have meaningful participation in the IEP/decision

making process. Focus on important procedural violations, but be careful about getting bogged down in the small stuff.

(11) Focus on the child and his or her needs and the evidence that supports what you want for your child.

(12) Evidence needs to be based on data as much as possible. Impressions or assumptions are not as credible if not based on data. For example, it is less persuasive to reject a school proposal if you have no information about the proposal and/or have not observed the program but are relying on the parent grapevine or the program's reputation. Use the school's data and any private data to show the child's progress or lack of progress over time and how the school responded over time. Compare information from year to year, such as the child's grades, test scores, IEP present levels of performance, IEP goals, and behavioral or anecdotal records to show patterns that demonstrate that the child is progressing or failing to progress (depending on the issue in the case). If you are trying to show the child is not benefiting from the school's program, it is also useful to chart the programs, services, and level of service in response to the lack of progress. If the child has not been progressing, the school should have been trying new strategies and/or increasing the intensity of services to address the lack of progress.

(13) Seek information about the research supporting the school's proposed program. Ask for the school's research, and investigate whether there is scientific support for the program yourself.

(14) Anticipate what arguments the school will use to defend its position and/or challenge your position. Make sure that you have evidence to support your position and to rebut the school's position and challenges.

(15) Prepare questions for your witnesses and the school's witnesses in advance. Try to link questions to the written evidence and to make sure you have established the underlying facts or foundation for questions. Don't assume facts that have not yet been introduced or proven.

(16) Don't assume that the hearing officer is an expert in the particular disability, program, or methodology. Provide information necessary for

the IHO to know the nature and extent of the child's needs or why the particular program you seek is necessary, how it works, and how it is supported by research or prior success.

(17) Remember that the free appropriate public education standard does not require the school to provide the best possible education.

(18) Avoid, as much as possible, getting into personal attacks or accusations about individuals' motivations or personality. Try to maintain a calm, courteous, and professional image.

(19) Prepare an opening statement and closing argument, based on the facts and the special education law.

(20) Parents have a right to obtain a written (or electronic) decision from the IHO, as well as to receive a record of the hearing at no cost. Find out how much time the hearing officer has to complete the decision under the state's special education regulations. Find out how much time is allowed after receipt of the hearing officer's decision for either party to appeal to court.

(21) As previously indicated, due process hearings are enormously complicated. The information shared here is only a brief introduction to some of the important steps in preparing for and conducting a hearing. Hearings are often like court trials. Special education law, as well as the court decisions interpreting it, is also complex. The strategies for what to ask for, what proof is needed, and how to conduct a hearing vary with every case. The information above is not intended as, nor could it provide, sufficient information to equip a parent to prepare or conduct a hearing on his or her own. Indeed, even an entire book devoted to this subject would not be able to accomplish that task adequately. The reader is strongly encouraged to consult his or her state's special education regulations for the broader rules relating to special education and the specific rules governing due process hearing procedures.

(22) It is also strongly recommended that parents considering or involved in a due process hearing seek representation from an attorney knowledgeable in special education law. If an appropriate

attorney cannot be obtained and/or assist in any case, parents are encouraged to seek consultation from knowledgeable special education advocates or others with special knowledge about the special education system, the needs of children with disabilities, and the due process system. Every state has a federally funded Parent Training and Information Center that can offer information and guidance on these matters. The Parent Training Center in your area can be found at www.taalliance.org, where there is a search engine for all of the Parent Training Centers in the United States. The National Disability Rights Network (www.ndrn.org) has federally funded disability advocacy organizations in each state. Even if they are unable to provide representation, they may be able to provide useful information and/or referral to other sources of support. The Council of Parent Attorneys and Advocates (www.copaa.net) also has a search engine for attorneys and advocates representing parents throughout the U.S., as do many of the advocacy groups or Web sites listed in the Web resources appendix at the end of the book. Finally, the school district and state Department of Education are required to provide parents with a list of low or no-cost legal resources providing assistance with special education matters, upon request.

CHAPTER 11

A Comparison of the IDEA and Section 504

S ection 504 of the Rehabilitation Act of 1973 is a civil rights law that makes it illegal to discriminate on the basis of disability in any program or activity receiving federal financial assistance. The exact language of Section 504 is very concise:

> No otherwise qualified individual with a disability in the United States . . . shall, solely by reason of her or his disability, be excluded from the participation in, be denied the benefits of, or be subjected to discrimination under any program or activity receiving Federal financial assistance or under any program or activity conducted by any Executive agency or by the United States Postal Service.[1]

Section 504 covers all public schools in the United States, as all public schools are recipients of federal financial assistance. Under some circumstances, Section 504 also covers private schools, but only if the private school is a direct recipient of federal dollars that fund programs or activities conducted by the private school. For example, if the private school receives federal funding to operate a specific training program or educational program, the school would be covered by Section 504. By contrast, if students in the school receive federally funded lunch subsidies but the school itself does not receive federal financial assistance for programming, the school might not be covered by Section 504.

Section 504 applies to any child with an identified physical or mental impairment that substantially limits a major life activity, including learning. It also covers individuals with a history of impairment, such as a child who had cancer, but is in remission, or a child that is regarded as having an impairment, although this is not true, such as a child that is HIV positive, but asymptomatic. The regulations implementing Section 504 provide a more detailed explanation of how schools receiving federal financial assistance must meet the needs of children with disabilities.[2]

As a general matter, because Section 504 does not use categories of disability or specific criteria for eligibility, a broader spectrum of children is eligible for Section 504 protections. In other words, many children with disabilities can be covered under Section 504 even if they do not meet the eligibility criteria for the Individuals with Disabilities Education Act (IDEA).

Under the Section 504 regulations, schools are obligated to identify and evaluate children suspected of having disabilities, as well as to conduct periodic evaluations of the students, including an evaluation at any time that the school proposes to change or terminate the student's Section 504 eligibility or plan.[3] Each school system is required to have a school wide Section 504 plan. The plan must describe the procedures for students to be determined eligible for Section 504 and the procedures for the development and implementation of Section 504 plans. The procedures, furthermore, must describe the protections the student is entitled to receive under Section 504 and must set out the safeguards and due process rights of children and their families if there are disputes concerning the student's eligibility or plan.[4] Under Section 504, students are entitled to receive a free appropriate public education (FAPE), though this entitlement is not defined in the same way as it is under the IDEA. Rather, under Section 504, the right to FAPE is defined as having equal access to the educational opportunities provided to students in regular education.[5]

Section 504 states that students must be served in the least restrictive environment appropriate to their needs and are entitled to receive such instructional services, related services, and accommodations as are necessary for them to have equal access to and benefit from the educational experience provided to other students.[6] Section 504 also requires that evaluations must be conducted in a manner that is nondiscriminatory and is appropriately designed and implemented to obtain accurate information concerning the child's disability and functioning.[7]

When a family is dissatisfied with a school's decisions about either the student's eligibility for Section 504 safeguards, the nature of the services or safeguards provided, or a school's decision to terminate Section 504 services or protections, the family may request a due process hearing against the school.[8] Parents can also file a complaint alleging violations of Section 504 with the Office for Civil Rights of the U.S. Department of Education. In addition, unlike under the IDEA, if a family believes its child has been discriminated against or injured by virtue of a school's violation of Section 504, the family may, under some circumstances, file a lawsuit in federal court, without necessarily going through a due process hearing first. (Under the IDEA, parents are generally required to have "exhausted their administrative remedy," which typically means they must go through a due process hearing before appealing to court. Increasingly, courts have linked Section 504 disputes to potential IDEA issues and required parents suing under Section 504 to go through the IDEA and/or Section 504 hearing process before going forward in court.) In addition, under Section 504, parents may have a right to sue for money damages. Generally, most courts do not recognize a right to sue for money damages under the IDEA, except for reimbursement for unilateral placements or for compensatory services.

In general, the IDEA provides a far more developed bureaucracy with a wide array of programs, services, and staff to address the needs of children with disabilities. By contrast, in most states and school districts, there is no parallel structure or bureaucracy for the delivery of Section 504 services. There are notable exceptions in some states and school systems, where Section 504 is widely used as an umbrella for serving some children with disabilities. Notably, the IDEA provides direct funding to school districts for the implementation of special education services, whereas there are no specific funds provided by the federal or state governments to pay for services that are called for under Section 504. Further, the statutory language and regulations implementing the IDEA are highly detailed and provide far-ranging (albeit sometimes insufficient) direction to school districts and parents regarding how the special education system is supposed to work. By contrast, Section 504 itself is only a paragraph in length and the regulations implementing Section 504 are much briefer than those regarding the IDEA.

The differences in available resources and detailed regulation do not automatically mean that either law is preferable. Each law has advantages for children with disabilities depending on the circumstances of the child, the school, and the particular issue. At the most general level, IDEA is more likely to be of use to children who require a greater intensity of specialized instructional services and/or related services, who have more complex needs, and/or when there is a greater need for specificity in planning for the child, protecting the child's procedural rights, or holding the school accountable regarding issues of implementation. By contrast, Section 504 is typically of greater utility if the child's needs are less complex, if the child has a disability that does not qualify him or her for special education, or when the child needs only accommodations, as opposed to special education.

Section 504 may also be preferable for children whose disabilities do qualify for protections under IDEA but whose condition requires only limited services or classroom accommodations. Section 504 may also be preferable if a lesser degree of bureaucracy, red tape, and paperwork is desirable. In addition, as some families are uncomfortable with the special education label or the stigma attached to involvement with special education, Section 504 may provide a viable way for a student to receive some additional assistance or protection without all of the trappings of the special education bureaucracy and labels.

Section 504 has a number of potential advantages when it comes to addressing children's needs. Evaluation requirements, for one, are less detailed and stringent than those under IDEA, so the evaluation process is often less rigorous. In addition, schools may be more willing to accept evaluations from outside evaluators as the basis for Section 504 eligibility than for IDEA eligibility. Because the Section 504 eligibility criteria are more amorphous than those under the IDEA, it is sometimes easier for a student to meet them. In addition, a child may be eligible under Section 504 based on the need for related services or accommodations, where the child would qualify for special education services only if he or she also requires some form of actual special education intervention. Thus, the population of students covered by Section 504 is broader than the population of students covered by IDEA.

In particular, children with disabilities can qualify for Section 504 protections and receive a 504 plan even if they require only related services or accommodations—and don't need special education services. The IDEA typically does not offer eligibility to students who only need related services or accommodations. (The only exception to this, regarding the IDEA, concerns students who are identified as having a speech and language disorder and require speech and language therapy but do not require special education intervention.)

Section 504 is also more likely to provide protection for children with health issues, such as asthma, diabetes, or seizure disorders, who may require medical management at school or accommodations regarding physical exercise or physical education classes, but do not require instructional services that would be sufficient to qualify them for IDEA eligibility. In addition, the IDEA does not provide any legal direction with respect to the issue of accessibility at public schools, whereas Section 504 expressly requires that there be physical or programmatic access, for all children with disabilities, such as for children who use a wheelchair.[9]

Some students might have a disability that is covered by the IDEA but not to a degree severe enough to warrant IDEA services. For example, a child may be diagnosed with a mild learning disability; although he or she might not meet the school system's criteria for eligibility for a learning disability under the IDEA, the child might qualify for the protections of Section 504.

In 1999, the Supreme Court issued a ruling which created a major limiting factor with respect to eligibility under Section 504 and the ADA. In *Sutton v. United Airlines*[10] the Supreme Court ruled that an airline pilot was not a person with a disability subject to the protections of the disability laws because his use of eyeglasses resulted in a mitigation or correction of his disability to a sufficient degree that, with his eyeglasses, he was no longer disabled. The *Sutton* decision was an interpretation of the Americans with Disabilities Act. Most schools did not adopt the "mitigating measures" standard limiting the eligibility of students with disabilities, but it has occurred in some instances. Examples of mitigating measures that may correct disabilities enough to make students functionally nondisabled could include eyeglasses, various medications, the use of assistive listening devices, or other corrective measures. However, on September 26, 2008, the Congress passed the Americans with Disabilities Amendments Act, which effectively reversed the *Sutton* decision, as well as several other court cases limiting the eligibility standards and scope of protection of the ADA and Section 504.

An advantage of Section 504, however, is that both this law and the Americans with Disabilities Act contain explicit language protecting individuals with disabilities from harassment or retaliation based on their disability and based on exercising their legal rights to secure the protections of these laws.[11] By contrast, the IDEA does not have any explicit safeguards for protection on the basis of disability from harassment, discrimination, or retaliation.

Disadvantages of Section 504 in comparison to the IDEA

Despite the greater flexibility, reduced bureaucracy, and lesser stigma of Section 504, it has a number of disadvantages in comparison to the services and safeguards of the IDEA. The very flexibility of Section 504, by virtue of the lesser degree of regulation, also means that Section 504 is more ambiguous as to what it requires. While this gives parents opportunities for creative argument that Section 504 should cover certain items that may not be explicitly listed in IDEA, the converse is also true. Because Section 504 is more ambiguous, schools may take a narrow reading of it or may limit the services or protections they are willing to provide.

In addition, some school districts don't understand Section 504 and fail to recognize its application fully or have a narrow interpretation of its requirements. Some school districts, for example, assume that Section 504 covers only children with physical or health impairments, without recognizing that it applies to children with any physical or mental impairment. Further, some schools believe Section 504 involves only accommodations for students when, in actuality, the regulations also include the potential provision of instructional services and related services. Not surprisingly, because of the absence of funding for Section 504 and the absence of a Section 504 bureaucracy in most school systems, schools often lack staff with a clear responsibility for Section 504 or a detailed understanding of how it works.

Another disadvantage to Section 504 is that, unlike the IDEA, it does not require the formal, detailed plans that are part of an individualized education program (IEP). Under the IDEA, these IEPs require the establishment of performance baselines, measurable goals, specified procedures and timelines for review, and a clear delineation of instructional and related services, aids, and supports to be provided. Section 504 regulations do not contain comparable specific directions for planning processes or for the contents of the child's Section 504 plan. Often, Section 504 plans describe what the child is expected to do, rather than the progress that the child is expected to make. Further, some Section 504 plans confuse a description of the staff's responsibilities with those of the student. For example, a Section 504 plan might state that the student will come to the nurse to receive medication, rather than stating that the nurse will be responsible for providing medication to the student.

In addition, under the special education system, all the special education, related services, and paraprofessional providers must meet specific state standards. While any educators providing services under Section 504 must meet the applicable standards of their state with respect to special or regular education, there are no specific Section 504 standards. This creates ambiguity with respect to the qualifications of those who may provide services. It also lowers the degree of accountability that schools might have with respect to delivery of Section 504 services. As a general matter, the Section 504 regulations provide less detailed standards for parents to hold schools accountable than do the IDEA plans. Further, although parents have the right to request a due process hearing for violations of Section 504, Section 504 hearing officers are typically appointed by the school districts and have fewer rules as to their competency and independence. Further, the absence of national standards on how Section 504 hearings are to be conducted results in confusion and ambiguity with respect to the procedures and safeguards available to parents in a Section 504 hearing. Again, this situation contrasts with the much higher degree of specificity and regulation governing the due process procedures under the IDEA.

With respect to children with behavioral challenges, the IDEA requires that the IEP include consideration of positive behavioral interventions and supports. It also contains an elaborate system for determining whether the child's behavior is related to his or her disability and specifies how the school may respond to behavioral infractions. By contrast, although the Office for Civil Rights interpretations of Section 504 have imposed some of the safeguards of the IDEA on Section 504 disciplinary procedures, there is far greater protection for children with behavioral challenges under the IDEA than under Section 504.

In sum, it is important that parents be aware of how each law functions and make informed choices about the potential advantages of each law regarding their child's needs at the particular time. It should also be clear, however, that parents do not have the option of simply flip-flopping back and forth between Section 504 and the IDEA regarding their child's eligibility. Decisions about eligibility under both laws are made by the school district with the participation of the parents, who have the right to challenge the school district's decision using the legal procedures that each law provides.

CHAPTER 12

The Psychology and Politics of Special Education: A Context

Perseverance is a great element of success. If you knock long
enough and loud enough at the gate, you are sure to wake up
somebody.

—Henry Wadsworth Longfellow

The special education system is ultimately shaped and regulated by special education laws and by the ways these laws are implemented and interpreted by the courts and by the federal and state departments of education and local school systems. The special education tableau is composed of much more than what is written in black and white, however. It also includes our views of the American educational system, our expectations for schools, our feelings about teachers, our willingness to commit resources, and even our feelings about people with disabilities. The law is not only subject to interpretation but also originates in and is implemented through the political process. Politics shape the contours of the law and dictate how resources are allocated at the state and federal level, and politics drive the decisions that are made at the school district and local school level. Who is on the school board, which interest groups are better organized and more vocal, who plays golf with whom, and a wide variety of other political and relationship based factors influence both system wide and child specific decision making.

Effective advocacy requires an awareness of the political and psychological factors that influence decisions. A parent struggling to get help for his or her child will benefit from knowing whether the school principal and director of special education are close friends or bitter enemies. A parent seeking to have his or her child included in regular education needs to know that the school board has a long term plan that puts a high priority on placing children with disabilities in regular education in particular schools in a step by step process over a number of years. A private clinician will benefit from knowing that the school psychologist recently had a contentious interaction with another private clinician and may be less forthcoming than he or she was previously. An advocate may be more effective if he or she is aware of a particular school district's prior history of working with or fighting against parents, up to and including battles in due process hearings and court. This chapter attempts to identify a variety of these factors and to show how they influence the federal, state, and local decision making process.

The issues raised here reflect my own perceptions, shaped by my experience both nationally and locally. I do not offer these thoughts to provide evidence or in an effort to prove them correct. Rather, I present them to assist others in gaining a perspective on how the system works and how to work most effectively within it (or, where necessary, against it).

At the outset, the special education system can be properly understood only in the context of the American educational system as a whole. Special education does not exist in a vacuum. Despite its bureaucratic separateness in some areas, an issue that will be addressed below, special education is a part of the overall school system and is influenced by all the issues that affect education in general. If the political system makes a decision to improve funding for education, that decision is likely to impact special education. If the nation begins pushing for more explicit outcome measures for all students, as embodied in the federal No Child Left Behind Act, that requirement will affect children with disabilities. Whether we hold the teaching profession in high or low regard will likely be reflected in our attitudes about special educators, as well. If there is a shortage of teachers and administrators, that will almost certainly present similar problems for staffing special education programs. Thus, an awareness of the issues confronting American education is helpful to an understanding of special education.

Changing times, changing responsibilities: The national expectation/ability gap

The generation of children who grew up in the 1950s to mid 1970s participated in an educational system that was highly regarded and viewed as an important cornerstone of our society. Our expectations concerning schools and teachers were far narrower than they are today. We expected schools to teach fundamental academic skills and to provide basic lessons in good citizenship. We assumed that teachers were entitled to respect and treated them accordingly. As a general matter, teachers were not only treated with respect by students but were assumed to have authority and the ability to exercise control. In the Kennedy era, educators were seen as key agents of social change, whether they were helping produce more scientists to keep up with the Russians, bringing educational opportunities to poor Americans through VISTA, or teaching children in developing countries through the Peace Corps. Historically, education was widely seen as a prestigious field. Those who chose it were regarded as embarking on a noble career. Schools and teachers were seen as a critical element in our ability to prosper as a nation.

For a variety of complex reasons, our attitudes about American education have shifted dramatically in the last 40 years. On the one hand, our expectations for what schools will be responsible for have increased exponentially. Schools are now responsible for providing free lunch programs, remedial reading, bilingual education, sex education, drug education, computer education, health education, vocational education, gifted education, character education, and—using superlatives that are at once overgenerous and divisive—special or exceptional education.

On the other hand, as the breadth and depth of our programmatic expectations have expanded, we have often failed to provide the funding or training to meet these increased expectations and we have become increasingly frustrated with the inability of American education to accomplish all that we expect. This, in turn, has led to ever more aggressive efforts to measure students, teachers, and school performance, coupled with more tangible and, at times, harsher consequences for those who fail to meet the new standards. For students, this situation has translated into the increased use of high stakes testing, which requires students in some states to achieve at a certain level in order to progress from grade to grade or even to graduate.

For schools, testing has meant that funding and, under some circumstances, even administrative control have been tied to the overall performance of a school's student population on certain district or state academic performance measures. For teachers, the increased emphasis on outcome measures has been increasingly tied to the need for more rigorous continuing teacher education and more rigorous and more frequent professional testing for teachers to be certified by the state.

Simultaneous with these increased programmatic responsibilities, there has been a shift in the relationship between the family and the school. The increased presence of dual career families and/or parents forced to work multiple jobs to make ends meet has meant that parents are often home less and less. At the same time, as our society has become more transient, extended family is less available to fill in when the parent(s) are not home. This means that families are less able to provide the level of academic support or social and character education that previously seemed prevalent or to ensure or reinforce the need for appropriate behavior at school. In fact, as a result of the many new pressures on families, some children may not even have a parent or caregiver present much of the time to provide supervision, let alone assistance or encouragement. These huge shifts in family structure and parenting roles have also had a profound impact on how children function at school, particularly concerning their attitudes toward authority figures. Educators can no longer assume that parents will support their efforts concerning behavior and discipline, sometimes because the parents are not available to do so, sometimes because they lack the desire or means to do so, and sometimes because they disagree with the educator's actions.

At the same time, children are now far more likely to have access to illegal drugs, alcohol, and weapons than they did in the 1950s. The issue of childhood drug and alcohol abuse has become an intractable problem in our society. Similarly, it seems that the frequency and severity of childhood mental illness and developmental disabilities are constantly growing. The schools are not equipped to deal with these problems effectively but cannot ignore them.

Regardless of research on the level and frequency of serious violence within American schools, the perception that violence is a growing problem has risen dramatically, particularly in response to the horrific tragedies in Colorado, Oregon, Kentucky, and elsewhere. This has led to an increased focus on safety and security and has required many schools to implement a variety of security measures, such as metal detectors and police patrols in the halls, that are inconsistent with our desire for open, comfortable school environments. Coupled with these efforts, schools have increasingly implemented "zero tolerance" policies, which command rigid and draconian punitive responses to a variety of disciplinary infractions, including drug and weapon violations, but which can also be triggered by less severe behaviors—including some that historically would not have been treated as seriously, such as a student's drawing cartoons with violent themes in his or her notebook. The perception that the schools are infested with drugs and weapons and are effectively out of control, whether accurate or not, has further contributed to a decline in the stature of American education and a loss of regard for the educational system.

The net effect of all these pressures is that schools and teachers are, in many respects, being set up to fail. In our society, the schools represent the most active, consistent, and wide reaching provider of services to children other than the family. As such, we have asked schools to assume responsibility for an incredibly wide range of problems that children and families are confronting. At the same time that we have raised expectations, we have failed to provide the resources, training, methodology, or authority that would be needed for schools to have a remote chance of success in these undertakings.

This expectation/ability gap has created a broad chasm between educators, parents, and the community, which colors many of our interactions involving education related issues. Even worse, the gap triggers a self fulfilling cycle of recrimination in which parents and community articulate expectations that cannot be met, leading to frustration and resentment by educators, which further aggravates the credibility/communication gap and leads to heightened conflict, rather than collaboration. As the educators become increasingly defensive, parents and the community become more aggressive in their demands for improved educator and student performance. This further undermines a sense of trust and collegiality and shifts the focus away from addressing key issues that are actually at the root of the problems the children, families, and schools are experiencing.

Internal pressures on American education

In addition to the societal pressures described above, a number of structural and historical pressures are also contributing to the struggles the educational system now faces. The first problem is lack of personnel. There is a shortage of new teachers coming into the educational system, while more experienced teachers are leaving at accelerated speeds. Various parts of the country are also facing an exodus of experienced school administrators, leading to shortages of veteran principals and other high level officials. It is no longer uncommon to find school principals and even higher level administrators who are in their thirties or forties. At times, this occurs not because the individual is exceptionally talented but because more experienced people cannot be found.

A second problem confronting regular education is the wide diversity of skill levels in a typical classroom. The increasing presence of children from a wide range of different language backgrounds further complicates the educational process and further challenges many classroom teachers.

> *Sam was a bright elementary school student with mild learning disabilities and deafness. He was an effective lip reader and used sign language. His parents wished for him to attend his neighborhood school. The school district resisted, claiming that it would be difficult to accommodate him in regular education and that he would miss too much of what was occurring in the classroom. Sam's neighborhood school served children who spoke more than twenty different languages as their primary language. Sam's parents were successful in their due process hearing against the school district, in part because the enormous diversity of linguistic and academic abilities in the school defeated the district's claim that Sam would not fit in and could not be accommodated.*

Efforts to address similar internal and external problems have led to an increased emphasis on collaborative teaching, in which several teachers may work with a group of students as members of a team. These problems have also resulted in increased reliance on paraprofessionals to assist teachers in managing larger class sizes or to help teachers handle the increasingly diverse needs of the students in their classes. While these strategies have worked well in some instances, in others they have produced tension and conflict. Further, the increased reliance on paraprofessionals in both regular and special education has introduced a group of adults who are often vested with enormous responsibility but given minimal training, are subject to limited regulation, and have diffuse job descriptions and accountability.

In response to these problems, some parents have become increasingly interested in having a greater role in their children's schools and in decisions about their children's education. Simultaneously, educational reform efforts have identified the importance of parental involvement in local level decision making, as a means of increasing parental participation and making schools more responsive to parents.

The net effect of these problems has resulted in the regular education system becoming overwhelmed and ill equipped to handle its responsibilities, yet facing ever increasing pressure to perform more successfully. One consequence of this dilemma is that administrators and educators sometimes become defensive about their collective and individual performance, resistant to real or perceived demands that increase their responsibilities even further, and hostile to increased parental involvement. Others respond with indifference, overwhelmed by the difficulty of successfully meeting the myriad demands.

Special education: The poor second cousin of American education

The problems facing American education impact all aspects of special education. Lack of funding, teacher shortages, disciplinary problems, and disputes over roles and responsibilities have as much effect on special education as they do on regular education. In addition to these problems, however, a variety of factors strain the special education system even beyond the pressures in regular education.

At the outset, the "specialness" of special education itself creates political problems that contaminate decisions within special education and in the overall educational system. Special education has different rules, which address everything from teacher training and parent participation to discipline. Special education in many states has separate funding streams and, in many schools, separate staff and separate administrative hierarchies.

Because children with disabilities are legally entitled to services that meet their individual needs, they may qualify for expensive services independent of the overall financial well being of a particular school or district. This dual system breeds hostility in some regular education administrators, teachers, and parents, and can create a tension filled arena in which regular and special education are perceived as competing interest groups. Consequently, decisions are not always based on the merits of a particular case, and the perception of "specialness" sometimes has a negative, rather than a positive, impact on the outcome.

This backlash is heightened by controversy surrounding special education funding. When the Individuals with Disabilities Education Act (IDEA) was passed in 1975, Congress promised that the federal government would provide 40 percent of the total cost of special education.[1] To date, this hasn't happened. Congress still provides less than 20 percent of the total cost of special education. While the 2004 IDEA paid lip service to reaching the 40 percent level, the actual commitment of funds did not occur. In fact, Congress agreed that schools could use 15 percent of their IDEA dollars to fund Early Intervention Services in regular education.[2] This had the effect of creating an indirect funding increase for regular education at the same time that reaching the 40 percent federal funding goal for special education remains far in the distance. As a result, states implemented their special education programs under what were essentially false pretenses. Whatever the actual financial impact of this federal underfunding might be, its political impact has been to generate additional resentment within the educational community. In some instances, it has caused special education to become the scapegoat for state and local school funding crises.

Mary has a neurological disorder that causes severe cognitive, communication, and motor problems. When she was in junior high, her parents wanted her to remain in regular education with her neighborhood peers. Her school district wanted her placed in a self contained life skills class in another school district. Over the course of a several year legal battle, the district was estimated to have spent well over $200,000 on legal fees and was getting political heat from the community regarding its handling of the case. At a school board budget meeting during the litigation, the panel members announced major budgetary problems, which they blamed in large measure on the increasing cost of special *education services in the district—and especially on the unusual costs of litigating this particular case.*

However, while the district's budget analysis revealed that special education expenses had indeed gone up dramatically, the analysis failed to report increased state funding it had received to underwrite the cost of special education in the same time period or that much of the litigation expense comes from insurance or sources other than the District's operating budget. In fact, the net cost of special education to the district was actually relatively constant, rather than increasing.

Unfortunately, in many communities, special education is being blamed for a wide variety of woes. These include budget problems, teacher and space shortages, and problems with school discipline. While it is true that special education expenditures consume a disproportionate share of total school spending on a per student basis compared to spending on students in regular education, these expenditures represent a necessary investment to address the needs of children with disabilities. It is the goal of the IDEA that this investment will pay off for the children with disabilities and our entire society by increasing the independence and self sufficiency of these students as they become adults.[3] In addition, although the IDEA is now over 30 years old, the special education system is in some respects still ramping up. As educators, parents, and professionals learn more about the evaluation process and about what kids need, more children are being identified who are in need of services. More children are receiving the services to which they are entitled. Simultaneously, parents, educators, and outside professionals have become increasingly aware of the schools' responsibilities under the IDEA and are better able to advocate for services for children in need. Moreover, the whole point of special education is that children with disabilities require more individualized and intensive services in order to benefit from their education in any meaningful way. Thus, the extra cost of special education was a reasoned investment that was good for the individual and for society. Further, this disproportionality is misleading as many students in regular education also receive expensive services, whether based on being on the football team or being in an Advanced Placement program with smaller student to teacher ratios.

Unfortunately, in some instances, investments in special education and regular education have become mutually exclusive. Instead of arguing for an expanded financial pot that meets the needs of all students, some people believe that funding for one program automatically takes away dollars from the others. This appears to be true, based on the political choices of the federal, state, and local governments. However, the public has the ability to make choices in our allocation of state and federal dollars—choices that could ensure higher or even "sufficient" funding for both regular and special education. Unfortunately, we have often acted as though there were a cap, when, in reality, the cap is imposed by politicians and the citizens who elect them.

The psychological and financial factors that produce a backlash concerning special education are further aggravated by its separateness. The existence of a parallel special education bureaucracy—complete with special rules, funding, and entitlements—which varies widely among states and school districts, creates its own set of problems. In some districts, special education teachers are not seen as accountable to the principal and may not be fully involved in the faculty. They may be shortchanged on the quality and size of their classrooms and may be shuffled from school to school due to the changing needs for classrooms from year to year. Collaboration between regular and special education teachers is sometimes inhibited because the special education teachers report through the special education hierarchy and may not be seen as colleagues by the regular educators and vice versa.

The clinical/educational complexities of dealing with disabilities also elevate the special educators to a perceived role of "expert." This promotes the notion that the educators' competence should not be questioned and their authority should not be challenged—potentially making it difficult for colleagues or parents to collaborate with them. Unfortunately, many educators are not experienced with collaboration. Some feel threatened by it. In addition, while the special educators may genuinely be experts in special education teaching methods, they are not always knowledgeable about the regular education curriculum. Conversely, the regular educators may be experts in the curriculum but untrained on special education methods. At times, meshing the two is problematic.

Yet another conflict is generated by the greater rights afforded to parents of children with disabilities in terms of access to information, participation, and legal review. The greater accountability required by the individualized education program (IEP) process (discussed in detail in Chapter 4) is seen by some special and regular educators as either a burden or an undesirable intrusion on their educational prerogatives. In addition, special education law gives parents the right to challenge school decisions more directly than in regular education. Indeed, in a bizarre way, the "specialness" of special education sometimes seems to generate more resentment from special educators than it does from regular educators because the "specialness" carries with it special obligations.

Unfortunately, the combination of adherence to the law, risk management, and the elevation of form over substance means that many schools (and the state and federal regulators) place excessive emphasis on procedural compliance, sometimes to the exclusion of substantive quality or even good judgment or common sense. In other instances, though, schools attain neither quality nor procedural compliance. According to the 2000 National Council on Disability report "Back to School on Civil Rights" not a single state in the nation fully achieved procedural compliance with the IDEA.[4] Were procedural noncompliance the only problem, the situation would be bad enough. Unfortunately, there is an equal or greater problem with a lack of quality services. There are major deficits with the quality and effectiveness of our special education system. The gap between best practice and actual practice is often great. Fundamentally, the needs of many children are either not being met at all or are being met at barely a maintenance level.[5] In fact, in the period prior to the passage of the 2004 IDEA, much was written about the poor outcomes for children in the special education system, including high drop out rates, underemployment and unemployment, heavy dependence on government aid, and increased rates of involvement with the criminal justice system.[6]

Against this backdrop, parents sometimes become concerned with a school's technical compliance or lack thereof, without regard for whether the overall program is positive and/or the relationship with the school is productive. This engenders confusion and bitterness among school staff members, which sets off a cycle of conflict that polarizes the relationships even further. The phenomenon is worsened because parents feel strongly about the needs of their child and sometimes have little patience for or sensitivity to the educators' obligation to address the needs of all the children simultaneously. Unfortunately, when parents complain, whether based on procedure or substance, they are sometimes met with a defensive reaction that causes them to feel victimized along with their children. These conflicts are daunting even to the most sophisticated and resilient parents, for the schools have vastly superior resources, access to information, and availability of legal assistance. Compounding this problem, hearing officers and judges sometimes assume that educators are acting in good faith and that parents are being unrealistic in their expectations and unreasonable in their demands.

Difficulties also result from the structure of special education in many schools. In many schools, special educators report to special education administrators and function somewhat independently from the regular education staff, even when they may be operating out of the same school building. This creates confusion concerning the chain of command. It also creates territoriality and confusion regarding which educator has primary responsibility for educating the child with a disability. When planning needs to occur, this departmentalization sometimes interferes with necessary communications between regular and special education staff.

Furthermore, because there are different rules pertaining to programming, planning, grading, and discipline for children with disabilities, a two-tier system sometimes operates, engendering resentment from regular education staff and the parents of regular education students. Conversely, special educators sometimes find regular educators to be rigid and unwilling to work collaboratively to serve the children with disabilities being included in their classrooms. Special educators sometimes experience an attitude that kids with disabilities are "their problem." Some regular educators simply want to shunt responsibility to the special educators, rather than assume any responsibility themselves.

Yet another conundrum for the special education system is that the staff is often behind the curve in terms of what the parents know about their children and their disabilities and about the services or technology needed to serve them. Even when good teacher training has been provided, many children have a disability or a combination of disabilities that are outside of the experience of a given educator. Given the vast number of different disabilities, illnesses, syndromes, and combinations of disorders, it would be literally impossible for any given educator to be familiar with every child's unique needs. Often, the parents, because they are focused on their child exclusively, learn more about the particular child's disability than the school staff may know. When the presumed experts may not be as expert as the parents, conflicts can erupt.

There can also be serious problems concerning technology. As the computer revolution leads day by day to advances in hardware and software that assist people with disabilities, there is no way that the school system can keep up, either in procuring the most current technology or in training staff to use it. At the same time, parents are understandably often doing their own research on what is available and correctly pushing the system to adopt the latest methods. Again, conflicts can arise as the educators lag behind the research, knowledge, and expectations of the parents—and as they try to respond to individual demands while fulfilling their obligations to students as a whole.

Compounding all of these problems is the reality of school board governance. School boards are elected locally. Though they are generally well intentioned and highly motivated individuals, school board members are unlikely to be educational experts. As a result, they often rely heavily on the local school district administration for direction regarding district policy. At times, it is difficult to sort out whether the board or the district superintendent is ultimately in charge. Because the boards are local, moreover, they are more vulnerable to local pressures. Often, by virtue of basic demographics, this means that special education services are not a high financial priority. After all, in a typical community, the special education population generally represents only about 12 percent of the total student body.[7] Furthermore, because of the complexities of special education services, private placement, due process, and discipline, special education may be seen as demanding a disproportionate amount of the board's time and effort. Thus, the decision makers closest to the controversy are sometimes less sensitive to the needs of children with disabilities and to the legal requirements of special education law.

These various problems highlight the many ways that the special education system has, by its structure and design, resulted in multiple points of conflict between parents and educators. In some instances, the conflicts are almost unavoidable, while in others they could be more effectively managed if the participants were more aware of the causes and impact of the issues and more open and deliberate about dealing with them. A number of strategies could help diffuse some of the problems.

E=MC² Advocacy Strategies: Using Politics and Psychology for Effective Advocacy

(1) Know the political and psychological climate. It is important that parents and advocates learn as much as they can about the political relationships, philosophy, and climate of the school and district. What is the school board's attitude toward special education? Are there board members who have children receiving special education services? Does the superintendent dominate the board, or is the board the dominant player? What is the relationship of the superintendent to the director of special education? Is the school system receptive to parental involvement or resistant to it? Is the local special education community active? Are parents pushing for more services? What is the district's financial position? (Note: Special education is especially at risk whenever there is a budget deficit.)

(2) A positive approach is always preferable. Recognize the many setups that are described above, and work to avoid the points of conflict wherever possible. Express open, honest, and frequent appreciation for the efforts of school staff. Work to identify common ground with the staff. Acknowledge the problem and express a desire to help. ("We know this is a resource problem, and we want to work with you to solve it.") Break bread with the staff, bring food to meetings, and give presents at holidays. Let the school staff know you appreciate what it does. Avoid public confrontations, particularly with individual line staff, as much as possible. Saving face is a real issue for all of us.

(3) Work to build internal allies. It is always easier to support a position when some of the people on the other side of the table agree with you. Cultivate relationships with the staff as much as possible. Try to stay in communication without having the communication seem oppressive or manipulative. Get involved in school activities (the PTA, field trips, school projects). Communicate the fact that you understand the pressures and challenges the staff faces.

(4) Build coalitions. There is strength in numbers. In most cases, the administration and board will be more responsive to a group of parents

than to an individual. Learn your rights. Train other parents. Develop a communication tree. Attend school board meetings regularly. When possible, elect parents to the school board who are sensitive to special education issues (or better yet, who are people with disabilities and/or parents of children with disabilities).

(5) The squeaky wheel gets the oil. Ultimately, decisions often favor those who are most willing to make their voices heard. When friendly interaction doesn't work, it is necessary to be persistent and to make it clear that the problem won't go away until it is adequately resolved. Go up the ladder, step by step, and don't give up. Call key decision makers. Enlist allies. Call the district administrators. Call the school board. Contact legislators. Convey a desire to collaborate and willingness to compromise, but also a commitment to achieving an adequate solution for your child.

13

How Laws Work: Who Has Trump?

The special education system is governed by a multitude of different laws, regulations, and judicial and administrative interpretations. It would be easier if there were a single set of rules applicable to everyone in the same way and collectively interpreted in a manner everyone could agree upon. However, neither the special education system nor any other aspect of our laws work that way. Because these laws will be used or interpreted by different people in different ways to suit their individual purposes, it is critical for parents and clinicians to understand the role and relationship of these different laws and interpretations in order to assure that they are used correctly and, where possible, to maximum advantage.

Further, laws and regulations consist of words that are subject to different interpretations. For example, the Individuals with Disabilities Education Act (IDEA) requires that children with disabilities should be "mainstreamed to the maximum extent appropriate." One interpretation of this statement would be that the key words are *maximum extent*, suggesting that mainstreaming should always, or almost always, occur. Another interpretation of this statement would focus on the word *appropriate*, suggesting that the degree of mainstreaming is individually determined by what is appropriate and that mainstreaming need not always occur.

Given all the confusion, this chapter will explain the different sources of legal direction by dividing them into four categories: (1) federal law; (2) state law; (3) judicial interpretation; and (4) agency interpretation.

Federal law

The United States Constitution is the most important source of legal direction in our country. All federal and state laws must be consistent with the U.S. Constitution. While there may be areas of federal or state law that are not addressed by the Constitution, when the Constitution provides direction, it controls any other law. The Fourteenth Amendment of the Constitution guarantees both equal protection of the law to all people and due process of law. The Constitution also sets forth a distribution of powers between the legislative branch (the Congress), the judicial branch (the federal courts), and the executive branch (the president and the administration). Further, the Constitution establishes in general terms a balance of power between the federal government and the states.

Congress is authorized to pass legislation necessary to carry out the business of the federal government and to effectuate those duties assigned to the federal government by the Constitution. Congress is not free to pass laws willy-nilly but must have some authority rooted in the Constitution for doing so. When Congress passes a law that is consistent with the provisions of the Constitution, that law applies to the entire country and must be followed. In a sense, federal laws give muscle to the skeleton provided by the Constitution. Federal laws are contained in the United States Code (USC).

Once a federal law is passed, the federal government must implement it. Generally, the federal agency responsible for the subject matter of the law reviews the law and develops regulations to implement it. A very elaborate system is used for the development of these regulations, in which the federal agency must publish proposed regulations, allow an opportunity for public comment, and then publish final regulations. Unless Congress overturns the regulations within a specified period of time after they are published in final form, the regulations become legally binding. Typically, these regulations provide even more detail about how a law will be implemented than the language of the law itself. If the federal laws are the muscles that allow the constitutional skeleton to be flexible, the regulations are the flesh that holds everything together and gives the law further meaning and definition. The federal regulations are contained in the Code of Federal Regulations (CFR).

Here, too, however, the regulations sometimes go beyond or contradict the literal words of the enabling legislation. For example, the IDEA amendments of 1997 stated that all children with disabilities were entitled to receive educational services, including those who were suspended, with no requirements for the number of days of suspension to trigger continuing services. The 1999 regulations that put the 1997 amendments into effect, however, stated that children with disabilities were entitled to receive continuing educational services *only* if they were suspended *for ten days or more* or expelled. By limiting education to those who were suspended for more than ten days or expelled but not to those who were suspended for fewer than ten days, the regulations added a significant qualifier that went beyond the words of the law itself. Similarly, the 1999 regulations added attention deficit/hyperactivity disorder and the 2006 regulations added Tourette Syndrome as "impairments," under the "other health impaired" eligibility category—even though there is no mention of those conditions in the IDEA statute. Still, unless the federal courts determine that a particular regulation is either inconsistent with the Constitution or with the enabling statute, the regulation has the force of federal law.

In some instances, federal laws have mechanisms for enforcement built in. In this regard, Section 504 is enforced by the Office for Civil Rights of the U.S. Department of Education but can also be enforced by individual requests for due process hearings and/or civil law suits in court.

The IDEA also has a mechanism for federal policing of its implementation—it involves U.S. Department of Education review of state special education plans and periodic monitoring of state activities.[1] However, the degree of federal monitoring and enforcement of the statute is very limited and has relatively little effectiveness in assuring state and local compliance. The most meaningful enforcement mechanism available to families under the IDEA is the right to request an impartial due process hearing. Unfortunately, as was discussed in Chapter 10, the due process procedure has many limitations and disadvantages.

The critical point here is that these laws are not self executing. There are no federal "special education police." The special education laws have meaning only to the extent that there is shared agreement as to what they require or, when there is disagreement as to what they require, to the extent parents are able to successfully prosecute a due process case or court action.

State law

The states are governed by federal law, by a state constitution, and by state laws. State statutes must be consistent with federal law and with their own state constitution. They must follow federal requirements and may address topics that are delegated to the states by federal law or that are not addressed by federal law. In exchange for receiving federal funding under the IDEA, the states are charged with implementing special education programs in a manner consistent with federal requirements. Because all states now accept federal IDEA funding, the states have all passed laws that incorporate, at least generally, the requirements of IDEA.

However, although the IDEA and the federal regulations implementing it are quite detailed, they also leave many questions up to the states. For example, the IDEA specifically assigns to the states the decision as to whether children aged 6 to 9 can be included in the "developmentally delayed" disability category, which applies by federal mandate to children aged 3 to 5. The IDEA also conveys to states the power to set a statute of limitations period for appealing due process decisions in court (but provides that, if the state does not have a specific statute of limitations for special education cases, the limitations period will be two years). A variety of other special education topics are either explicitly or implicitly delegated to the states, ranging from the names of the IEP meetings to the specific criteria for teacher certification. However, the states may not adopt laws that contradict federal law or provide a lower threshold of protection to the child. The IDEA requirements are incorporated into states statutes, with the various state specific provisions and variations allowed under the IDEA (or occasionally that may be arguably inconsistent with federal law).

Just as the federal agencies charged with implementing federal law are responsible for issuing federal regulations that interpret and give definition to federal law, the state agency responsible for implementing a particular state law typically issues state regulations that explain the law. If the state agency follows the appropriate procedure in issuing these regulations, the regulations have the force of law in that state unless or until a court rules otherwise. With respect to special education, each state has an agency responsible for education and a subagency responsible for special education. This agency may be called the State Department of Education, the Department of Public Instruction, the State Board of Education, or something similar.

It should be noted that the IDEA refers to these state agencies collectively as "State Education Agencies." Each state education agency (SEA) has an office or department responsible for special education, which may be known as the Office of Special Education, the Office of Exceptional Education, the

Bureau of Special Education, and the like. In any event, this bureaucracy is charged with implementing the federal and state special education law, setting state special education policy, distributing federal and state special education funds, monitoring local compliance with federal and state law, and, in some instances, administering the special education mediation and due process systems.

In a sense, state regulations are the bottom rung of the statutory/regulatory ladder. The U.S. Constitution is preeminent, followed by federal law, federal regulation, state constitutions, state statutes, and finally, state regulation. For practical purposes, however, SEAs and local school districts tend to pay the most attention to state regulations and the state's policies and forms, which set forth the specific definitions and procedures that schools use on a day to day basis. Typically, if teachers and administrators are familiar with any law at all, they are more likely to be familiar with the state regulations than with state law or federal law or regulations. This makes sense, as the teachers and administrators are more directly involved with and accountable to the SEA than they are to the federal government. However, this does not mean that state or federal law should be ignored. To the contrary, although the local school staff may be more familiar with state regulation, the state regulations are sometimes inconsistent with state and/or federal law or may be interpreted or implemented locally in a way that violates federal law. Where these conflicts occur, federal law should ultimately prevail. Because of the potential for inconsistency between federal law, state law, and state regulation or local implementation, it is critical that people involved in special education be well versed in all these matters and able to articulate the controlling federal or state requirements when needed.

Judicial interpretation

Special education disputes may arise because the parties disagree about the nature or extent of the child's needs or because they disagree about what the law requires for the child. These two types of disputes can be described as fact based or law based disputes. A fact based dispute might involve, for example, a parent's perception that a child is struggling academically or socially, when the school believes the child is actually doing well. By contrast, a law based dispute might involve differing interpretations of what the law requires the school to do for that child based on disagreement over the term *free appropriate public education*, even though the parents and school agree about how the child is doing. In either instance, what the law requires may come into play. This inevitably raises the question of what the law means.

As was described earlier, all laws are subject to interpretation, a task made more complex by the reality that the law itself may be ambiguous or internally inconsistent. It is the job of the hearing officer or judge to reach a final conclusion as to what the facts are, to make a judgment about what the law means, and then to apply the law to the facts in order to reach a conclusion.

Because the words of the laws themselves are often subject to differing interpretation, the interpretations offered by the judges themselves become a form of law. Our legal system is governed by the legal doctrine of *stare decisis*, which means that courts are generally bound to follow relevant interpretations that have been previously issued by other judges. The court decisions theoretically serve to fill in the gaps in our understanding of what the laws mean, providing guidance as to how the law should be applied in new situations we encounter. For example, even before the IDEA required it, courts held that schools must make sure the behavioral problems of children with disabilities are not related to their disability before deciding to employ regular education discipline. In this way, the laws gain further meaning and should be more clearly understood. The doctrine of *stare decisis* is not absolute, however. Lower courts often find ways to reinterpret or apply prior decisions to modify or overrule prior court decisions.

Within the federal court system, court cases—including appeals of special education due process decisions—start at the federal district court, or trial court, level. Every state has at least one federal district court, while larger states may be divided into several districts, each with its own federal district court. Decisions by federal district courts are binding only with respect to the specific case that the court is hearing but may be persuasive or influential in helping other courts to analyze or understand a particular issue. If either party is dissatisfied with the outcome of a federal district court decision, that party may appeal the decision to the United States Circuit Court of Appeals for that region. The circuit courts are also known as appellate courts. There are currently 13 federal circuit courts. A decision by a federal circuit court of appeals controls precedent not only in that case but also with respect to all similar cases in that circuit. In effect, once the circuit court has ruled on an issue, that ruling becomes the law for that circuit.

If either party is dissatisfied with the decision of the circuit court of appeals, it may appeal to the U.S. Supreme Court. The Supreme Court has the option to accept an appeal or reject it. If the Supreme Court rejects it, the decision of the circuit court is automatically affirmed. Typically, the Supreme Court will accept a case only if it presents a very important legal question and there is a conflict concerning that question in the decisions of different circuit courts. The Supreme Court can decide the issue in favor of either party or can remand the issue to the trial or circuit court for further consideration. If the Supreme Court issues a final decision, that decision becomes the law of the land. The Supreme Court's decisions typically do not focus on resolution of factual disputes, but rather on resolving differing interpretations of the law. Although the Supreme Court also generally subscribes to the doctrine of *stare decisis*, it is not uncommon for the Supreme Court to modify or overturn even its own prior rulings.

Federal courts always have the right to interpret federal laws. Because both the IDEA and Section 504 are federal laws, the federal courts are permitted to deal with them. Typically, however, the federal courts will only address state law questions if a state law claim is filed in conjunction with a federal law claim. Even then, for interpretation of the state law claim, the federal court will rely on any available precedent by that state's courts concerning that issue. The federal court may also get involved in a state law issue if there is an allegation that a state law violates federal law.

Disputes concerning the interpretation or implementation of federal laws may also be filed in state courts. When this occurs, the state court will look to federal court interpretations in an effort to interpret the federal law in a manner consistent with the federal courts. However, if there is a federal law claim involved, a party may seek to remove a case from state court into federal court. In effect, the federal courts are generally the final arbiters of federal law issues.

Agency interpretation

The agencies responsible for implementing the law typically have some ongoing role in interpreting it and in using those interpretations to guide their work. The U.S. Department of Education Office of Special Education Programs is responsible for interpreting and implementing the IDEA at the federal level. Similarly, each SEA is responsible for interpreting and implementing the IDEA at the state level. Even with the benefit of laws, regulations, and judicial interpretations, there are many aspects of the law that result in policy statements that the responsible agency issues. These policy statements are intended to answer questions; fill in blanks; clarify points of ambiguity, confusion, or conflict; or subtly influence how a law is interpreted to shift it in a new direction. Policy statements are intended as guidance to the people covered by the law. For example, a U.S. Department of Education policy memorandum that interprets the rules for disciplining children with disabilities is relevant to all states and to all children with disabilities in the nation's schools. States and school districts are not absolutely required to follow these policy statements in the same way that they would have to follow the law. However, they are expected to treat them seriously, especially because the policy statements often influence how the courts will analyze or respond to a legal question.[2]

Each SEA is similarly responsible for interpreting its state's special education law and regulations. Its interpretations must be considered by school districts and will influence how the courts interpret the laws and regulations of that state. In the hierarchy of laws, regulations, and court decisions, agency interpretations are at the bottom of the list. Nonetheless, federal agency interpretations play an important rule in understanding the IDEA generally, and state agency interpretations play a significant role in how school districts implement their own state's regulations. Sometimes, it is possible to influence how the state is dealing with a special education issue more easily by obtaining a favorable agency interpretation than it is to try to amend the statute or regulations.

14

Conclusion

The special education system and the laws that govern it are ever changing. The Individuals with Disabilities Education Act (IDEA) will be due for reauthorization and potential amendment in 2009, though it is unlikely that the U.S. Congress will conclude any action to amend it until at least 2010. Regardless of what may occur with the federal legislation, funding, and judicial interpretation of the IDEA, children with disabilities require appropriate, high quality education in the least restrictive environment to meet their needs. The problems of insufficient financial resources, lack of effective programming, and inadequate training of school staff persist. The difficulties parents face in navigating the system and ensuring that their children's rights are protected and that their children receive the education they need are ongoing. The need for greater collaboration between parents and educators and a system that is more welcoming of parental participation remains critical. Currently, the special education system fails many children and too often sets up damaging conflict between teachers and parents, which works to the detriment of all, but, most importantly, hurts the child.

This advocacy guide has provided information about the current law, the special education system, and practical ways for working to obtain appropriate services for children with disabilities. As the law changes and evolves, parents, clinicians, and advocates will need to be aware of these changes and incorporate them into their efforts on behalf of the children for whom they are advocating. However the law changes, much of the practical information and strategies discussed here will remain relevant. I hope that the information will empower parents and others to work for the services that children need and to advocate more effectively for those services. At the same time, this guide has highlighted the need for systemic improvement in special education programs, increased funding and teacher training, and enhanced protections for children and their parents. The empowerment of parents to act on behalf of their individual children will hopefully translate into broader advocacy in support of systemic improvement in special education, both locally and nationally.

Notes

Introduction

1. 348 F. Supp. 866 (D.C. 1972).

2. 343 F. Supp. 279 (E.D. Pa 1972).

3. 20 USC §1400(c)(4).

4. *Journal of School Health* 70, no. 9 (Nov. 2000): 371–376.

5. Albert Einstein, (quotation) copyright Xplore Inc.,Brainymedia, Brainymedia.com.

6. *Atomic Physics* (film), copyright J Arthur Rank Organization, limited 1948. www.aip.org/history/einstein/voice1.htm.

7. Michio Kaku, *Einstein's Cosmos: How Albert Einstein's Vision Transformed Our Understanding of Space and Time (Great Discoveries)*. (New York: W.W. Norton and Company, Inc. 2004).

Chapter 1: An Overview of Legal Protections for Children with Disabilities

1. 34 CFR 300.512 (a)(1).

2. 34 CFR §104.35(a).

Chapter 2: Eligibility

1. 34 CFR §300.7(a)(1)–(b)(13).

2. 34 CFR §300.8(b).

3. Office of Special Education Programs Data Dictionary (1992); 22 OSEP Ann. Rep. pt. II (2000).

4. 34 CFR §300.304(c)(6).

5. 34 CFR §300.320(a)(2)(i), (ii); Elizabeth Dane, *Painful Passages: Working with Children with Learning Disabilities* (Washington, D.C.: NASW Press, 1990), 27.

6. 34 CFR §300.7(c)(4)(i).

7.   20 USC §1400(C)(5)(A)(ii).

8.   *Timothy W. v. Rochester, N.H., Sch. Dist.*, 875 F.2d 954, 962 (1st Cir. 1989).

9.   *Timothy W.*, 875 F.2d at 958.

10.   20 USC §1401(3)(B).

11.   20 USC §1414(b)(2)(B); 20 USC §1414(b)(3)(A)(ii); 20 USC §1414(b)(3)(B).

12.   20 USC §1401(29); *Roncker v. Walter*, 700 F.2d 1058, 1063 (6th Cir. 1983).

13.   34 CFR §300.39(b)(3).

14.   20 USC §1412(a)(5).

15.   34 CFR §300.8(c)(4)(ii).

16.   34 CFR §300.8(c)(4)(ii).

17.   34 CFR §300.8(c)(4)(B), (C).

18.   Carl R. Smith, "Behavioral and Discipline Provisions of IDEA '97: Implicit
      Competencies Yet to Be Confirmed," *Exceptional Children* 66 (2000): 410–411.

19.   34 CFR §300.8(c)(10).

20.   American Speech-Language-Hearing Association, *Audiological Assessment of
      Central Auditory Processing: An Annotated Bibliography* (Rockville, MD: 1990),
      32.

21.   20 USC §1414(b)(6)(A).

22.   20 USC §1414(b)(6)(B).

23.   34 CFR §300.309.

24.   34 CFR §300.309(c)(2).

25.   34 CFR §300.309(a)(2)(ii).

26.   34 CFR §300.309 (a)(2)(ii).

27.   34 CFR §300.304(b)(1); 34 CFR §300.320.

28.   34 CFR §300.8(c)(9).

29.   *U.S. Dept. of Educ. Joint Policy Memorandum*, 18 IDELR 116 (1991).

30.   *Letter to Cohen*, 20 IDELR 73 May 13, 1993; 21 IDELR 73 March 14, 1994.

31.   34 CFR §300.8(c)(9).

32.   American Academy of Pediatrics Clinical Practice Guideline: Diagnosis and
      Evaluation of the Child with Attention Deficit/Hyperactivity Disorder, 1158–
      1170 (2000); American Academy of Child and Adolescent Psychiatry, Practice
      Parameters for the Assessment and Treatment of Children, Adolescents, and
      Adults with Attention Deficit/Hyperactivity Disorder, 4 (1997).

33. 21 IDELR 73 (1994); *U.S. Dept. of Educ. Joint Policy Memorandum*, 18 IDELR 116 (1991).

34. 21 IDELR 73(1994); 34 CFR §300.34(c)(5); 34 CFR §300.300.39(b)(1); 20 USC §1401(a) and §1402(26)(A).

35. 20 USC §1414(b)(3)(A)(ii); 20 USC §1414(d)(3)(A)(iv); 34 CFR §300.311(c)(1); 34 CFR §300.324(a)(1)(iv).

36. 34 CFR §300.8(c)(9).

37. 20 USC §1412(a)(25)(A)–(B); Pub. L. No. 108-446, 118 Stat. 2647; 34 CFR §300.174(a).

38. 20 USC §1412(a)(25)(A)–(B).

39. *Berlin Brothersvalley Sch. Dist.*, EHLR 53:124 (OCR 1998); *San Ramon Valley Unified Sch. Dist.*, 18 IDELR 465 (OCR 1991).

40. American Psychiatric Association, *Diagnostic and Statistical Manual of Mental Disorders: DSM-IV-TR* (Washington, D.C. 2005).

41. The IDEA defines autism as "(i) a developmental disability significantly affecting verbal and nonverbal communication and social interaction, generally evident before age three, that adversely affects a child's educational performance. Other characteristics often associated with autism are engagement in repetitive activities and stereotyped movements, resistance to environmental change or change in daily routines, and unusual responses to sensory experiences. (ii) Autism does not apply if a child's educational performance is adversely affected primarily because the child has an emotional disturbance, as defined in paragraph (c)(4) of this section. (iii) A child who manifests the characteristics of autism after age three could be identified as having autism if the criteria in paragraph (c)(1)(i) of this section are satisfied." 34 CFR 300.8(c)(1).

42. Committee on Educational Interventions for Children with Autism, Division of Behavioral and Social Sciences and Education, National Research Council, Educating Children with Autism (Washington, D.C.: National Academy Press, 2001), 23–31.

43. 34 CFR §300.8(c)(11).

44. 34 CFR §300.8(a)(2).

45. "The term [special education] includes . . . speech-language pathology services, or any other related service, if the service is considered special education rather than a related service under State standards." 34 CFR §300.39(a)(2)(i).

46. Kevin N. Cole, Paulette E. Mills, and Darcy Kelley, "Agreement of Assessment Profiles Used in Cognitive Referencing," *Language, Speech, and Hearing Services in Schools* 25 (1994): 25–26.

47. 34 CFR §300.8(c)(2).

48. 34 CFR §300.8(c)(3).

49. 34 CFR §300.8(c)(5).

50. 34 CFR §300.8(c)(7).

51. 34 CFR §300.8(c)(8).

52. 34 CFR §300.8(c)(12).

53. 34 CFR §300.8(c)(13).

54. 34 CFR §300.111(d).

55. 34 CFR §300.324(a)(iv).

Chapter 3: The Evaluation and Reevaluation Process

1. 34 CFR §300.301; 34 CFR 300.303(a).

2. 34 CFR §300.300(a); 34 CFR 300.300(a)(3).

3. 34 CFR §300.503(a)(2) and (b).

4. 34 CFR §300.305(a)(l)(i).

5. 34 CFR §300.301(c)(l)(i).

6. 34 CFR §300.226.

7. 34 CFR §300.226(c).

8. 34 CFR §300.111(a).

9. 34 CFR §300.305(a) and 300.111(a).

10. 34 CFR §300.304(b) and (c)(1)–(4):

    "(b) Conduct of evaluation. In conducting the evaluation, the public agency must—

    "(1) Use a variety of assessment tools and strategies to gather relevant functional, developmental, and academic information about the child, including information provided by the parent, that may assist in determining—

    "(i) Whether the child is a child with a disability under §300.8; and

    "(ii) The content of the child's IEP, including information related to enabling the child to be involved in and progress in the general education curriculum (or for a preschool child, to participate in appropriate activities);

"(2) Not use any single measure or assessment as the sole criterion for determining whether a child is a child with a disability and for determining an appropriate educational program for the child; and

"(3) Use technically sound instruments that may assess the relative contribution of cognitive and behavioral factors, in addition to physical or developmental factors.

"(c) Other evaluation procedures. Each public agency must ensure that—

"(1) Assessments and other evaluation materials used to assess a child under this part—

"(i) Are selected and administered so as not to be discriminatory on a racial or cultural basis;

"(ii) Are provided and administered in the child's native language or other mode of communication and in the form most likely to yield accurate information on what the child knows and can do academically, developmentally, and functionally, unless it is clearly not feasible to so provide or administer;

"(iii) Are used for the purposes for which the assessments or measures are valid and reliable;

"(iv) Are administered by trained and knowledgeable personnel; and

"(v) Are administered in accordance with any instructions provided by the producer of the assessments.

"(2) Assessments and other evaluation materials include those tailored to assess specific areas of educational need and not merely those that are designed to provide a single general intelligence quotient.

"(3) Assessments are selected and administered so as best to ensure that if an assessment is administered to a child with impaired sensory, manual, or speaking skills, the assessment results accurately reflect the child's aptitude or achievement level or whatever other factors the test purports to measure, rather than reflecting the child's impaired sensory, manual, or speaking skills (unless those skills are the factors that the test purports to measure).

"(4) The child is assessed in all areas related to the suspected disability, including, if appropriate, health, vision, hearing, social and emotional status, general intelligence, academic performance, communicative status, and motor abilities."

11.   34 CFR §300.304(c)(6).

12.   34 CFR §300.304(c)(1)(ii).

13.   34 CFR §300.304(c)(1)(i).

14.   S. Rep. No. 94-168, at 28 (1975).

15.   34 CFR §300.304(c)(3).

16.   34 CFR §300.304(c)(1)(iv).

17.   34 CFR. §300.304(c)(l)(v).

18.   34 CFR §300.303(a).

19.   34 CFR §300.300(c).

20.   34 CFR §300.503(a)(2).

21.   34 CFR §300.303(b)(l).

22.   34 CFR §300.303(b)(2).

23.   34 CFR §300.305(d)(2).

24.   34 CFR §300.502(c).

25.   34 CFR §300.502(b).

26.   34 CFR §300.502(b)(2)(i).

27.   34 CFR §300.502(d).

28.   34 CFR §300.101(c).

29.   34 CFR §300.532; *Letter to Cohen*, 213 IDELR 105 (OSEP 1987); *Letter to McClanahan*, 28 IDELR 481 (OSEP 1997); *Santa Rosa (TX) Indep. Sch. Dist.*, 23 IDELR 1153 (OCR 1995).

30.   *Letter to Parker*, 18 IDELR 963, 964–965 (OSEP 1992).

31.   20 USC §1412(a)(25)(A)–(B): "The State educational agency shall prohibit . . . educational agency personnel from requiring a child to obtain a prescription for a substance covered by the Controlled Substances Act . . . as a condition of attending school, receiving an evaluation . . . or receiving services under this chapter." However, this provision does not "create a Federal prohibition against teachers and other school personnel consulting or sharing classroom based observations with parents or guardians regarding a student's academic and functional performance, or behavior in the classroom or school, or regarding the need for evaluation for special education or related services."

Chapter 4:   Free Appropriate Public Education and the IEP Process

1.   34 CFR §300.101, 112, and 114.

2.   *Polk v. Susquehanna Intermediate Unit 16*, 853 Fed 2d 171 (3d Cir. 1988).

3.   *J. L. v. Mercer Island School District* 2007 WL 2253304 (W.D. Wa.).

4.   34 CFR §300.101(c)(1).

5.   34 CFR §300.101(c)(1).

6.   34 CFR §300.323; 34 CFR §300.321; 34 CFR §300.322.

7.   34 CFR §300.322.

8.   34 CFR §300.320.

9.   34 CFR §300.39.

10.   34 CFR §300.114, 116, 117.

11.   34 CFR §300.39; 34 CFR §300.320(a)(4).

12.   20 USC §1414(d)(1)(B).

13.   34 CFR §300.520.

14.   34 CFR §300.520.

15.   34 CFR §300.321(b)(3).

16.   34 CFR §300.321(f).

17.   34 CFR §300.21(e).

18.   34 CFR §300.321(e).

19.   34 CFR §300.322(b)(1)(i); 34 CFR §300.321(b).

20.   34 CFR §300.320(a)(4).

21.   34 CFR §300.322(a); 34 CFR §300.322(c); 34 CFR §300.322(d).

22.   34 CFR §300.306(a).

23.   34 CFR §300.320 (a)(27)(i)(A).

24.   34 CFR §300.324(a)(1).

25.   34 CFR §300.320(a)(1).

26.   34 CFR §300.320(a)(3)(ii).

27.   34 CFR §300.324(a).

28.   34 CFR §300.324(a)(2)(i).

29.   34 CFR §300.324(a)(2)(ii), (iii), and (iv);
        34 CFR §300.324(a)(2)(v).

30.   34 CFR §300.5; 34 CFR §300.6.

31.   34 CFR §300.324(a)(6).

32.   34 CFR §300.320(a)(4).

33.   34 CFR §300.320(a)(7).

34.   34 CFR §300.320(a)(7).

35.   34 CFR §300.324(a)(2)(v).

36.   20 USC §1414 (d)(1)(A)(i)(V); §1414(d)(1)(A)(i)(IV)(cc).

37.   34 CFR §300.324(a)(2)(i).

38.   34 CFR §300.323(c)(i); 34 CFR §300.323(c)(2);
        34 CFR §300.323(a).

39.   34 CFR §300.17; 34 CFR §300.323(d)(1)(2).

40.   34 CFR §300.518.

41.   34 CFR §300.533.

42.   34 CFR §300.39(b)(3).

43.   34 CFR §300.106 and 34 CFR §300.107.

44.   34 CFR §300.106.

45.   34 CFR §300.106(a)(3).

46.   National Research Council, Committee on Educational Interventions for Children with Autism, Division of Behavioral and Social Sciences and Education, *Educating Children with Autism* (Washington, D.C.: National Academy Press, 2001), 219.

47.   34 CFR §300.107(a).

48.   34 CFR §300.107(b).

Chapter 5:   Special Education and Related Services

1.   34 CFR §300.17.

2.   34 CFR §300.39(a)(1).

3.   34 CFR §300.39(a)(2).

4.   34 CFR §300.39(b)(3).

5.   34 CFR §300.31(a).

6.   34 CFR §300.34(a).

7.   34 CFR §300.34(c)(4).

8.   34 CFR §300.24(a).

9.   34 CFR §300.34(b)(1).

10.   34 CFR §300.34(b)(2).

11.   *Irving Independent School District v. Tatro*, 468 U.S. 883 (1984); *Cedar Rapids Community School District v. Garret F.*, 526 U.S. 66 (1999).

12.   34 CFR §300.34(c)(13).

13.   34 CFR §300.34(c)(7).

14.   34 CFR §300.34(c)(10).

15.   34 CFR §300.34(c)(2).

16.   34 CFR §300.34(c)(14).

17.   34 CFR §300.34(c)(8).

18.   34 CFR §300.34(c)(6).

19.   34 CFR §300.34(c)(15).

Chapter 6:   Least Restrictive Environment

1.   34 CFR 300.114(a)(2).

2.   34 CFR 300.115(a)(b)(2).

3.   34 CFR §300.116(a).

4.   34 CFR §300.321(a)(2).

5.   34 CFR §300.116(b).

6.   34 CFR §300.116(c).

7.   34 CFR §300.116(d)(e).

8.   34 CFR §300.320(A)(a)(4).

9.   34 CFR §300.116(d).

10.   34 CFR §300.116(e).

11.   34 CFR §300.307; 34 CFR §300.117.

12.   34 CFR §300.321(a)(2).

13.   34 CRF §300.320(a)(4); 34 CFR §300.324(a)(3).

14.   34 CFR §300.320(a)(l)(i) and (a)(2)(i)(A) and (a)(4).

15.   34 CFR §300.116(a)(1).

16.   34 CFR §300.327.

17.   34 CFR §300.321(a)(5).

Chapter 7: Private Placement

1. 34 CFR §300.115.

2. 34 CFR §300.148(a).

3. 34 CFR §300.148(c).

4. 34 CFR §300.148(d).

5. 34 CFR §300.148(e).

6. *Burlington School Committee v. Commonwealth of Massachusetts*, 471 U.S. 359 (1985).

7. *Carter v. Florence County School District*, 510 U.S. 7 (1993).

8. 34 CFR §300.131(a).

9. 34 CFR §300.137.

10. 34 CFR §300.137(c).

11. 34 CFR §300.138 and 34 CFR §300.139.

12. 34 CFR §300.140.

13. 34 CFR §300.136.

14. 34 CFR §300.141 and §300.142.

Chapter 8: Behavior Management and Discipline

1. 34 CFR §300.304(c)(4).

2. 34 CFR §300.305(a)(2)(ii); 34 CFR §300.304(c)(1)(ii).

3. 34 CFR §300.324(a)(2)(i).

4. 34 CFR §300.324(a)(3)(i).

5. 34 CFR §300.536.

6. 34 CFR §300.530(b)(2); §530(d)(4).

7. 34 CFR §300.530(d)(4).

8. 34 CFR §300.530(e).

9. 34 CFR §300.530(d).

10. 34 CFR §300.530(b)(2).

11. 34 CFR §300.530(f).

12. 34 CFR §300.533.

13. 34 CFR §300.530(e)(1)(i).

14. 34 CFR §300.530(e)(1)(ii).

15. 34 CFR §300.530(f).

16. 34 CFR §300.518.

17. 34 CFR §300.533.

18. 34 CFR §300.532(c).

19. 34 CFR §300.530(g)(2).

20. 34 CFR §300.532(b)(2)(ii).

21. 34 CFR §300.531.

22. 34 CFR §300.534(a).

23. 34 CFR §300.534(b).

24. 34 CFR §300.534(c).

25. 34 CFR §300.534(d)(2).

26. 34 CFR §300.534(d)(2)(ii)(iii).

Chapter 9: Special Issues Concerning Transition and Graduation

1. 20 USC §1400(c)(5)(A).

2. 34 CFR §300.320(b).

3. 34 CFR §300.43(a).

4. 34 CFR §300.321(b)(1).

5. 34 CFR §300.321(b)(2).

6. 34 CFR §300.321(b)(3).

7. 34 CFR §300.320(b).

8. 34 CFR §300.101(a); 34 CFR §300.102(a)(3).

9. 34 CFR §300.101(c).

10. 34 CFR §300.101(c)(2).

11. 34 CFR §300.320(c).

12. 34 CFR §300.320(b)(2).

13. 34 CFR §300.324(c)(1).

14. 34 CFR §300.320(a)(7).

15. 34 CFR §300.102(a)(3)(iii); 34 CFR §300.503(a)(i).

16. 34 CFR §300.507.

17.   34 CFR §300.518.

18.   34 CFR §300.102(a)(3)(i).

19.   34 CFR §300.102(a)(3)(ii).

20.   34 CFR §300.305(e)(2).

21.   34 CFR §300.305(e)(3).

22.   34 CFR §300.507(a)(2); 34 CFR §300.511(e).

Chapter 10: Procedural Safeguards, Mediation, and Due Process

1.   34 CFR §300.501(a); 34 CFR §300.322(f);
        34 CFR §300.320(a)(3)(ii).

2.   34 CFR 300.322(b).

3.   34 CFR §300.322(a).

4.   34 CFR §300.322(c).

5.   34 CFR §300.503.

6.   34 CFR §300.503.

7.   34 CFR §300.504.

8.   34 CFR §300.321(a)(6).

9.   34 CFR §300.322.

10.   34 CFR §300.303(a)(2).

11.   34 CFR §300.503.

12.   34 CFR §300.502(c).

13.   34 CFR §300.502(b).

14.   34 CFR §300.300(b).

15.   34 CFR §300.300(b)(4).

        The U.S. Department of Education has adopted a new rule that gives parents an
        absolute right to withdraw their consent for their child to receive special education
        at any time after the child enters special education. This means that parents may
        decide to remove their child from special education and have him or her return
        to regular education status even if the school does not agree with the decision.
        However, if the parents exercise this right, the school is not legally responsible
        for providing a free appropriate public education nor for all the procedural
        requirements of the special education process.

16.   34 CFR §300.300(a)(3); 34 CFR §300.300(c)(1)(ii).

17. 34 CFR §300.322.

18. 34 CFR §300.501(a); 34 CFR §300.322(f); 34 CFR 300.320(a)(3)(ii); *Schaffer vs. Weast*, 546 U.S. 49 (2005).

19. 34 CFR §300.518.

20. 34 CFR §300.530.

21. 34 CFR §300.533.

22. 34 CFR §300.506.

23. 34 CFR §300.506(a).

24. 34 CFR §300.506(b)(6).

25 34 CFR §300. 512(a)(1).

26. 34 CFR §300.506(b)(7).

27. 34 CFR §300.510(b).

28. 34 CFR §300.506(b)(7).

29. 34 CFR §300.510.

30. 34 CFR §300.510(a)(1)(ii).

31. 34 CFR §300.510(a)(1).

32. 34 CFR §300.510(a)(3).

33. 34 CFR §300.510.

34. 34 C.F.R. §300.510(e).

35. 34 CFR §300.3510(b)(4).

36. 34 CFR §300.511(c).

37. 34 CFR §300.511(c).

38. 34 CFR 300.507(d).

39. 34 CFR 300.507(e) & (f).

40. 34 CFR §300.512.

41. 34 CFR §300.512(a)(1).

42. 34 CFR §300.512(a)(4).

43. 34 CFR §300.512(a)(5).

44. 34 CFR §300.512(c)(2).

45. 34 CFR §300.507(b).

46.   34 CFR §300.516(a).

47.   34 CFR §300.516(b).

Chapter 11:   A Comparison of the IDEA and Section 504

1.   29 USCA §794(a).

2.   34 CFR §104.34.

3.   34 CFR §104.32.

4.   34 CFR §104.33; 34 CFR §104.36.

5.   34 CFR §104.33.

6.   34 CFR §104.34.

7.   34 CFR §104.35.

8.   34 CFR §104.36.

9.   34 CFR §104.21.

10.   527 US 471 (1999).

11. 42 USC §12203.

Chapter 12:   The Psychology and Politics of Special Education: A Context

1.   Tyce Palmaffy, "The Evolution of the Federal Role," in C. E. Finn, A. J. Rotherham, and C. R. Hokansen, eds., *Rethinking Special Education for a New Century* (Washington, D.C.: Fordham Foundation and Progressive Policy Institute, 2001), 1.

2.   20 USC §1413(f)(i).

3.   20 USC §1400(d)(l)(A).

4.   National Council on Disability, *Back to School on Civil Rights: Advancing the Federal Commitment to Leave No Child Behind* (Washington, D.C.: 2000). This document can be found on NCD's Web site: www.ncd.gov/newsroom/publications/2000/backtoschool_1.htm.

5.   President's Commission on Excellence in Special Education, *A New Era: Revitalizing Special Education for Children and Their Families* (Washington, D.C.: 2002), 18; this publication can also be accessed online at www.ed.gov/inits/commissionsboards/whspecialeducation/reports/index.html. Wade F. Horn and Douglas Tynan, "Time to Make Special Education 'Special' Again," *Rethinking Special Education for a New Century,* 46.

6. *Back to School on Civil Rights*, 18; Wade F. Horn and Douglas Tynan, "Time to Make Special Education 'Special' Again," 46; *A New Era*, 45; 20 USC §1400(c)(12)(A).

7. "Foreword," *Rethinking Special Education for a New Century*, v.

Chapter 13: How Laws Work: Who Has Trump?

1. 20 USC §1412(a); 20 USC §1416.

2. IDEA 2004 provides that the U.S. Department of Education may not issue regulations or policy interpretations that violate or contradict the requirements of the IDEA itself. See 20 USC §1406(b) and (d). In addition, the department's responses to requests for clarification of policy are informal, not legally binding, and limited to the specific facts presented. See 20 USC §1406(e).

Important Web Sites

B elow are Web sites that offer important information for parents, teachers, and others interested in learning about the rights of children with disabilities:

Federal government information

To order free copies of federal laws and regulations, visit www.edpubs. ed.gov.

U.S. Department of Education Office of Special-Education Programs

For links to multiple government-policy statements and resources on the IDEA, visit http://idea.ed.gov.

For information on the U.S. Department of Education Office of Special Education Programs, visit www.ed.gov/about/offices/list/osers/osep/index. html.

Section 504

For information specifically on section 504, visit the U.S. Department of Education Office of Civil Rights at www.ed.gov/policy/rights/guid/ocr/ disabilityoverview.html .

To file a complaint for a violation of Section 504, go to www ed.gov/ about/offices/list/ocr/complaintintro.html.

Federally funded technical support sites

The following are important support sites funded by the federal government:

- National Center on Secondary Education and Transition (NCSET) (www.ncset.org)
- What Works Clearinghouse (http://ies.ed.gov/ncee/wwc)

General information on special education and disability issues

The following Web sites are listed in alphabetical order:

- Closing the Gap: Assistive Technology Resources for Children and Adults with Special Needs (www.closingthegap.com)
- Council of Parent Attorneys and Advocates (www.copaa.net)
- Monahan and Cohen (www.monahan-cohen.com). This is the author's law firm.
- National Disability Rights Network (www.ndrn.org). This is an "umbrella" organization for state protection and advocacy systems
- National Information Center for Handicapped Children and Youth (www.nichcy.org)

Disability and advocacy groups

The following is a selective list of important organizations for people with disabilities; it is listed in alphabetical order.

- The ARC (www.thearc.org). This is an association for people with intellectual and developmental disabilities
- American Bar Association, Commission on Mental and Physical Disability Law (www.abanet.org/disability)
- Autism Society of America (www.autism-society.org)
- Brain Injury Association of America (www.biausa.org)
- Children and Adults with Attention Deficit/Hyperactivity Disorder (www.chadd.org)
- Great Schools (www.greatschools.net)

- Learning Disabilities Association of America (www.ldanatl.org)
- National Alliance on Mental Illness (www.nami.org)
- National Association for Down Syndrome (www.nads.org)
- National Down Syndrome Society (www.ndss.org)
- National Federation of Families for Children's Mental Health (www.ffcmh.org)
- Nonverbal Learning Disability Association (www.nlda.org)
- Tourette Syndrome Association (www.tsa-usa.org)
- United Cerebral Palsy Association (www.ucp.org)
- Wrights Law (www.wrightslaw.com)

Access to parent information center, special education attorneys and advocates

- ABA Commission on Mental and Physical Disability law, Disability Lawyers Directory (www.abanet.org/disability/disabilitydirectory/home.shtml)
- Council of Parent Attorneys and Advocates (www.copaa.net)
- LD Online (www.ldonline.org/yellowpages). This site is listed under the "Learning Media Yellow Pages"
- National Disability Rights Network (www.ndrn.org)
- ALLIANCE—Technical Assistance Alliance for Parent Centers (www.taalliance.org)
- Wrightslaw, Yellow Pages for kids (www.yellowpagesforkids.com)

To research legislation currently under consideration or other legislative activity, visit the Library of Congress at www.thomas.gov.

Higher education disability sites

- Association on Higher Education and Disability (www.ahead.org)
- Health Resource Center Online Clearinghouse on Postsecondary Education for Individuals with Disabilities (www.heath.gwu.edu)

Acronyms Commonly Used in Special Education

Note that the names for various meetings and other terms—and the resulting acronyms and initialisms—vary from state to state. This is not a comprehensive list, and some terms and acronyms may be different in your state.

ABA	Applied Behavioral Analysis
ABC	Antecedents, Behavior, and Consequences
ADA	Americans with Disabilities Act
ADD	Attention Deficit Disorder
AD/HD	Attention Deficit/Hyperactivity Disorder
APE	Adaptive Physical Education
ASL	American Sign Language
AT	Assistive Technology
AUG COM	Augmentative Communication
BIP	Behavior Intervention Plan
CAPD	Central Auditory Processing Disorder
CD	Communication Disorder
CFR	Code of Federal Regulations
D/B	Deaf-blindness
DD	Developmental Delay
D/HOH	Deaf/Hard of Hearing
DP	Due Process

DTT	Discrete Trial Training
EC	Early Childhood
ED	Emotional Disturbance
EI	Early Intervention (ages 0–3)
EIS	Early Intervening Services (services prior to special education)
ESY	Extended School Year
FAPE	Free Appropriate Public Education
FBA	Functional Behavior Analysis
FC	Facilitated Communication
FERPA	Family Educational Rights and Privacy Act
HI	Hearing Impairment
HOH	Hard of Hearing
IAES	Interim Alternative Educational Setting
IAEP	Interim Alternative Educational Placement
IDEA	Individuals with Disabilities Education Act
IDEIA	Individuals with Disabilities Education Improvement Act (Parts A, B, C effective 7/1/05)
IEE	Independent Educational Evaluation
IEP	Individualized Education Program
IFSP	Individual Family Service Plan (for children ages 0–3)
IHO	Impartial Hearing Officer
ITP	Individualized Transition Plan (part of an IEP for students 16 and older)
LD	Learning Disability
LEA	Local Educational Agency (school district)
LEP	Limited English Proficiency
LRE	Least Restrictive Environment
MD	Multiple Disabilities
MDC or MDR	Manifestation Determination Conference or Manifestation Determination Review
MI	Multiple Impairment
MR	Mental Retardation
NCLB	No Child Left Behind
NLD (NLVD)	Nonverbal Learning Disability
OCD	Obsessive Compulsive Disorder
ODD	Oppositional Defiant Disorder

OHI	Other Health Impairment
OI	Orthopedic Impairment
O&M	Orientation and Mobility Services
OSEP	Office of Special Education Programs, U.S. Department of Education
OT	Occupational Therapy
PBIS	Positive Behavior Intervention System
PBM	Positive Behavior Management
PBS	Positive Behavior Support
PDD	Pervasive Developmental Disorder
PECS	Picture Exchange Communication System
PH	Physically Handicapped
PLOP	Present Level of Performance
PT	Physical Therapy
RTI	Response to Intervention
S/C	Self-Contained Classroom
Sp Ed.	Special Education
SEA	State Educational Agency
SLD	Specific Language Disability
SL	Speech/Language Disorder
S/L	Speech/Language Therapy
SLP	Speech/Language Pathologist
TBI	Traumatic Brain Injury
TDD	Telephone Device for the Deaf
TEACCH	Treatment and Education of Autistic and Related Communication Handicapped Children
TS	Tourette Syndrome
VI	Visual Impairment
504	Section 504 (Rehabilitation Act of 1973)

C

Sample Letters

On the following pages are five sample letters that parents may use when requesting due process hearings, records, evaluations, or placing a child unilaterally into a private school. The bold text forms the basic structure of the letter; the information within brackets is factual content that must be added anew for each letter; the material in plain text is a suggestion for how to proceed with your argument.

Request for an Impartial Due Process Hearing

Check state regulations, timelines, forms, and your state's Department of Education Web site for appropriate terminology and to whom to send the letter. Each state has its own procedures and timelines for due process hearings.

[Date]
[Your street address]
[Your city, state, zip code]
[Your email address]
[Your fax number, if applicable]

VIA FACSIMILE [include fax number] and CERTIFIED MAIL/RETURN RECEIPT REQUESTED. [Keep confirmation receipt from fax and/or certified mail number in your files.]

[Name of superintendent, special education director, etc.]
[District name and number]
[Street address]
[City, state, zip code]

Dear [superintendent, special education director,
state department of education, etc.]:

Re: [student's name]

[student's date of birth]

[name of school child attends]

I am the parent of [child's full name]. We reside at [provide your full address]. On behalf of my [daughter/son], I am requesting an impartial due process hearing for the following reasons:

List the reasons you are filing for a due process hearing—for example, failure to provide an appropriate placement, services insufficient to meet my child's needs, failure to educate my child in the least restrictive environment, etc.

For each area, provide a brief description of how the school did not meet your child's needs—for example, the classroom did not address my son's emotional needs; the school provided my child only 30 minutes a week of speech and language services, even though my private report showed he/she needed extensive services, etc.

Information supporting our complaint includes, but is not limited to, the following examples:

Provide a brief description of evidence supporting your complaints.

We may request the opportunity to amend the due process hearing request if necessary. As relief, we would like the district to provide the following:

Tell the district how you want the problem to be solved.

I am interested in mediation but do not wish to delay the appointment of an impartial hearing officer.

[This request for mediation is optional, but often desirable.]

Sincerely,

[Print your full name]

Record Request

Check state regulations and your state's Department of Education for appropriate terminology, the timeline within which the school must respond, and to whom to address the letter. Some record requests should be for all files, while others may request specific documents. Note that the school may impose a "reasonable" charge for copying the school records.

[Date]
[Your street address]
[Your city, state, zip code]
[Your email address]
[Your fax number, if applicable]

VIA FACSIMILE [fax number] and CERTIFIED MAIL/RETURN RECEIPT REQUESTED *[Keep confirmation receipt from fax and/or certified mail number in your files.]*

[Name of superintendent, school principal, or record custodian]
[School district name and number]
[Street address]
[City, state, zip code]

Dear [superintendent, principal, or record custodian]:

Re: [full name of student]

I am requesting a complete copy of the records you have on my [son/daughter], [child's name]. [She/He] is in the [grade] at the [name] School. I am requesting all special education and regular education records; all evaluation reports and eligibility meeting records; IEP reports; Section 504 reports; internal memoranda and email correspondence; grades; achievement test scores; attendance records; correspondence; behavioral reports; anecdotal records; and teacher records. I am also requesting the records of every related service provider or evaluator who has been involved with [child's name] and the records of any staff who provides services through the special education cooperative or intermediate service unit.

We look forward to receiving these records within the next [provide number] days. If you have any questions, please do not hesitate to contact me.

Sincerely,

[Print your full name]

Request for an Evaluation

Check state regulations, timelines, forms, and your state's Department of Education Web site for appropriate terminology, the amount of time the district has to complete its evaluation, and to whom to send the letter.

[Date]
[Your street address]
[Your city, state, zip code]
[Your email address]
[Your fax number, if applicable]

VIA FACSIMILE [provide fax number] and CERTIFIED MAIL/RETURN RECEIPT REQUESTED *[Keep confirmation receipt from fax and/or certified mail number for your records.]*

[Name of superintendent, school principal, or special education director]
[School district name and number]
[Street address]
[City, state, zip code]

Dear [superintendent, principal, or special education director]:

Re: [full name of student]

My [son/daughter] attends [name of school] and is in the [____] grade. I am requesting that the district evaluate my child and determine if [he/she] is eligible for special education services. My child has been struggling with

Name specific problems you have observed—for example, problems with reading, handwriting, making friends, etc.

I understand that the district will first decide if it will evaluate my child or not and will notify me of its decision within [_____] days. If the district agrees to an evaluation, a meeting will be held to discuss what areas need to be evaluated, and my written consent will be obtained for testing to begin.

If you have any questions, please do not hesitate to contact me. I look forward to hearing from you.

Sincerely,

[Print your full name]

Request for an Independent Evaluation

Check state regulations and with your state's Department of Education for the person to whom to send the request, the timelines, and the process if the district agrees to fund an independent evaluation or denies the request.

[Date]
[Your street address]
[Your city, state, zip code]
[Your email address]
[Your fax number, if applicable]

VIA FACSIMILE [provide fax number] and CERTIFIED MAIL/RETURN RECEIPT REQUESTED *[Keep confirmation receipt from fax and/or certified mail number for your records.]*

[Name of superintendent, school principal, or special education director]
[School district name and number]
[Street address]
[City, state, zip code]

Dear [superintendent, principal, or special education director]:

Re: [full name of student]
   [student's address]

The school team has evaluated my [son/daughter]. At this time, I am requesting that the district provide an independent evaluation at district expense in the following areas:

Provide a detailed list of the areas that you believe require an independent evaluation.

I am making the request for the following reasons:

State the disagreement clearly—for example. I disagree with the findings that my child is cognitively impaired; the occupational therapist stated that my son did not need services, but I see him struggling to finish his homework nightly, etc.

I understand that you have [___] days to respond to my request.

If you have any questions, please do not hesitate to contact me. I look forward to hearing from you.

Sincerely,

[Print your full name]

Unilateral Placement Notice Letter

Check state regulations and with your state's Department of Education for appropriate terminology and to whom to send the letter. The letter must be sent at least ten business days prior to the child's enrollment in the private program or at the most recent individualized education program (IEP) meeting prior to enrollment. See your state's regulations for other exceptions.

[Date]
[Your street address]
[Your city, state, zip code]
[Your email address]
[Your fax number, if applicable]

CERTIFIED MAIL/RETURN RECEIPT REQUESTED *[Keep certified mail number for your records.]* Or deliver the letter in person and obtain a signed receipt.

[Name of superintendent]
[School district name and number]
[Street address]
[City, state, zip code]

Dear [superintendent, principal, or special education director]:

Re: [full name of student]

   [name of school]

   [grade]

   [ID number, if any]

We are writing to inform you that effective [provide exact date], we will be unilaterally enrolling [name of student] at [name of school], a private school, and are requesting that the cost of this placement be at school district expense.

We are rejecting the school district's placement for our child because

State general reasons, such as [name of child]'s needs have not been appropriately identified; [name of child] has not been provided with appropriate IEPs; [name of child] has been denied sufficient services; [name of child] has not been offered an appropriate placement; [name of child] has been denied appropriate methodologies; and/or because [name of child] has not made progress.

Please consider this letter as our formal request for the school system to assume financial responsibility for the cost of this private placement, pursuant to the requirements of the IDEA.

Sincerely,

[Print your full name]

Index